WORST-CASE
SCENARIOS

WORST-CASE

SCENARIOS

Cass R. Sunstein

HARVARD UNIVERSITY PRESS

Cambridge, Massachusetts · London, England

2007

A Caravan book. For more information, visit www.caravanbooks.org

Library of Congress Cataloging-in-Publication Data

Sunstein, Cass R.
Worst-case scenarios / Cass R. Sunstein
p. cm.
Includes bibliographical references and index.
ISBN-13: 978-0-674-02510-3 (alk. paper)
ISBN-10: 0-674-02510-5 (alk. paper)
1. Risk perception.   2. Policy sciences.   3. Climatic changes—
Government policy—United States.   4. Terrorism—Government
policy—United States.   5. Ozone layer depletion—Government
policy—United States.   I. Title

HM1101.S864   2007
320.60973—dc22   2006052942

For Bill Meadow

CONTENTS

WORST-CASE
SCENARIOS

INTRODUCTION

How do human beings and their governments approach worst-case scenarios? Do they tend to neglect them or do they give them excessive weight? Whatever we actually do, how *should* we deal with unlikely risks of catastrophe?

In the aftermath of the attacks on 9/11, Vice President Dick Cheney set out what has become known as The One Percent Doctrine: "We have to deal with this new type of threat in a way we haven't yet defined . . . With a low-probability, high-impact event like this . . . if there's a one percent chance that Pakistani scientists are helping al Qaeda build or develop a nuclear weapon, we have to treat it as a certainty in terms of our response."[1]

For especially horrific outcomes, it is tempting to think that a 1 percent chance should be treated as a certainty. In so suggesting, Vice President Cheney took the same position as many people who are confronting a low probability of disaster. No less than environmentalists who focus on species loss, climate change, and genetic modification of food, Vice President Cheney urged that governments should identify, and attempt to prevent, the worst-case scenario. Indeed, another vice president, Al Gore, implied a related principle for climate change—because the risk of a terrible catastrophe is real, we ought to respond aggressively to it. Many environmentalists enthusiastically embrace the Precautionary Principle, which is specifically designed for situations in which we cannot know that harm will occur. According to the Precautionary Principle, threats to the environment need not be established with certainty. Even a small risk of a catastrophic or irreversible harm is enough to require a serious response.

But consider an obvious objection to this position. A 1 percent chance of a terrible outcome is a lot better than a certainty of a terrible outcome. In order to figure out what to do, you should multiply the probability of the outcome by its magnitude. If you face a 1 percent chance of losing $10,000, you should take fewer precautions than if you face a 90 percent chance of losing $10,000. Even with losses that do not involve money, and that are hard to turn into monetary equivalents, it is important to attend to both the probability of harm and the magnitude of harm. If you face a 1 percent chance of getting sick, you should act differently from how you would act if you faced a 90 percent chance of getting sick. People who are sensible, or even sane, do not treat a 1 percent risk of loss the same as a certainty of loss.

Suppose that you have a health problem of some kind—serious heart disease, a brain tumor, failing eyesight, severe and chronic back pain—and your doctor tells you that an operation is 99 percent likely to solve the problem and to have no bad side-effects. Will you decline the operation if the doctor emphasizes that in 1 percent of cases things go quite wrong? Probably not. Whatever you do, you are most unlikely to treat a small chance of a bad outcome as equivalent to a certainty of a bad outcome. You will focus not just on the nature of the worst case but on the probability that it will come about. Perhaps you will decide to create a special "margin of safety," or buffer zone, against the worst outcomes. But even if you do so, you will probably think a lot before deciding on the right margin of safety, and you will pay a great deal of attention to the probability of harm. The same point holds for governments. For public officials no less than the rest of us, the probability of harm matters a great deal, and it is foolish to attend exclusively to the worst-case scenario.

Suppose there is a 99 percent chance that a new law will increase national security, and a 1 percent chance that it will decrease national security; a 99 percent chance that a reform of the health care system will improve both health and the economy, and a 1 percent chance that reform will significantly increase unemployment; a 99 percent chance that a voucher system for education will make schools better, and a 1 percent chance that schools will get worse. If government initiatives are rejected whenever they entail a 1 percent chance of a bad outcome, we will have far too few initiatives. In many contexts, governments, just like ordinary people, take their chances on the worst-case scenario—and they are entirely right to do so.

These points create real problems for any one percent doctrine. Ordinarily it is a big mistake to ignore the difference between a 1 percent chance and a certainty. But pause over what it would mean if Al Qaeda *were* able to acquire nuclear weapons for use against the United States and its allies. For a truly catastrophic outcome, a 1 percent chance may not be so radically different from a much higher chance—and it is tempting to consider responding as if it were a certainty. To see the point, imagine a 1 percent chance that New York City, or the entire East Coast, would be completely destroyed. Or imagine a 1 percent risk of worldwide calamity from climate change—with hundreds of millions of deaths from malaria and other climate-related diseases, countless extinctions, the melting of the polar ice sheets, catastrophic flooding in Florida, New York, Paris, Munich, and London. Or imagine a 1 percent chance of a devastating collision between a large asteroid and our planet. If the worst-case scenario is awful enough, we might well treat a small probability as if it were much larger.

But on reflection, is this really wise? One problem is that responses to worst-case scenarios can be both burdensome and risky—and they can have worst-case scenarios of their own. We need to investigate the burdens and risks of the responses, not simply the scenarios. In the context of national security, an aggressive response to a 1 percent threat may create a new threat, perhaps higher than 1 percent, of producing its own disaster. A preemptive war, designed to eliminate a small risk of a terrible outcome, might create larger risks of a different but also terrible outcome. If the United States attacked an unfriendly nation to eliminate the (low probability?) danger that it poses, the attack would likely create a certainty of many deaths, and a (low?) probability of many more.

The Bush administration resisted significant steps to halt climate change, pointing to the burdens and costs of the regulatory actions that some people believe to be required. Suppose that climate change does, in fact, create a 1 percent risk of catastrophe at the very least—and that an aggressive response to climate change, calling for massive changes in energy policy, creates a significant chance of imposing serious hardships on many nations, including not just the United States but India and China as well. Perhaps those hardships would entail significant increases in unemployment and hence poverty. If the world devotes resources to climate change, perhaps it will not be able to use those resources to combat more serious problems.[2] To take another example: We could easily imagine responses to the AIDS crisis, such as quarantines, that would impose unacceptable burdens on people who are infected or who are at risk of becoming infected. To know whether and how to respond, we must look at the consequences of possible responses—not only at the existence, probability, and size of the danger.

In this book, I try to make progress on issues of this kind. I have three specific goals. The first is to understand people's responses to worst-case scenarios and in particular their susceptibility to two opposite problems: excessive overreaction and utter neglect. As we shall see, both problems affect individuals and governments alike. The second goal is to consider how both individuals and public officials might think more sensibly about situations involving low-probability risks of disaster. Insisting on a wide viewscreen, one that emphasizes the likelihood and magnitude of the risks on all sides, would be a good place to start. The third goal is to explore the uses and limits of cost-benefit analysis, especially when dealing with harms that will not come to fruition in the near future. Cost-benefit analysis is at best a proxy for what really matters, which is well-being rather than money; but sometimes proxies can be helpful.

Throughout I shall use climate change as a defining case, both because it has immense practical importance and because it provides a valuable illustration of the underlying principles. But I shall also refer to other sources of very bad worst-case scenarios, including terrorism, depletion of the ozone layer, genetic modification of food, hurricanes, and avian flu. My hope is that the basic analysis can be adapted to diverse problems, including many not yet on the horizon. The discussion is organized around five general themes.

Intuition and analysis   People's reactions to risks, and to worst-case scenarios, come through two different routes.[3] The first is intuitive; the second is more analytical. Our intuitive reactions tend to be rapid and based on our personal experience. Those who have had a recent encounter with violent crime, an automobile accident, or a serious health scare will often fear a bad outcome in a roughly similar situation, whether or not their fear has any objective basis. By contrast, those who have no relevant experience may believe that an unlikely event is unworthy of attention. If a risk is perceived to fall below a certain threshold, it might not affect our behavior at all.

Our intuitions can lead to both too much and too little concern with low-probability risks. When judgments are based on analysis, they are more likely to be accurate, certainly if the analysis can be trusted. But for most people, intuitions rooted in actual experience are a much more powerful motivating force. An important task, for individuals and institutions alike, is to ensure that error-prone intuitions do not drive behavior.

Overreaction and neglect   Intuitive judgments about probability often depend on whether a bad outcome can be readily imagined—whether it is cognitively "available." Before the attacks of 9/11, almost no one had imagined hijackers turning airplanes into flying bombs. The absence of recent airplane hijackings made people feel far more secure than they ought to have—the phenomenon of "unavailability bias." As a result, the terrorist threat was badly neglected. On the other hand, in the aftermath of a highly publicized event people are often far more fearful than they ought to be—the phenomenon of "availability bias." An available incident can lead to excessive fixation on worst-case scenarios—just as the absence of such an incident can lead to an unjustified sense of security.

This problem is compounded by the fact that when people's emotions are engaged, they tend to ignore the question of probability altogether. They focus on the bad outcome or on the worst that might happen, without thinking enough about how unlikely it is. (Best-case thinking—which is the curse, or blessing, of unrealistic optimists—is a related problem.) When governments impose excessive precautions in the face of some risks, they are often falling victim to "probability neglect"—wrongly treating highly improbable dangers as if they were certainties. By contrast, people often believe that they are "safe" in the sense that the worst-case scenario may be dismissed or need not be considered at all. This too is a form of probability neglect, because the assumption is that when a situation can sensibly be described as "safe," there is no risk at all. In fact, human beings face risks of different degrees of probability. It is a pervasive and damaging mistake to think that "safety" comes with an on-off switch.

Worst cases everywhere   In some contexts, people are acutely aware of the burdens imposed by attempting to eliminate worst-case scenarios; but in other contexts, they are not attuned to those burdens at all. In regulatory policy, for example, those who urge extensive precautions against the worst cases often disregard the possibility that those very precautions can inflict losses and even create risks of their own. Risks, and bad worst cases, may be on all sides. Preemptive wars—designed to eliminate threats before they can materialize, including the 2003 Iraq invasion and Israel's 2006 attack on Hezbollah—have been defended on the ground that delays may increase the magnitude of the relevant threat. If a nation waits while its adversary plots and prepares, a delay might be deadly. But preemptive wars will ensure many deaths—and such wars can increase, rather than decrease, overall dangers to national security.

Often people, and nations, take undue precautions against worst-case scenarios simply because they disregard the burdens and risks of those precautions. But often people, and nations, neglect worst-case scenarios because they are unduly attentive to the burdens imposed by precautions. It is important to look at both sides of the ledger.

Risk and uncertainty   With these points in mind, we can make a good deal of progress in understanding why, and when, people fail to respond sensibly to worst-case scenarios—and what might be done about these problems.

The first step is, of course, to specify the bad outcomes and try to assess their probability. By multiplying outcomes by their probability, we can produce the "expected value" of various courses of action. Sometimes science enables us to identify both outcomes and probabilities within a sharply restricted range. Public health officials might have reason to believe, for example, that the probability of a worst-case outbreak of the avian flu is above 0 percent but below 5 percent; climatologists might conclude that the probability of catastrophic climate change is above 1 percent but below 5 percent. With such information in hand, we are in a position to establish the magnitude and likelihood of gains and losses from various courses of action, including staying the current course ("business as usual"). Perhaps a margin of safety should be created to protect against the worst cases; but as we shall see, it is important to know what we lose by creating that margin of safety. If a patient, suffering from life-threatening cancer, learns that surgery and chemotherapy are 75 percent likely to produce at least a decade of additional life, his choice will probably be easy. Sometimes public officials are in a similar position. Equipped with a sense of the imaginable outcomes, of their probability, and of the burdens and risks of responding to them, we will often be in a good position to know what to do.

When probabilities cannot be assigned to the worst-case scenario, the analysis is harder. Suppose that officials or scientists have no idea about the likelihood of a terrible outcome, or that they are able to specify only a wide range—believing, for example, that the risk of a catastrophic climate change is over 1 percent but below 20 percent. Even when probabilities cannot be assigned, a great deal of progress can be made if we ask how much is lost by eliminating the worst-case scenario and by specifying the difference between the worst case and next-worst case. As we shall see, the problem of irreversibility raises distinctive challenges. The simplest point is that it makes sense to do an extra amount in order to maintain flexibility for the future.

Well-being, money, and consequences   It is impossible to know how to handle worst-case scenarios without having a sense of the relevant consequences. But once we identify consequences, we still need to do much more thinking before we can decide how to respond. Consequences do not speak for themselves; human beings have to evaluate them. Science may tell us what specific effects climate change is expected to have on human and animal life; but only moral evaluation of those effects is needed to enable us to decide what, exactly, should be done in response.

In offering guidance for handling hard problems, I emphasize the goal of increasing social well-being, usually without attempting to specify that controversial idea. (I use the term "well-being" interchangeably with the term "welfare.") Often we can make a lot of progress on worst-case scenarios without reaching the hardest or most foundational issues. In ordinary life, we do this all the time. If a really bad outcome will almost certainly not occur, and if we lose a lot by trying to prevent it, precautionary steps will not have much appeal. If the worst-case scenario cannot be ruled out, and if it is easy to ensure that it will not occur, we will take precautions. Sensible governments behave the same way, and many good decisions about risks—in such diverse domains as national security and environmental policy—are made on the basis of a fairly simple inquiry into the relevant variables. People who have different conceptions of well-being, or who are not sure how to think about the most serious controversies, can often agree that one course of action makes sense and that others do not. In short, an understanding of the nature of the potential outcomes and their likelihood may well make it possible for people to achieve what we might call an "incompletely theorized agreement" on the appropriate course of action—that is, an agreement about what to do without any kind of agreement on the theory that underlies our conclusion.[4]

Often, of course, life produces much harder questions. It is now standard practice for economists and other policy analysts to turn various effects, including risks to life and health, into monetary equivalents. As we shall see, cost-benefit analysis of this kind helped to spur extremely aggressive efforts to protect the ozone layer. For that problem, the United States turned out to be the most pro-regulatory nation on the face of the earth—under the leadership of President Ronald Reagan, not generally known for being pro-regulatory. But in the United States, at least, cost-benefit analysis has raised serious cautionary notes about some proposed efforts to protect against climate change.

The idea of cost-benefit analysis raises many questions, both technical and less technical, about whether and how to turn risks and worst cases into monetary equivalents. What matters is well-being, not money, and money is a poor proxy for well-being.[5] Nonetheless, I shall offer a qualified defense of cost-benefit analysis—not with the preposterous suggestion that it always tells us what to do but with the more modest claim that in deciding what to do, cost-benefit analysis will often provide us with valuable information. Of course we need to know what, exactly, the monetary figures represent. Do they reflect more in the way of premature death and serious illness? Do they refer to higher prices for consumer products? To lower wages? Qualitative as well as quantitative information is important. But in deciding how to respond to worst-case scenarios, monetary equivalents can provide some valuable discipline.

We need to consider distributional questions too. Who is helped and who is hurt by any effort to eliminate worst-case scenarios? The question is especially pressing for the problem of climate change, where people in poor regions, above all India and Africa, are most vulnerable. But the distributional question bears on many other potential disasters as well, such as AIDS and avian flu. We also need to separate the question of regulation from the question of subsidy. It would not make sense to adopt regulations that force the citizens of a poor nation to pay $100 each to eliminate a risk of 1/500,000. But it might well make sense for wealthy nations to transfer resources to citizens of such a nation, to enable them to take more and better steps to eliminate the risks they face.

For advocates of cost-benefit analysis, a particularly thorny question is how to handle future generations when they are threatened by worst-case scenarios. According to standard practice, money that will come in the future must be "discounted"; a dollar twenty years hence is worth a fraction of a dollar today. (You would almost certainly prefer $1,000 now to $1,000 in twenty years.) Should we discount future lives as well? Is a life twenty years hence worth a fraction of a life today? I will argue in favor of a Principle of Intergenerational Neutrality—one that requires the citizens of every generation to be treated equally. This principle has important implications for many problems, most obviously climate change.

Present generations are obliged to take the interests of their threatened descendents as seriously as they take their own.

But the Principle of Intergenerational Neutrality does not mean that the present generation should refuse to discount the future, or should impose great sacrifices on itself for the sake of those who will come later. If human history is any guide, the future will be much richer than the present; and it makes no sense to say that the relatively impoverished present should transfer its resources to the far wealthier future. And if the present generation sacrifices itself by forgoing economic growth, it is likely to hurt the future too, because long-term economic growth is likely to produce citizens who live healthier, longer, and better lives. I shall have something to say about what intergenerational neutrality actually requires, and about the complex relationship between that important ideal and the disputed practice of "discounting" the future.

The plan   The organization of this book follows the themes just traced. Chapter 1 sets the stage by exploring risk perceptions, and our responses to worst-case scenarios, with close reference to two of the most important threats of our time: terrorism and climate change. With respect to terrorism, American reactions are greatly heightened by three identifiable mechanisms: availability, probability neglect, and outrage. With respect to climate change, American reactions are greatly dampened. Because most Americans lack personal experience with serious climate-related harms, and because those harms are perceived as likely to occur in the future and in distant lands, Americans have been unwilling to spend much money to prevent them. As we shall see, terrorism and climate change present instructive polar cases: The first is peculiarly likely to produce close attention to worst-case scenarios, while the latter is especially unlikely to do so. An understanding of Americans' divergent reactions to these two risks illuminates worst-case thinking in general.

Chapter 2 offers a different kind of comparison. The Montreal Protocol, designed to protect the ozone layer, has been a sensational success story. It has largely eliminated ozone-depleting chemicals and ensured that the ozone layer will eventually return to its natural state. The United States, the world's largest emitter of such chemicals, took the lead in urging an aggressive response to the problem of ozone depletion. By contrast, the Kyoto Protocol, designed to protect against climate change, presents a mixed picture at best. It has been firmly rejected by the United States, the world's largest emitter of greenhouse gases. It does not impose restrictions on emissions from the developing world, even though China is likely to be the world's largest greenhouse gas emitter in the near future. And it is likely to be violated by many of its signatories, including several European nations. The task is to explain the radically different fates of these two efforts to come to terms with potentially catastrophic environmental problems.

Part of the explanation lies in the dramatically different approaches of the United States, based on a domestic assessment of the consequences of the two protocols. Part of the explanation lies in the different incentives of most of the planet's nations. The problem of ozone depletion could be handled relatively easily, in a way that promised to deliver huge benefits at low cost. The same could not be said for climate change. The United States and China have a lot to gain from the emission of greenhouse gases, and disproportionately little to fear from climate change. Taken together, chapters 1 and 2 offer concrete lessons about how a successful agreement for climate change might be made more probable, and how such an agreement might be structured. The discussion also offers some broader lessons about how and when societies are likely to respond to worst-case scenarios.

Chapters 3 and 4 turn to the question of how to deal with such scenarios. Chapter 3 explains that notwithstanding its international influence, the Precautionary Principle is incoherent; it condemns the very steps that it requires. To see the point, imagine if we adopted a *universal* One Percent Doctrine, forbidding any course of action that had a 1 percent chance of causing significant harm. The likely result would be paralysis, because so many courses of action would be forbidden. (Even doing nothing might be prohibited; human beings who do nothing—assuming we can agree what that means—will probably end up pretty unhealthy. Will they even eat? What will they eat?) But narrower and better precautionary principles can be devised. In particular, I identify a Catastrophic Harm Precautionary Principle, designed to provide guidance for dealing with extremely serious risks. This principle emphasizes the need to attend to both the magnitude and the probability of the harm. It also emphasizes that when catastrophic risks come to fruition, they often have even more serious consequences than we foresee, because of a process that has been called "social amplification." Properly understood, a Catastrophic Harm Precautionary Principle should counteract the dual problems of overreaction and neglect.

Chapter 4 explores the question of irreversibility and in particular the argument for an Irreversible Harm Precautionary Principle, suited to such problems as ozone depletion, protection of endangered species, destruction of cultural artifacts, and of course climate change. One problem here stems from the need to specify the idea of irreversibility, which can be understood in several different ways. Another problem is that precautionary steps may be irreversible too, even if they merely involve expenditures. But the central point remains: Sensible individuals and societies are willing to spend a great deal to preserve their own flexibility in the future. Chapters 5 and 6 investigate costs and benefits. As Chapter 5 explains in detail, what matters is well-being, and even when the costs of regulation exceed the benefits, regulation might promote well-being. But cost-benefit analysis is useful nonetheless. Whether we care about individual autonomy or social welfare, there is good reason to consider people's "willingness to pay" to avoid risks, including those risks associated with worst-case scenarios—at least when regulation forces people to pay for the benefits they receive. But it is important to ask whether people are adequately informed and whether they suffer from the kinds of cognitive defects emphasized in Chapter 1. If people lack information, or if they process information poorly, we cannot rely on their willingness to pay to reduce statistical risks. At the same time, people's judgments as consumers differ from their judgments as citizens, and this difference complicates the economic case for cost-benefit analysis. An additional problem involves social deprivation: If deprivation has led people to adapt to serious risks, believing them to be an inevitable part of life, then we cannot defend a decision to expose those people to those risks by saying that they prefer the way that they now live. These various points help to clarify the current debate over risk regulation in poor countries. Of course it is preposterous to say that the inhabitants of one nation are "worth less" than the inhabitants of another. But as we shall see, it is not preposterous to say that a rich nation rightly spends more to reduce a mortality risk of 1 in 100,000 than a poor nation does.

Chapter 6 explores one of the most vexing questions of all: valuation of the future. I argue on behalf of a Principle of Intergenerational Neutrality that requires existing generations to give careful consideration to the consequences of their decisions for those who will follow. But this principle does not resolve the debate over whether to "discount" future events or their monetary equivalents. Some of the time, future generations are helped, not hurt, by a decision to discount, because the future is damaged if the present impoverishes itself. But for some problems, cost-benefit analysis with discounting can lead to severe violations of the Principle of Intergenerational Neutrality. As we will see, that form of analysis can impair well-being and cause serious problems of distributional unfairness. These problems should be addressed directly— a point that has implications for climate change in particular.

By way of conclusion, I emphasize the possibility of self-help and investigate some of the links between personal behavior and the judgments of government officials.

CHAPTER ONE

OF TERRORISM AND CLIMATE CHANGE

When I was a child, and facing some difficult situation, my mother would often ask, "What's the worst that could happen?" This was an extremely comforting question. True, the worst was bad, but it wasn't all that bad. I might miss a few days of school from a nasty cold. My Little League baseball team might lose a game or I might strike out every time I went to bat. I might flunk a math quiz. A friend might decide he didn't really like me.

In retrospect, I am not at all sure why my mother's question was so comforting. Maybe my answers were unimaginative. My cold might turn out to be mononucleosis, in which case I would miss months of school. I could get hit by a wild pitch and be badly hurt. What if I flunked not just one test but a lot of tests, and developed test-related anxieties that would have damaging long-term effects? Perhaps I would lose not one friend but all of them.

But maybe I wasn't so unimaginative after all. More likely, I understood my mother to be asking, "What's the worst that could happen, realistically speaking?" Evidently, I felt essentially safe, and so I created an implicit probability-related boundary on worst-case scenarios—not even pausing to consider (or rapidly ruling out) risks that were extremely unlikely to materialize. Or maybe I responded not only to my mother's words but also to the feeling that accompanied them—her own sense of safety, her certainty that nothing was so terrible about "the worst that could happen." Because my mother evidently felt that the worst case was not so bad, I felt that way too. Her confidence was contagious.

In most domains, however, thinking about the worst that could happen is far from comforting, and those who emphasize bad possibilities mean to energize people, not to soothe them. In defending the war against Iraq, President George W. Bush tried to focus the nation's attention squarely on a worst-case scenario: "Imagine those 19 hijackers with other weapons and plans, this time armed by Saddam Hussein. It would take one vial, one canister, one crate slipped into this country to bring a day of horror like none we have ever known."[1] To say the least, President Bush was not trying to assuage people's fears.

In 2006, *Time* magazine ran a cover story on climate change with this title: "Be worried. Be very worried." For climate change, those who emphasize worst-case scenarios are attempting to shake people from complacency and spur them into immediate action. In fact, a popular movie from 2004, *The Day after Tomorrow*, had major if short-term effects on risk perceptions associated with climate change, simply because it emphasized the worst that could happen.[2] Former Vice President Gore's 2006 documentary *An Inconvenient Truth* is full of worst-case scenarios, and it is effective partly for that reason.

What is true for public policy is true for ordinary life as well. If your child is struggling in school or has to be hospitalized, you will not be calmed by considering what might go most wrong. Recently I refused to allow my teenage daughter, a strong swimmer, to take a long swim on her own; I knew that the risk was less than trivial, but the mere fact that I was able to visualize a bad outcome was enough for me. (I was unable to defend myself to my daughter, who rightly emphasized that there was no real danger; but she indulged me.) If you are deciding whether to take a job in Paris, to marry, or to go to a restaurant in a marginal neighborhood, attention to the worst case is not going to calm you down. Many people refuse to go to doctors and ignore incipient medical problems because they fear the worst-case scenario. Indeed, an active debate about how often people should be tested for cancer has been fueled by evidence that such testing produces real anxiety, which itself can lead to health problems.[3] As parents, candidates for public office, and terrorists know, an excellent way to trigger people's concern and to change their beliefs and behavior is to draw attention to the worst imaginable outcome.

Should governments always tell people about the worst-case scenario? Consider this example. The National Environmental Policy Act (NEPA) requires government agencies to discuss the environmental effects of proposed courses of action. By requiring discussion of those effects, NEPA is supposed to have important democratic functions. A plan to build a nuclear power plant in New York or a new highway in Hawaii, or to allow oil drilling in Alaska, could have many environmental consequences. The theory behind NEPA is that before the plan goes forward, the public should be able to learn about those consequences and to have its say. Government attention should itself be focused on those consequences, to ensure that they are not neglected before the final decision is made. Now suppose that the worst-case scenario for one of these projects is truly horrific, though highly unlikely. Must the government discuss it publicly?

In the 1980s, federal courts thought so. In Galveston Bay, Texas, the Army Corps of Engineers proposed to approve an oil distribution center and deepwater port. Many people were troubled by a single question: What would be the effect of a total cargo loss by a supertanker, resulting in a massive oil spill? The government said that it need not investigate that highly improbable outcome. A federal court disagreed, ruling that a worst-case analysis was mandatory under the law.[4] In so saying, it pointed to a federal regulation specifically requiring government to explore worst-case scenarios.

Responding to this decision and others like it, the Council on Environmental Quality, operating under President Ronald Reagan, acted aggressively. It deleted the requirement of worst-case analysis, and it issued a new regulation governing incomplete or unavailable information. The new regulation, still on the books, requires attention only to reasonably foreseeable adverse impacts. For low-probability risks of catastrophe, discussion is required only if "the analysis of the impacts is supported by credible scientific evidence, is not based on pure conjecture, and is within the rule of reason." If we view its decision sympathetically, the government did not want people's imaginations to run wild—or to allow scare tactics, or sheer speculation, to derail legitimate or promising projects. A more skeptical observer would say that the government sought to protect its decisions from public scrutiny by concealing the possibility of real disaster.

Predictably, this regulation was challenged in court. The case involved a development project that had, as a worst-case scenario, the complete devastation of a local herd of mule deer. The Supreme Court upheld the regulation.[5] The Court said that the worst-case requirement had attracted "considerable criticism." If the government discusses a worst-case scenario in public, people might well fixate on it, even if it is most unlikely to come to fruition. If people fixate on that bad outcome, they might have serious qualms about a proposed course of action, even if it promises huge benefits and even if the small risk really should be ignored.

Compare the medical setting, where a doctor's decision to mention the worst-case scenario might lead a patient to refuse an operation that, in the end, is by far the best course of action. The Council on Environmental Quality was trying to ensure that in evaluating government projects, adults think like sensible patients, or like children do when their parents calmly ask them "What's the worst that can happen?"—focusing on realistically likely outcomes, not on wildly speculative ones.

Safe or Unsafe

In deleting the requirement of worst-case analysis, the government was responding to a much broader point about how human beings think. People often treat situations as "safe" or "unsafe," without seeing that the real question is the likelihood of harm. Much of the time, human beings ignore low-probability, high-consequence events, giving them far less attention than they deserve. But when people experience or see a relevant bad outcome, their concern frequently becomes exaggerated. Here we find a basis for both indifference to worst-case scenarios and wild overreactions to them. Consider this remarkable comment from Kai Erikson on the effects of natural disasters:[6]

One of the bargains men make with one another in order to maintain their sanity is to share an illusion that they are safe, even when the physical evidence in the world around them does not seem to warrant that conclusion. The survivors of a disaster, of course, are prone to overestimate the perils of their situation, if only to compensate for the fact that they underestimated those perils once before; but what is worse, far worse, is that they sometimes live in a state of almost constant apprehension because they have lost the human capacity to screen the signs of danger out of their line of vision.

What is most notable about this passage is the sharp division between ordinary people, who "share an illusion that they are safe," and those recently subject to a natural disaster, who "sometimes live in a state of almost constant apprehension." Part of the reason for the illusion of safety is that our judgments about risks are often based on our own experience; and by definition, a low-probability event is one that we are unlikely ever to have encountered. Another factor is that people tend to edit out low-probability risks, treating them as zero-probability risks. Life would be impossible if we focused on the wide range of unlikely disasters that we encounter on a daily or even hourly basis. People who are sensible, or healthy, do not often think about those possible disasters.

The tendency not to dwell on low-probability events is fortified by the human propensity for unrealistic optimism.[7] About 90 percent of drivers believe they are better than the average driver and less likely to be involved in a serious accident.[8] As a result of unrealistic optimism, many low-level risks barely register at all. Unrealistic optimism can also breed best-case thinking even when the probability is ridiculously low. Lotteries are successful partly for this reason. Consider this account: "They didn't really know what the odds—1 in 76 million—mean. Big dreams are easier than big odds; to be precise, in the 11 p.m. drawing, there is only one possible winning combination out of 76,275,360 . . . Clarence Robinson, a manager at Macy's, said: 'One in 76 million people, right? It's just a number. I'll win.'"[9]

A related factor is that people tend to reduce cognitive dissonance by treating low-level risks as if they are insignificant, not worthy of attention. Facing occupational risks, workers often disregard worst cases as a result.[10] When we think we are "safe," even though we face a statistical risk, our judgments might well be motivated by an effort to avoid the anxiety that comes from a daily appreciation of the inevitability of risk and the potential of disaster.

At the individual level, a decision to disregard low-level risks is hardly irrational. Most people lack the information or skill that would permit fine-grained judgments, and when the probability of the worst-case scenario really is low, it may be sensible to treat it as if it were zero. True, people do and should buy insurance against low-probability catastrophes (at least if the price is right); and they should take precautions against some such risks as well. But it is not so bad to "screen the signs of danger out," if only because of the anxiety that will likely be produced by a failure to screen, and because thinking about all worst-case scenarios all of the time is at best unpleasant. We may do much better to consider ourselves "safe" and to disregard small risks, because the distress created by focusing on them outweighs any benefit that might come from acting to reduce their likelihood.

But risks can suddenly come "on screen," making people believe that where they once were safe, they are now unsafe, in the sense that they are threatened by the worst-case scenario. In the United States, the most obvious example is the aftermath of the attacks of 9/11, when many people who ignored the worst-case scenario associated with flying suddenly had that risk very much in view.

Experimental work strongly supports the conclusion that when people are not ignoring worst-case scenarios, they tend to respond excessively to them.[11] Consider the domain of insurance. When the probability of harm is below a certain threshold, people treat the risk as essentially zero. They are willing to pay very little or even nothing for insurance in the event of loss. But when the probability exceeds a certain level, people are willing to pay a significant amount for insurance—an amount that greatly exceeds the expected value of the risk. These responses support the intuitive suggestion that some risks are simply off-screen, whereas others, statistically not much larger, can come on screen and produce big changes in people's behavior. When told that the probability of being killed in an automobile accident is only 0.00000025 per trip, 90 percent of people said that they would not wear seatbelts—a finding apparently based on a judgment that so small a probability is essentially zero.[12]

True, people should wear their seatbelts, if only because doing so is not much trouble, and wearing them can reduce a significant risk over the course of a lifetime. But there is a real difference between the perspectives of individuals and the perspectives of public officials. A worst-case scenario that may be rationally ignored at the individual level (a 1/500,000 risk, say) deserves a good deal of attention when it is faced by 250 million people. Policymakers and regulators, who deal with big populations, must take low probabilities seriously. Even when ordinary people can reasonably treat tiny risks as if they were zero, the analysis is altogether different for those whose business is to reduce risks.

Two Polar Cases

An understanding of how people react to low-probability risks has concrete implications for two of the most important risks of our time: terrorism and climate change. In terms of American reactions, these two threats represent polar cases. The worst-case scenarios associated with terrorism were barely visible on September 10, 2001. But after the attacks of 9/11, they became highly salient and have motivated a great deal of private and public action ever since—some of it necessary, some of it sensible, some of it absurd. The worst-case scenarios associated with climate change, by contrast, have yet to affect the behavior of most American citizens or their national government, notwithstanding prominent and even tireless efforts by those concerned about the problem. In trying to understand the relevant differences here, we should be able to learn a great deal about both private and public reactions to worst-case scenarios.

Both sets of risks are potentially catastrophic.[13] The attacks of 9/11 killed almost three thousand people, an unquestionably large number; but other forms of terrorism, perhaps involving biological or nuclear weapons, could conceivably kill a million people or more.[14] Some of the worst-case scenarios associated with climate change involve many millions of deaths from starvation and disease as a direct or indirect result of warmer temperatures.[15] Human beings face a number of catastrophic risks, but terrorism and climate change rank among the most serious.

The two risks share an additional feature: the difficulty of assigning probabilities to the worst-case outcomes. Officials cannot reasonably say that the risk of a catastrophic terrorist attack in the next ten years is somewhere between, say, 5 percent and 20 percent.[16] According to the One Percent Doctrine sketched by Vice President Cheney, a small chance of a disastrous harm deserves serious attention, in part because we may not be able to know if the risk is truly 1 percent, or 5 percent, or 10 percent, or 20 percent, or 80 percent. What do you think are the chances of a serious terrorist attack in the United States in the next five years? How much confidence do you have in your answer? Specialists are able to do better than most of us, but they too cannot confidently assign probabilities.

Although scientific knowledge is advancing, the picture is not altogether different for climate. In one (admittedly dated) view, the risk of catastrophic effects by 2100 is somewhere between 2 percent and 6 percent.[17] But some people believe that we lack sufficient information to assign a probability to this risk; there are simply too many imponderables.[18] In the case of terrorism and climate change, nations may be operating in the domain of uncertainty rather than risk, in the sense that they are able to identify the worst outcomes without being able to specify the likelihood that they will occur. Both terrorism and climate change, then, present potentially catastrophic threats whose probability cannot be specified with great confidence; and if the worst-case scenarios do come to fruition, they will likely affect many people at the same time.

With respect to terrorism, Americans have been fixated on worst cases. With respect to climate change, on the other hand, Americans have been essentially oblivious to worst cases. What accounts for this difference? As we shall see, terrorism-related risks are likely to attract attention because of three independent factors: cognitive availability, probability neglect, and outrage. Because the attacks of 9/11 are cognitively available and highly salient, many people believe that a future attack is likely. This idea in turn triggers strong emotions, causing many Americans to neglect the question of probability altogether as they focus on the nature of the terrible outcomes. Public fear is heightened by outrage directed toward an identifiable perpetrator, Osama Bin Laden, and his allies.[19] Taken together, fear and outrage are intense visceral emotions that dampen the public's attention to the question of probability.

American politicians have influenced this process. Prominent officials have regularly focused attention on the risk of terrorism, amplifying the salience of the threat and the public's outrage at the initial attacks. Such officials have acted as worst-case entrepreneurs, attempting to ensure that people consider the worst that might happen. They have been exceedingly successful in that regard. Perhaps they have been right to do so; perhaps the nation is significantly safer as a result. Of course, some officials have had a real stake in emphasizing worst-case scenarios. At least in the years immediately following the attacks of 9/11, President George W. Bush, and undoubtedly other Republicans as well, gained in popularity after every reminder, in news coverage and elsewhere, of the terrorism risk—and they gained among Democrats and independents, not merely within their own party.

With respect to climate change, the situation is entirely different. No salient event has heightened public concern, and indeed most people lack personal experience that would make the relevant risks seem immediate or even real, as opposed to speculative and hypothetical.[20] Climate change usually does not trigger strong emotions, and many people wonder whether significant harm is likely. The sources of climate change are obscure and multiple, and they lack faces; hence outrage, which amplifies public reactions to risk, is absent. And to the extent that Americans see *themselves* as contributors to climate change, they are inclined to diminish the magnitude of the danger. The worst-case scenarios are perceived to be far away in both time and space, suffered mostly by people in other nations and over the longer term. For all of these reasons, Americans feel little visceral emotion on the subject of climate change.

Through their words and deeds, national leaders might be able to focus public attention on the risk of climate change. But for the most part they have not yet done so. We can find a few worst-case entrepreneurs in the domain of climate change, but their voices are rarely loud, and the cognitive, social, and political dynamics are not working in their favor.

My goal in this chapter is not to suggest any particular approach to the problems of terrorism and climate change or to endorse any view about how to rank or compare the two problems. Some people believe that terrorism is self-evidently the more serious one, and that climate change poses highly speculative risks for which it is appropriate to "wait and learn."[21] Perhaps the problem of climate change is manageable, exaggerated, or out of our hands. People committed to such judgments may find no puzzle at all in the divergent American reactions. They are simply reasonable.

Those who believe that climate change is self-evidently the more serious problem might be tempted to explain the divergent reactions by reference to the power of well-organized interests in the United States. Perhaps powerful groups, armed with a lot of money, have worked hard and successfully to dampen public concern about climate change. Or perhaps the problem lies in some combination of selfishness, ignorance, myopia, and obtuseness on the part of those responsible for American law and policy. But for present purposes, I put these issues largely to one side and explore the divergent reactions without making any claims about how these risks should be assessed in principle. In due course, I shall have something to say about the appropriate treatment of the two sets of risks, with recommendations for climate change policy in particular.

Whatever one's views about how to assess the two threats, the question of risk perception and the disparate reactions to worst-case scenarios should be interesting for their own sake. It would be most surprising if people's judgments about risks of this kind were unerring or if they closely tracked the most accurate understanding of the facts. Society's demand for risk regulation raises important puzzles of its own; and the supply is affected by the demand. If we are able to understand American reactions to terrorism and climate change, we should be able to learn a lot about risk perception and public fear more generally.

One implication is clear: The United States is unlikely to take significant steps to reduce greenhouse gases unless the perceived costs of risk reduction are much decreased, an available incident triggers fear of significant and imminent harm, or sustained analysis suggests that the risk is very serious. Altruistic or self-interested people, in the private or public sphere, would do well to take these points into account in any effort to increase the likelihood that the public will respond to climate change—or to any other source of alarming worst-case scenarios.

Beliefs and Practices Involving Climate Change

The American public does not want to spend significant resources to reduce greenhouse gases. Of course it expresses general approval, in the abstract, of such reductions. (In the abstract, and without attention to costs, who would disapprove of reducing greenhouse gas emissions?) But most Americans believe that the United States is not at serious risk, certainly in the short-term, and they believe that the real threat is faced by people in other nations. They express little support for large increases in the price of energy or gasoline, even if such increases would reduce the risks associated with climate change.

These statements do not, of course, capture all of the important details.[22] On the one hand, large majorities of Americans were found as early as 2000 to favor the Kyoto Protocol (88 percent), to believe that the United States should reduce its greenhouse gas emissions (90 percent), to support an increase in fuel economy standards (79 percent), and to favor government regulation of carbon dioxide as a pollutant (77 percent).[23] In the same year, a slim majority also supported a tax on "gas guzzlers" (54 percent).[24] Restrictions on power plants, designed to limit greenhouse gas emissions, were strongly supported (61 percent).[25]

On the other hand, strong majorities were opposed to a gasoline tax (78 percent) and to a business energy tax (60 percent) designed to reduce greenhouse gas emissions.[26] In 2000, the environment ranked only sixteenth among the most important problems in the nation; of these, climate change was ranked twelfth of thirteen environmental issues (below urban sprawl).[27] Notwithstanding the vast publicity given to climate change in recent years, polls showed broadly similar conclusions in 2006, with Americans ranking the environment twelfth on a list of the most important problems— below immigration, health care, and gas and heating oil prices. Among environmental problems, climate change was ranked ninth, well below damage to the ozone layer (a problem that has long been handled through regulatory controls).[28] Another 2006 poll found that strong majorities of Americans oppose an increase in taxes on electricity and gasoline as an attempt to reduce climate change.[29]

In the same year, a different poll found that 59 percent of Americans would support an increase in the gasoline tax to reduce the threat of climate change, but the magnitude of the increase was not specified.[30] In late 2005, Americans showed far less concern for environmental disasters than for many other hazards, including attacks on nuclear power plants.[31]

Recent polls continue to show that about 70 percent of Americans support the Kyoto Protocol.[32] But when such polls offer "no opinion" as an option, that option receives about 35 percent support, and the protocol itself is favored by only 42 percent. Remarkably, about 43 percent of Americans in 2006 believed that President George W. Bush supported the protocol; when informed that he opposed it, support dropped from 70 percent to about 48 percent. Asked if "global warming is a significant enough problem such that America should be willing to limit job growth to address it," only 35 percent said yes, while 55 percent said no. Of course, public opinion is not static, and there are some signs that the concern of American citizens has been increasing in recent years. But the percentage of people believing that climate change is "critical" actually decreased from 46 percent in 2002 to 37 percent in 2004, and when people are asked to compare the problem with others, it is rarely even close to the top.

Though Americans show some concern about climate change, they are willing to sacrifice little to reduce the associated risks. Most do not believe that climate change poses a serious threat in the near future, and hence they do not think that they, or their friends and family members, face a real risk in the short-term.[33] About two-thirds of Americans reject the view that climate change will pose a threat in their lifetimes.[34] Americans express some support for programs that, as they perceive them, do not impose costs on the public but pass those costs along to some abstraction such as "companies" or "automobile manufacturers" or "power plants." But when the costs are seen as requiring out-of-pocket expenditures, their enthusiasm for legal controls on greenhouse gases diminishes dramatically.

In 2003, Americans showed less concern about climate change than did the citizens of Germany, Switzerland, Japan, Ireland, Great Britain, Mexico, Brazil, Portugal, Canada, Denmark, Norway, Chile, and Poland.[35] In 2001, citizens in Europe in general and Britain in particular ranked the environment as the largest global threat—above poverty, natural disasters, famine, AIDS/HIV, and even war.[36] A strong majority of Britons (63 percent) polled in 2004 ranked climate change as the most important environmental issue in the world.[37] In the same year, terrorism was ranked as the "most serious threat to the future well-being of the world" by 48 percent of those polled, but global warming came in second, at 25 percent—about double the number for population growth and AIDS/HIV.[38] It is an understatement to say that the issue of climate change has far less salience in the United States. In 2006, Americans were found to have a lower level of concern about climate change than citizens of the fourteen other nations involved; significantly higher rates of concern were shown in Russia, Spain, Nigeria, Japan, India, France, Pakistan, and Turkey, among others.[39]

In terms of legal mandates, the United States has done essentially nothing to reduce the emission of greenhouse gases. The goal of government action to date has been largely to collect information about emissions levels and encourage further research.[40] Under President George W. Bush, one of the nation's principal goals was an 18 percent improvement in greenhouse gas intensity between 2002 and 2012, with intensity measured as emissions per unit of gross domestic product (GDP).[41] But this goal has been an aspiration, not a requirement; and in a growing economy, significant reductions in greenhouse gas intensity can be accompanied by extremely large increases in greenhouse gas emissions.[42]

To be sure, substantial resources are being devoted to research.[43] In recent years, over $5 billion has been appropriated for climate change programs and energy tax incentives.[44] More than $2 billion has specifically been appropriated for the Climate Change Science Program and the Climate Change Research Program, both designed to analyze existing trends and to explore possible solutions.[45] Since 1992, the Department of Energy has been required to estimate aggregate greenhouse gas emissions in the United States, and annual reports are available.[46] These estimates are mandated by the United Nations Framework Convention on Climate Change, signed by the United States; the Framework Convention includes no emissions reduction mandates, in large part because the United States strenuously resisted them.

One of the more ambitious current programs involves company-by-company reporting of actions taken to reduce greenhouse gas emissions, but this program itself remains voluntary,[47] in sharp contrast to the reporting requirements in other federal legislation.[48] The United States lacks a company-by-company Greenhouse Gas Inventory, comparable to the Toxic Release Inventory that has played such a large role in reducing toxic emissions.[49] At the international level, the most aggressive program in which the United States now participates is the "methane to markets" agreement,[50] but it makes only a modest contribution to greenhouse gas reductions.[51] No regulatory limits are imposed on greenhouse gases from fossil fuels, motor vehicles, or any other source, notwithstanding efforts to persuade the government to impose such limits.

State and local governments have been undertaking some action on their own. In December 2005, the governors of seven states signed a Memorandum of Understanding, designed to create a regional "cap-and-trade" plan to reduce power plant emissions.[52] The mayors of over two hundred cities, comprising over 43 million Americans, have pledged to meet city-level goals corresponding with the requirements of the Kyoto Protocol.[53] In June 2005, Governor Arnold Schwarzenegger pledged to reduce California's greenhouse gas emissions to 1990 levels by 2020, a pledge that helped produce the West Coast Governor's Global Warming Initiative, which includes California, Washington, and Oregon.[54] California has enacted legislation to reduce emissions of greenhouse gases from automobiles, with a 22 percent reduction target by 2012 and a 30 percent reduction target by 2016. In 2006, California enacted legislation that would require state-wide emissions to be capped at 1990 levels by 2025—a step that would require a 25 percent cut from the levels that would be expected without regulation.

These various initiatives go well beyond the actions of the national government, and it remains a puzzle why some state and local governments are so much more concerned about the problem than federal officials. One possibility is that in some parts of the country citizens are genuinely alarmed about climate change and willing to reward leaders who propose to do something about it. In California, Governor Schwarzenegger may well have found that his popularity, and his prospects for reelection, were enhanced by taking a strong stand in favor of regulation. Another possibility is that the relevant measures are largely symbolic; and even if more than that, they may be unlikely to inflict significant costs on citizens. In California, citizens and officials may be optimistic about the ability to achieve reductions without imposing real burdens; they may also be aware that if burdens turn out to be real, California's legislature will relax its mandates. The important point is that, taken as a whole, measures now proposed by state and local governments are not projected to reduce emissions by a significant amount.

Perhaps unsurprisingly, greenhouse gas emissions in the United States have been increasing in the very period when climate change has received attention both domestically and abroad. Greenhouse gas emissions went up no less than 15.8 percent between 1990 and 2004.[55] In 1990, carbon dioxide emissions were 5,002.3 million metric tons; in 2004, they were 5,973.0 million metric tons, a jump of 19 percent. To be sure, greenhouse gas *intensity* has declined a significant 21 percent in the same period. But because of greater energy use, per capita emissions have actually risen over this period by 1.2 percent—an increase that, alongside population growth, accounts for the rise in aggregate emissions.

Fossil fuel combustion is by far the largest contributor to greenhouse gas emissions in the United States, accounting for 98 percent of carbon dioxide emissions. Greenhouse gas emissions from fossil fuels have been growing in most sectors, with a 1.7 percent increase between 2003 and 2004. While methane emissions were reduced by 10 percent in 2004, total greenhouse gas emissions increased by 1.7 percent in the same year, the largest increase on record from any nation. All the principal sectors—residential, commercial, industrial, and transportation-related uses—remain free from national regulation.

By contrast, in Bulgaria, Estonia, Latvia, the Czech Republic, Lithuania, Hungary, Poland, Russia, Ukraine, Iceland, Luxembourg, the United Kingdom, Sweden, and Germany, substantial reductions in greenhouse gas emissions occurred between 1990 and 2003. As we shall see in Chapter 2, the reductions in these nations conceal some important complexities. But one fact is simple enough: The United States has not taken any significant steps to diminish greenhouse gas emissions.

Beliefs and Practices about Terrorism

With terrorism, the picture is altogether different. After the 9/11 attacks, the risk of terrorism has been consistently ranked among the most pressing problems facing the United States.[56] With respect to the war on terror, Americans disagree on a great deal. But they agree that the risk of terrorism is both serious and real, and they favor expensive precautions to reduce that risk. In 2006, the Pew Research Center found that defending the nation from terrorism was a "top priority" for 80 percent of Americans—a higher percentage than for any other problem.[57] In the period shortly after the 9/11 attacks, 88 percent of Americans believed that it was either very likely or somewhat likely that there would be "another terrorist attack within the next few months"—with about half of Americans worrying about the possibility that a family member might "become a victim of a terrorist attack," and over 40 percent worrying that "terrorist attacks might take place where [they] live or work."[58]

Later studies have continued to show a high level of concern, with many people believing that an imminent attack is likely.[59] In August 2006, nearly half of respondents described themselves as "somewhat" or "very" worried that they, or someone in their family, would be a victim of terrorism.[60] Nearly half also said that it was somewhat or very likely that there would be a terrorist attack in the United States "in the next several weeks." In 2006, there was actually an increase, from the year before, in the percentage of Americans saying that they were "very worried or somewhat worried" that they or someone in their family would "become a victim of terrorism."[61] The level of concern is lower now than it was in the immediate aftermath of the 9/11 attacks, but public fear will leap again if any future attack occurs.[62] Americans believe they face a serious threat of a terrorist attack in the not-distant future, and they fear that their loved ones are at risk. This belief makes Americans quite willing to support substantial measures to reduce the terrorist threat.

With strong backing from public opinion, the federal government has taken massive steps to reduce terrorism-related risks. Vice President Cheney's One Percent Doctrine captures much of the nation's actual practice. The most expensive measures have been the wars in Afghanistan and Iraq. As of September 2005, $212 billion had been allocated from the United States Treasury for the war in Iraq, and aggregate costs were estimated at $255 billion to the United States, $40 billion to Coalition partners, and $134 billion to Iraq, for a total global cost of $428 billion.[63] As of May 1, 2006, the appropriations were nearing $300 billion[64]—ensuring that the cost of the Iraq War to the United States has now surpassed the total expected cost of the Kyoto Protocol, which, based on plausible assumptions, would have been $325 billion.[65] Of course the motivations for the Iraq war are contested and numerous; my only point is that without the perceived threat to the United States, the nation would not have supported it. There is a great deal more in the way of costly activity, including new legislation[66] and numerous regulations.[67] For present purposes, the details are not important. What matters is that the government is attuned to worst-case scenarios, and it is willing to expend a great deal, in the way of energy and resources, to ensure that they do not come to fruition.

Beliefs and Regulation

Divergent judgments about climate change and terrorism help to account for governmental behavior. Of course there are many possible relationships between public attitudes and official responses (see Table 1). We can easily imagine cases in which both the public and its representatives insist on risk reduction, especially if the focus is on worst-case scenarios. After the attacks of 9/11, this was certainly the case with the war on terror. The same can plausibly be said about certain steps to reduce air pollution.[68] In other contexts, such as acid deposition (sometimes called "acid rain"), the public does not demand risk reduction, but officials favor it; they are permitted to take certain steps because the public does not oppose

Table 1 Relationships between public attitudes and official responses.

	Officials want risk reduction	Officials do not want risk reduction
Public demands risk reduction	War on terror after 9/11	Superfund legislation (governing abandoned hazardous waste dumps)
Public does not demand risk reduction	Controls on ozone-depleting chemicals; acid deposition regulation	Controls on greenhouse gases; airline security before 9/11

them, and electoral retribution is unlikely.[69] With respect to ozone-depleting chemicals, the public did not exactly demand regulation, but public interest in it was considerable, and officials acted in a way that reflected public concern (see Chapter 2).

Very different issues arise when the public demands some kind of regulatory response that officials would not favor on their own. The Superfund statute, designed to regulate abandoned hazardous waste sites, is a case in point. The publicity given to the apparent disaster at Love Canal in the 1970s made a statutory response almost inevitable, even though some officials were opposed, either publicly or privately.[70] In a famous episode in the 1990s, the public once again favored environmental regulation, this time because of the health hazards allegedly associated with the pesticide Alar, which was sprayed on apple trees and had been detected in apple juice.[71]

But sometimes neither the public nor officials demand a response to a real or apparent risk. This is a plausible account of the recent situation with respect to climate change, and it certainly explains the state of airport security before the 9/11 attacks. At that time, not many people, in or out of government, were arguing for more stringent security measures at airports. The fact that the 9/11 terrorists could get concealed box cutters through metal detectors or baggage x-ray machines indicates how lax security had become.[72]

Of course these stylized categories ignore important variations. We can identify cases in which the public does not merely fail to demand risk reduction but would affirmatively punish risk reduction efforts at the polls. Aggressive security measures at airports before 9/11 would probably have fallen into this category, simply because such measures would have been deemed a significant and unnecessary inconvenience in response to a highly speculative threat. By 2000, the hijackings of the 1970s and 1980s were mostly forgotten, and the risk seemed at best abstract. Any effort to impose restrictions of the sort that have become customary today would have seemed ludicrous and invasive. When citizens face a large burden from risk reduction, they and their government tend to ignore or downplay worst-case scenarios. Many citizens would almost certainly resist a large increase in the gasoline tax, even if the increase were defended by reference to environmental concerns, energy self-sufficiency, or some combination of the two.

We can also imagine cases in which officials would seek to block regulation even if the public demands it, or would insist on a more tepid, less costly, and more symbolic response than the public would like. When the public became concerned about toxic releases from chemical plants, for example, the legislative response involved disclosure requirements rather than regulatory controls. We could also imagine cases in which the public helps to spur regulation, perhaps through consumer behavior that reduces its cost, but in a way that does not exactly conflict with the desires of officials.

The category of "officials" contains a great deal of diversity. In Table 1, the term is meant to refer to those with some kind of formal position, and thus includes mayors, governors, presidents, national and state legislators, and bureaucrats in various levels of government. Disagreements or even conflicts arise among state and national governments, and career bureaucrats often hold different opinions from elected officials, as indeed they did in the case of both national security and climate change.

And of course the public itself is hardly monolithic. Within the United States, the citizens of California have been unusually concerned about the risks of climate change. Internal divisions among the citizenry can greatly complicate the political economy of risk reduction, not least when well-organized private groups move government responses in their preferred directions. In the context of terrorism, the airline industry played a significant role in preventing more extensive security procedures before 9/11.[73] Powerful organizations have also discouraged aggressive measures to control greenhouse gas emissions.[74]

Public opinion is affected by the acts of both officials and well-organized groups, and it shifts over time, often in response to the statements and actions of influential people in the private and public sectors. Worst-case campaigns waged in the media can diminish or heighten public concern by manipulating the variables of availability, probability neglect, and outrage. In the aftermath of 9/11, leaders could have dampened the public's concern, especially as time passed, by giving assurances that the risk of another attack was low and by comparing terrorism-related risks to those encountered in ordinary life. Even in 2001, for example, Americans were fifteen times more likely to die in a motor vehicle accident than as a result of a terrorist attack; seven times more likely to die of alcohol-related causes; five times more likely to die of HIV; and five times more likely to die as a result of accidental poisoning or exposure to toxic substances. Since the 1960s, the number of Americans killed by international terrorism is about the same as the number killed by lightning or by accidents caused by deer.

American leaders did not emphasize these facts. President Bush instead pointed to worst-case scenarios, suggesting that we are "still not safe" and that ours is "a nation in danger."[75] By contrast, other nations, including Israel, have to some extent "normalized" terrorism-related risks for the general population. Tourists often react far more dramatically to violent events than do people who regularly live in the affected area.[76]

To be sure, "normalizing" airplanes that fly into tall buildings, killing thousands of people, is much more difficult than "normalizing" suicide bombers, whose destructive acts are fairly localized. But in the war on terror, prominent officials have played a large role in activating public concern, invoking the 9/11 attacks to stress the need for protective measures. Whether or not such measures are justified, they make a contribution of their own to the beliefs and desires of the public. Aggressive security measures at airports, for example, may well serve to intensify public fear in a way that can heighten the demand for further precautions.

With respect to climate change, most influential national leaders, far from activating concern, have attempted to downplay it. Of course the malleability of public opinion has its limits, and terrorism is far more likely to trigger visceral fear than is climate change. Nevertheless, we can imagine a situation in which the objective facts were the same but the responses of American leaders were different. Under these conditions, the public's concern about climate change might increase, and its worry about terrorism might decrease, to the point where attitudes are not quite so divergent. Public opinion is a product in part of the simple facts of the situation—above all, the fact of the 9/11 attacks—but also of political responses to the underlying risks.

Benefits, Costs, and Rational Choice

When thinking about risk and its regulation, citizens engage in at least some kind of weighing of costs and benefits. If people conclude that they have a lot to gain and little to lose from taking precautions against worst-case scenarios, they will favor precautions. Leaders will respond to what citizens believe, though their judgments will be influenced by a separate analysis of their own. Perhaps the cost-benefit ratio is simply higher for reducing certain terrorist threats than for reducing the risks of climate change. Let us see if we can explain Americans' divergent reactions to terrorism and climate change in this way.

Benefits   Americans might well believe that they have far more to gain from efforts to reduce the risks of terrorism than from efforts to reduce the risks of climate change. Perhaps they think that catastrophic worst-case scenarios are more likely for the former than for the latter. Much depends on the specific measures proposed, of course. But the simplest claim here would be that even if significant climate change is already occurring, its effects will not be truly significant in the United States.[77] If we doubt the risk of serious harm, we might well resist regulatory responses. Perhaps the best response to existing concerns involves continued research, especially if little is gained by acting now rather than a few years from now.[78]

With respect to terrorism, by contrast, it is senseless to say that the risk is not real or that the threat is too speculative to warrant immediate action. Particular risk-reduction strategies might be questioned—on the ground, for example, that certain surveillance programs will not significantly reduce the chance of terrorist attack and that whatever information is gained is more than offset by a loss of civil liberties.[79] But it is hard to argue that the best approach to terrorism is "learn, then act."

By contrast, current evidence strongly suggests that Americans believe they have relatively little to gain from efforts to control climate change. In 2006, a large majority of Americans said both that climate change is "already happening" and that it does not pose a "serious threat" to them or their way of life.[80] In 2000, a sample of people was asked, "Which of the following are you most concerned about? The impacts of climate change on . . . (1) you and your family; (2) your local community; (3) the U.S. as a whole; (4)

people all over the world; (5) non-human nature; or (6) not at all concerned."[81] Nearly 70 percent of respondents answered (4) or (5), and only 13 percent answered (1) or (2). In the view of most Americans, the principal risks are faced by those in other nations, or future generations, or the environment in general.[82] The immediate health effects of climate change are not believed to be large enough to motivate behavior.

In a cross-national study of perceptions of risk associated with terrorism, Americans estimated their *personal* chance of serious harm from terrorism in the next year as 8.27 percent—a significant risk.[83] For the average healthy American, even the most serious mortality risks are far lower than that. About 40,000 people die annually from automobile accidents in each year, for example, meaning that the average American faces a mortality risk of 1 in 7,500, or .015 percent. The 8.27 percent figure is almost certainly wildly inflated,[84] but if Americans believe they face a personal risk of this magnitude from terrorism in the next year, aggressive protective measures will be forthcoming.

For climate change, Americans perceive the risk as far lower. The findings of some specialists support this view. For example, a respected study in 2000 found that extremely little would be lost by a ten-year delay in emissions reductions.[85] Perhaps this judgment was wrong or is now out of date.[86] But even if it is wrong, doubts about the personal benefits of policies to reduce climate change help to explain divergent public reactions. The pattern of regulation is influenced by this fact.

Costs Perhaps those who show greater concern about terrorism believe, at least intuitively, that the costs of controlling climate change are likely to be very high—far higher than the costs of reducing the threat of terrorism. When costs are visible, the argument for responding to worst-case scenarios is weakened, and people are likely to seek extremely good evidence that these low-probability events are worth worrying about.

Cost comparisons are difficult in the abstract, and everything depends on the particular steps at issue. The Iraq War has turned out to be extremely expensive, easily exceeding $300 billion for the United States alone and dwarfing the expected cost of the Kyoto Protocol. We can imagine a few modest steps to control greenhouse gases that would have been quite cheap. But at the time the decision was made to invade Iraq, perhaps the public believed that significant reductions in the risk of terrorism could be undertaken at a reasonable cost—in light of the perceived immediacy of the threat—and perhaps people do not think this is true of steps to limit climate change. In this kind of informal cost-benefit analysis of risk reduction, the public's perception of the magnitude of the likely costs is doing a great deal of work.

In the late 1990s, about 63 percent of Americans agreed with the following statement: "Protecting the environment is so important that requirements and standards cannot be too high and continuing environmental improvements must be made regardless of cost."[87] In the same vein, 59 percent supported the Kyoto Protocol, with only 21 percent opposed.[88] But 52 percent of Americans said that they would refuse to support the Kyoto Protocol if it would cost an extra $50 per month for an average American household.[89] And only 11 percent of Americans would support the treaty if the monthly expense rose to $100 or more.[90] How can we explain strong majority support for environmental improvements "regardless of cost" and strong majority rejection of those improvements when the cost is high?

The answer lies in the fact that people are not, in fact, willing to spend an infinite amount for environmental improvements.

When the costs are squarely placed in front of them, people begin to weigh costs and benefits, and their enthusiasm for regulatory expenditures diminishes. Americans believe that car companies should be required to take steps to reduce greenhouse gas emissions, but they are not willing to spend much, if anything, on increased gasoline prices. Surveys in Europe suggest that significant numbers of citizens are willing to pay something to reduce the risks of climate change, but even there the amount is not extremely high.[91] Among all people between the age of 15 and 64, only about 20 percent are willing to pay more for gasoline to reduce environmental harm, and among that group the average willingness to pay is an increase of 2.4 percent, or 11.5 cents per liter.

If the risk of climate change could be significantly reduced for $10 million, or with an annual tax increase of $1 on every American, much more would be done to combat climate change. In the 1990 Clean Air Act, the government's extremely aggressive steps to control acid deposition became possible only after the creation of an ambitious emissions trading program that reduced the anticipated costs of emissions controls; hence those who would otherwise be inclined to oppose the program found it acceptable.[92] For citizens as well as leaders, an intuitive assessment of costs and benefits plays a large role in determining the level of precautions actually sought.

American costs, foreign benefits   The most serious damage from climate change is not expected to be felt in the United States.[93] According to some estimates, American agriculture will actually be a net winner as a result of climate change.[94] In other accounts, Americans as a whole will be net losers, but not nearly to the extent of other nations.[95] These estimates square with public perceptions, for Americans believe that other nations have more to lose from climate change than the United States does, and this belief affects their willingness to pay for regulatory protections. A "revealed preference" study of American taxation and foreign aid suggests that Americans value a non-American life in the poorest nations at 1/2000 of the value they put on an American life.[96] If Americans believe that people in India and South Africa, rather than in Florida and New York, are at serious risk, they will be far less likely to act.

Some systematic analyses suggest that indeed the United States stands to lose much more, and to gain much less, from aggressive regulation than European nations do.[97] The particular numbers are disputed, of course, but a prominent study finds that for the United States, the likely costs of the Kyoto Protocol greatly exceed its likely benefits.[98] The picture for the world as a whole is complicated, with Europe anticipated to be a net gainer and Russia likely to gain an especially large amount.[99] Those nations that have shown enthusiasm for the Kyoto Protocol are responding in large part to the fact that they expect to gain a great deal and to spend relatively little. Almost all Eastern European nations have easily met their obligations under the Kyoto Protocol, because their emissions allowances greatly exceed their likely emissions.[100] When the costs of managing behavior are so low, regulation seems attractive, assuming that leaders and citizens believe that the risks of failing to take action are real.

At the present time, some influential people believe that the United States will be able to handle the costs of climate change as it occurs, and that expensive precautions are hard to justify simply from the standpoint of national interest. If this is so, then intuitive cost-benefit balancing helps to explain the official position of the government. Looked at in this way, aggressive regulation seems to be a way of benefiting other countries, one that is not self-evidently in the interest of the United States. Precautions against terrorism are another matter. While other nations are likely to benefit, the principal beneficiary of these protections is the United States itself.

Present costs, future benefits   Consider the following question: "Do you think climate change is an urgent problem that requires immediate government action, or a longer-term problem that requires more study before government action is taken?" Many more Americans believe that the problem is "longer-term" than believe it is "urgent."[101] They think the largest costs of risk reduction will be felt immediately, whereas the benefits will be received mostly by people in the future. Whatever their stated moral commitments, citizens are usually unwilling to pay a great deal to help those who will follow them. Perhaps they assume that if risks will not be incurred for many decades, they might not be incurred at all, simply because technological advances will provide a currently unforeseen solution. Perhaps they are being unrealistically optimistic, or reducing cognitive dissonance, by believing that a probabilistic harm in the future will not come to fruition at all, or will not be particularly bad if it does.

Perhaps current citizens are rationally discounting the future, believing that harms in fifty years do not deserve the same attention as harms today, simply because a dollar now is worth more than a dollar in a half-century. Perhaps they are using an implausibly high discount rate to assess future benefits. Or they might be simply self-interested, treating future generations as a kind of foreign country. Thomas Schelling argues that "greenhouse gas abatement is a foreign aid program, not a saving-investment problem of the familiar kind."[102] If political actors are responsive to their citizens, they are unlikely to impose high current costs for long-term gains. By the time the largest benefits of risk reduction are generally felt by the public, those politicians will be out of office and indeed long dead.

Here, then, is a big difference between the risk of terrorism and the risk of climate change. Every politician has a strong incentive to take steps to prevent terrorist attacks. If such an attack occurs "on my watch," the likelihood of political reprisal is high. The danger of such an attack is immediate. By contrast, a climate-related "incident" on the watch of any current politician is an unlikely possibility. Hurricanes are perhaps a counterexample, but whether any particular hurricane is a product of climate change is a subject for debate. To justify public concern, or the imposition of immediate costs, such a politician must trigger moral commitments, which may not be so easy to do. If moral commitments do not operate as an impetus for costly controls, a politician who attempts to regulate greenhouse gases might be imposing costs on current voters for the benefit of future people who will never be able to reward that particular politician with their electoral support. Such politicians might well be heroic, or may have an eye on the judgments of history; but statesmen of that particular sort are rare.

Rational choice?   We now have the ingredients of a tempting explanation for divergent American reactions to terrorism and climate change. With respect to climate change, many people dispute the benefits of aggressive regulation and see the costs as high, certainly for the United States. The benefits are perceived as likely to be enjoyed disproportionately by other nations and not in the near future. The analysis is very different for terrorism, where Americans are painfully aware of the worst-case scenarios, perceive themselves as peculiarly at risk compared with other nations, and believe that the benefits of risk reduction will be felt in the United States and by current generations. For some efforts to reduce the risk of terrorism, Americans have raised serious questions about whether the benefits justify the costs; but they agree that many expensive measures are worthwhile.

But this explanation is far from adequate. On September 10, 2001, terrorism was hardly a high-priority item for Americans. Indeed, the year before the attacks, literally zero percent of the public counted terrorism as the nation's leading problem.[103] By contrast, many specialists believed, for a period preceding the attack, that the risk of terrorism was foolishly neglected in light of a rational assessment of costs and benefits—and hence that the 9/11 attacks were a kind of "predictable surprise."[104] In this view, the neglect was a product of "unavailability bias," in which the absence of readily available incidents of harm made people unreasonably indifferent to the risk. The worst-case scenario was foolishly ignored. Yet in the eighteen months following the 9/11 attacks, between 15 and 20 percent of the public continued to name terrorism as the nation's most important problem—and the "fluctuations closely track[ed] the frequency of television news stories concerning terrorism."[105] Here, too, is a tribute to the power of cognitive availability.

Maybe the post-9/11 reaction is simply a form of rational updating, or rethinking, on the part of Americans; the attacks themselves certainly provided new information about the immediacy and magnitude of the threat. In the case of ordinary citizens, this account is plausible. But as an explanation for the behavior of the United States government, much more was involved, because officials had the information to justify quite aggressive security measures well before 9/11. To understand the missing ingredients, we must venture into the realm of human cognition.

Rational Fear and Emotional Responses

Judgments about risks come through two different pathways.[106] Often people's judgments are rooted in their own experience. Has a bad outcome come to fruition in the recent past? Has that outcome been experienced personally—as in an encounter with violent crime or a brush with serious illness? If an outcome has not been experienced personally, is it nonetheless highly visible in the media or a subject of daily conversation? Alternatively, judgments might emerge from statistical accounts of one or another kind. People might learn, for example, that a shift to a diet low in cholesterol can decrease the risk of heart disease by 10 percent, or that a reduction in sulfur dioxide emissions is likely to reduce asthma attacks by 40 percent, or that lowered sun exposure is likely to decrease the risk of skin cancer by 30 percent. While people's judgments are affected by both of these pathways, personal experience is typically far more effective in motivating behavior.

Here is an autobiographical example. I have a serious allergy to shrimp, crab, and lobster. The allergy was discovered in early childhood, in an incident that I cannot remember. As a child and an adult, I simply avoided these foods, never suffering an allergic reaction. A few years ago, I ordered a vegetarian dish at a pretty bad Chinese restaurant in Wisconsin and had to be rushed to the hospital with a life-threatening breathing problem. Apparently seafood had been mixed with the vegetables. Since that experience, my allergy has played a far more prominent role in my food choices—by, for example, making me reluctant to order vegetarian dishes at perfectly good Chinese restaurants. Sometimes I am ridiculously risk averse—declining to eat dishes that, realistically speaking, are entirely seafood-free. On occasion I will feel a shot of alarm after eating something that is assuredly not seafood but that somehow reminds me of shrimp or crab. Before the incident a few years ago, my decisions were based on a calm and essentially sensible statistical analysis. A memorable personal experience now plays a key role in what even I can see as pretty odd thoughts and behavior.

The difference between judgments based on experience and judgments based on analysis has been linked to two "systems" of cognitive operations by which human beings evaluate risky situations.[107] System I is fast, associative, and intuitive; System II is slow, deliberative, and analytic. The two systems may well have different locations in the human brain.[108] The whole field of neuroeconomics, which focuses on fear in particular, attempts to investigate that question. Current findings suggest that the amygdala—located deep within the temporal lobes—makes people alert to danger before the prefrontal cortex gets involved.[109]

The underlying neuroscience is not undisputed, but the distinction between the two systems is useful whether or not identifiable brain structures are involved. The central point is that people have immediate and often visceral reactions to products, activities, and situations, and the immediate reaction operates as a mental shortcut for a more deliberative or analytic assessment of the underlying issues. Sometimes the shortcut can be overridden, or corrected, by System II.

A worst-case scenario that triggers System I is particularly likely to influence the conduct of both consumers and voters. In fact, System I is often the source of worst-case thinking. It might lead people to be terrified of flying in airplanes or of large dogs. Once System II becomes involved, it might create a deliberative check, ensuring an eventual conclusion that the risks are trivial. My own reaction to what-is-probably-not-but-might-conceivably-be-shrimp is easily understood in these terms. System I may fasten attention on worst-case scenarios, leading people to take special steps to avoid them. System II can help them see that the likelihood of a terrible outcome is actually quite low—not worth extensive precautions.

Alternatively, System I might be relatively unconcerned with a worst-case scenario, because visceral reactions are not triggered; a System II analysis may be required to motivate action. System I might not respond to the risks associated with sunbathing, but System II might cause people to avoid sun exposure after some kind of analysis of the risk. System I might not be alarmed by the prospect of catastrophic climate change, or genocide in Darfur, but System II might try hard to kick System I into action; and even if it fails, System II can produce some action on its own.

Considerable evidence suggests that immediate emotional reactions often help to explain people's response to risks. Reports about "mad cow disease," for example, produce far more fear in the public than reports about bovine-spongiform encephalopathy (BSE) or Creutzfeldt-Jacob disease (CJD)—both variants of this rare condition. The two more formal, less graphic descriptions of the disease dampen concern.[110]

When asked to assess the risks and benefits associated with certain items, people tend to say that risky activities provide low benefits and that beneficial activities create low risks. Consider the case of nuclear power. Those who believe that the risks of nuclear power are high often believe that its benefits are small; those who believe that its benefits are large often believe that its risks are low. An emotional reaction to nuclear power may well come first and help to direct judgments of both risk and benefit.[111] When people are asked to make these assessments under time pressure, the inverse correlation between benefit judgments and risk judgments is even more pronounced, with people all the more likely to say that nuclear power is low benefit/high risk or high benefit/low risk rather than low benefit/low risk or high benefit/high risk.[112] And when people are told about the high benefits of some activity or item, such as nuclear power or pesticides, they tend to conclude that the risks are therefore low (even when they are provided with absolutely no information about risks).[113] These findings strongly suggest that System I is at work when people are making judgments about risk levels.[114]

For many Americans, the idea of terrorism conjures up intense images of disaster, as the idea of climate change does not.[115] White House officials under President Bush asked executive personnel to use the term "climate change" in preference to "global warming," evidently believing that "climate change" is more abstract and neutral than "global warming"—though the latter does not appear to be especially frightening to most people.[116] Warmer may even be better, especially during a rough winter in Chicago or Boston. By contrast, the 9/11 attacks made the terrorist threat easy to imagine and in an important sense quite personal.

Of course emotional responses are not simply given; they have sources. We could easily imagine a society, not unrecognizably different from our own, in which terrorism produces far less concern than it now does and in which climate change produces far more. If events potentially related to climate change were familiar and salient, and if events related to terrorism were not, the divergence in reactions would run in the opposite direction. We do not have to use our imagination to see this: Before the attacks of 9/11, Americans were not much worried about terrorism; and among some groups of Americans, climate change already produces intense concern, almost certainly equal to or greater than that associated with terrorism.

To understand why this inversion is unusual, we need to examine some details about how, exactly, terrorism produces an acute reaction and climate change does not. The explanation involves greater attention to three factors that I have briefly mentioned: availability, probability neglect, and outrage.

Availability

In thinking about risks, people rely on certain rules of thumb ("heuristics") that serve to simplify their inquiry.[117] When using these mental short-cuts, people answer a hard question by substituting an easier one.[118] Should Americans be fearful of hurricanes, nuclear power, AIDS, mad cow disease, alligator attacks, sniper attacks, or avian flu? To answer this question, people try to think of relevant examples.[119] If images of the threat come easily to mind, people are far more likely to be frightened and concerned than if they do not. Consider a simple study showing people a list of well-known people of both sexes and asking them whether the list contains more names of women or more names of men. In lists in which the men were especially famous, people thought there were more names of men, whereas in lists in which the women were more famous, people thought there were more names of women.[120]

A risk that is familiar, like terrorist attacks in the aftermath of 9/11, will be seen as more serious than a risk that is less familiar, like the diabetes risk associated with obesity. The salience of the threat is important as well. Seeing a family's house burning down has much more impact on our reactions than reading about it in the newspaper.[121] Because tornadoes are an easily imagined cause of death, people think they cause far more harm than less vivid causes of death, such as asthma attacks, which in fact occur with a far greater frequency (here a factor of 20).[122] So too, recent events have far more impact than do those that have receded into the past.

When rare events actually occur, they often have a far greater effect on people's subsequent decisions than can be justified by objective analysis.[123] But when rare events are merely possible, and have not yet occurred, people's behavior is far less affected than an objective analysis warrants. The reason is that the events are, by definition, rare—and not having encountered them, people conclude that such events can be safely ignored. Reacting to their personal experience, people show a pattern of both underreaction and overreaction to rare events, with the overreaction occurring in the immediate aftermath of a personal encounter with the threat.

Whether people buy insurance for natural disasters is greatly affected by recent experiences.[124] If floods have not occurred in the immediate past, people who live on flood plains are far less likely to purchase flood insurance.[125] In the aftermath of an earthquake, insurance for earthquakes rises sharply, but it declines steadily from that point forward, as vivid memories recede.[126] For disaster planning in general, personal experience is a good predictor of whether people will take precautionary steps.[127] One study found that personal involvement in a previous evacuation was the strongest predictor of whether households would evacuate in hurricanes Hugo and Andrew.[128] Those who have experienced disasters were more willing to believe they were personally at risk.[129] They were also more likely to make adaptive plans.[130]

But personal experience can also lead people to assume, wrongly, that all will be well. While households that had been in the direct path of Hurricane Andrew were much more likely to plan to evacuate during subsequent hurricane threats, those in a high-risk area that Andrew narrowly missed showed an increased likelihood to ignore evacuation orders for later storms.[131]

Some studies suggest that personal experience is less important than what has been called hazard intrusiveness—the frequency with which a hazard is thought about and discussed.[132] Even after an event has occurred, it may not be salient if people's attention is diverted by the ordinary events and concerns of daily life. But if a threat is made salient through social interactions, media attention, or other means, mitigation and preparatory measures are more likely. The likelihood of evacuation in the face of hurricane warnings is strongly correlated not with general predisaster concern but with the extent to which recipients of a warning believe they will be personally harmed.[133] Because of unrealistic optimism and people's tendency to have an illusion of control over hazards, an available example may well be a necessary way to trigger a fear of personal harm. A clear implication is that vivid pictures of previous storm damage may well be a good way of promoting precautionary measures.

An illuminating study, with important implications for divergent reactions to terrorism and climate change, attempted to test the effects of imagery on perceived judgments of risk.[134] The study asked subjects to read about an illness (Hyposcenia-B) that "was becoming increasingly prevalent" on the local campus. In one condition, the symptoms were vague and hard to imagine, involving an inflamed liver, a malfunctioning nervous system, and a general sense of disorientation. In another condition, the symptoms were concrete and easy to imagine, involving muscle aches, low energy, and frequent severe headaches. People were asked to visualize a three-week period in which they had the disease and to write a detailed description of what they imagined. After doing so, people were asked to assess, on a ten-point scale, their likelihood of contracting the disease. Probability judgments were very different in the two groups: People with the easily-imagined symptoms were far more inclined to believe they might get the disease.

During the SARS scare, Americans perceived terrorism to be a far greater threat to themselves and others than SARS; Canadians perceived SARS to be a greater threat to themselves and others than terrorism.[135] At the time the study was done, Canadians had experienced no incidents of terrorism but several cases of SARS, whereas Americans had experienced a serious terrorist attack but no cases of SARS. People seem to believe, not irrationally, that what has happened before is often the best guide to what will happen again.[136] But this kind of thinking can lead to excessive fear or excessive neglect. The problem of neglect is especially serious when citizens face a potentially catastrophic risk that has not come to fruition in the recent past.[137]

If availability plays a large role in people's risk-related judgments, then we might have a simple explanation for the asymmetry in American reactions to terrorism and climate change: The vividness of the attacks of 9/11 drives people's probability judgments about terrorism, whereas no such incident caused by climate change is available to them. Consider what would have happened if in 2000 a candidate for public office had made the risk of terrorism a central issue in a political campaign. Voters would have thought the candidate had an odd sense of priorities—focusing on a distant and un-realistic possibility that did not resonate in any way. Or suppose that in 2000 a member of Congress had aggressively argued for much of the same legislation that followed the attacks of 9/11, including the Patriot Act, increased security measures at airports, and new presidential authority to detain suspected terrorists for years without trial. Congress would have immediately rejected any such effort; and any legislator who argued for it would probably have been characterized as an alarmist and a serious threat to civil liberties. In 2000 the public was no more focused on terrorism-related risks than on the risks associated with climate change. The attacks of 9/11 made all the difference.

Risk-reduction legislation is often fueled by identifiable crises that bring worst-case scenarios vividly to mind. A chemical accident at Bhopal, India, focused media attention on safety issues and led members of Congress to pass right-to-know legislation calling for disclosure of toxic releases.[138] The relevant legislation could not possibly have been enacted without the highly publicized Bhopal disaster.[139] Corporate Average Fuel Economy (CAFE) standards, requiring improved gas mileage for motor vehicles, were a product of the Arab oil embargo and the nationally publicized "energy crisis" of the late 1970s; without the crisis, the fuel economy legislation would have been unimaginable.[140]

Often the available incidents are a product of presentations by influential actors. *Silent Spring* by Rachel Carson helped to inspire the entire environmental movement, including legislation to impose national controls on pesticides and other threats to the natural environment.[141] With its vivid narratives of the harm caused by pesticides to birds and other wildlife, Carson's book may well have played a role in establishing the Environmental Protection Agency.[142] Carson did not offer a dry analysis of the costs and benefits of pesticides; she made particular events highly salient to her readers.

Within the United States, public concern about risks usually tracks changes in the actual fluctuations of those risks. But on occasion public concern, fed by vivid images that do not reflect actual changes in levels of danger, outruns the actual facts.[143] At certain points in the 1970s and 1980s, extreme leaps in concern about teenage suicide, herpes, illegitimacy, and AIDS occurred without significant changes in the size of the underlying threat. The determining factor was media attention on a few vivid cases.[144] We cannot yet say whether the media response to the 9/11 attacks has been excessive, insufficient, or optimal. But it was unquestionably a function of a highly salient event.

Those who operate as worst-case entrepreneurs show an intuitive understanding of the importance of availability and salience. By its very nature, the voice of an influential politician comes with huge amplifiers; when public officials bring an incident before the public, it is likely to spread far and wide and will often be taken as an indication of a larger problem. Because of the magnitude of the harm, the terrorist attacks of 9/11 would inevitably loom large no matter what President George W. Bush chose to emphasize. But he and his staff referred to the attacks on countless occasions, frequently to emphasize the reality of seemingly distant threats and the need to incur significant costs to counteract them.[145] In the years immediately following the attacks, President Bush had a large incentive to invoke them. A reminder of the attacks led Americans to show stronger popular support for him—and the increase in support occurred among people inclined against him as well as those inclined in his favor.[146] Even a general reminder of their own personal mortality led both Republicans and Democrats to show stronger support for President Bush.[147]

With climate change, no salient incident triggers public concern. The evidence linking Hurricane Katrina with climate change is contested and disputable, and most Americans have not concluded that the hurricane was in any sense "caused" by climate change.[148] In answering this question posed in 2005, "Do you think the severity of recent hurricanes is most likely the result of global climate change, or is it just the kind of severe weather events that happen from time to time?" only 39 percent responded that the hurricanes were a product of climate change; 54 percent answered that severe weather events just "happen."[149] If a vivid incident were to occur, the likelihood of an American response would increase immediately. Worst-case entrepreneurs point to a long list of possibilities. If climate change is abrupt, or if a dramatic event (such as the melting of the polar ice caps) does occur, the availability heuristic might well spur aggressive responses.

But consider another possibility. Climate change might well turn out to be gradual, unaccompanied by events that can easily be tied to the emission of greenhouse gases. A costly response might well be unlikely even if it is justified, simply because the problem never becomes sufficiently salient. The risk of inaction would be compounded by the fact that no nation could respond adequately on its own—a point I shall explore in more detail in Chapter 2.

Probability Neglect

As a result of the availability or unavailability of a salient event, people's assessment of probability can be highly inaccurate. But sometimes people venture little assessment of probability at all, especially when strong emotions are involved. What affects thought and behavior is the worst-case scenario itself, not the likelihood that it will occur—even though that probability should matter a great deal.

Consider a study involving children and adolescents, in which the following question was asked:[150] "Susan and Jennifer are arguing about whether they should wear seat belts when they ride in a car. Susan says that you should. Jennifer says that you shouldn't . . . Jennifer says that she heard of an accident where a car fell into a lake and a woman was kept from getting out in time because of wearing her seat belt . . . What do you think about this?" In answering that question, many subjects did not think about probability at all. One exchange took the following form:[151]

A: Well, in that case I don't think you should wear a seat belt.

Q: (Interviewer) How do you know when that's gonna happen?

A: Like, just hope it doesn't!

Q: So, should you or shouldn't you wear seat belts?

A: Well, tell-you-the-truth we should wear seat belts.

Q: How come?

A: Just in case of an accident. You won't get hurt as much as you will if you didn't wear a seat belt.

Q: Ok, well what about these kinds of things, where people get trapped?

A: I don't think you should, in that case.

These answers are odd, even comical; the child is evidently refusing to answer the question. But the answers are hardly unrecognizable. Some of the time, both children and adults alternate between bad scenarios without thinking a great deal about the question of probability. The point applies to hope as well as fear; vivid images of good outcomes will crowd out consideration of probability, too.[152]

Probability neglect received its clearest empirical confirmation in a striking study of people's willingness to pay to avoid electric shocks.[153] One experiment attempted to see whether varying the probability of harm would matter more or less in settings that trigger strong emotions than in settings that seem relatively emotion-free. In the "strong emotion" setting, participants were asked to imagine that they would participate in an experiment involving some chance of a "short, painful, but not dangerous electric shock." In the "emotion-free" setting, participants were told that the experiment entailed some chance of a $20 penalty. Participants were asked to say how much they would be willing to pay to avoid participating in the relevant experiment. Some participants were told that there was a 1 percent chance of receiving the bad outcome (either the $20 loss or the electric shock); others were told that the chance was 99 percent.

For those facing the relatively emotion-free injury—the $20

penalty—the difference between the median payment for a 1 percent chance and the median payment for a 99 percent chance was predictably large: $1 to avoid a 1 percent chance, and $18 to avoid a 99 percent chance. Those facing electric shock, by contrast, were willing to pay $7 to avoid even a 1 percent chance of shock, but only $10 to avoid a 99 percent chance. Apparently people will pay a significant amount to avoid an emotionally-laden hazard, and the amount they will pay does not vary greatly whether the probability of the hazard is very high or very low.

Consider several findings in the same vein:

- When people discuss a low-probability risk, their expressed concern rises even if the discussion consists mostly of apparently trustworthy assurances that the likelihood of harm really is tiny.[154]
- People are willing to pay more for flight insurance to cover losses resulting from "terrorism" than they are willing to pay for flight insurance to cover losses resulting from "all causes."[155]
- People show "alarmist bias." When presented with competing accounts of danger, they tend to move toward accepting the more alarming account.[156]
- In experiments designed to test levels of anxiety in anticipation of a painful electric shock of varying intensity, the probability of the shock had no effect. "Evidently, the mere thought of receiving a shock is enough to arouse individuals, but the precise likelihood of being shocked has little impact on level of arousal."[157]

Probability neglect provides a great deal of help in understanding the divergent American reactions to terrorism and climate change. An intense, often highly visual reaction to the thought of a terrorist attack can easily crowd out judgments about probability. The same is hardly true of climate change. At the present time, the American public does not connect climate change with particular bad outcomes.

Outrage

In George Orwell's *1984,* political leaders focused public fear and outrage on Emmanuel Goldstein, a former and now-despised Party member. During the Two Minutes of Hate, the Party made Goldstein the outlet for emotions that would have been more plausibly directed at the failures of the regime. Osama Bin Laden was never a friend to the United States or a member of any of its parties, and to say the least, he is a genuine enemy. But there can be little doubt that the war on terror has been spurred by what we might call the Goldstein Effect—the ability to intensify public concern by giving a definite face to the adversary, specifying a human source of the underlying threat.[158]

To be sure, the risk of terrorism does and should trigger outrage, whatever the magnitude of the risk.[159] The point is that if terrorism can be associated with a particular person or group, the outrage will intensify. This approach has generally succeeded with Osama Bin Laden. It was also successful with the invasion of Iraq in 2003, when the Bush administration made Saddam Hussein a casualty of the Goldstein Effect. To make these claims, it is of course unnecessary to question the demonization of Osama Bin Laden and Saddam Hussein; those who are demonized may actually be demons.

People are especially responsive to an identifiable perpetrator, just as they are especially responsive to an identifiable victim. Stalin understood the point well: "A single death is a tragedy. A million deaths is a statistic." In 1993, worldwide concern was riveted on Baby Jessica—an eighteen-month-old child who had fallen down a well. After an extensive effort, Jessica was saved, and when she turns twenty-five she stands to inherit a trust fund of one million dollars, mostly from gifts. By contrast, mere statistical victims—those without faces or narratives—elicit much less in the way of public concern. One of the most urgent tasks for political actors genuinely concerned with worst-case scenarios is to mobilize public concern about risks that seem to threaten faceless victims.

What is true for victims is true for perpetrators. If a wrongdoer has a clear identity—a face and a narrative—the public is far more likely to support an aggressive response. Such a perpetrator is difficult to find in the context of climate change. Warmer temperatures are a product of the interaction between nature and countless decisions by countless people in the private and public domains. To the extent that nature itself is responsible, or perceived as responsible, public concern is greatly dampened.[160] If nature is put to one side, contributors to climate change include not merely numerous companies in the United States and around the world but each one of us, through our daily activities and consumption. There are no obvious demons here—no human beings who actually intend to produce the harms associated with climate change. In the case of terrorism, a "we/they" narrative fits the facts; in the context of climate change, those who are the solution might well be the problem.

Some people have tried to use the Goldstein Effect against American leaders, charging them with negligence or even recklessness.[161] When President Bush rejected the Kyoto Protocol in 2001, many European citizens and their leaders were indeed outraged.[162] But no one could claim that President Bush actually *sought* to bring about climate change. In the next decades, activists might be able to enlist the Goldstein Effect against the United States and China, which are likely to be the largest contributors to greenhouse gas emissions. But nations lack faces.

More generally, a great deal of evidence suggests the pervasive importance of outrage to people's reactions to risk. Several studies test this question with the hypothesis that certain low-probability risks, such as those associated with nuclear waste radiation, produce outrage, whereas other low-probability risks, such as those associated with radon exposure, do not. The most striking finding is that even when the risk was statistically identical in the nuclear waste (high outrage) and radon (low outrage) cases, people in the nuclear waste case reported a much greater perceived threat, and a much higher intention to act to reduce that threat.[163] Indeed, the effect of outrage on people's reaction was about the same effect as a 4,000-fold increase in the statistical risk.[164] Efforts to communicate the meaning of differences in risk levels, by showing comparisons to normal risk levels, reduced the effect of outrage—but even after those efforts, outrage had nearly the same effect as a 2,000-fold increase in risk.[165] Outrage almost certainly contributed to "right-to-know" legislation involving chemical releases.[166] Terrorism is a high-outrage threat—indeed it may be the highest-outrage threat—and hence the public response is likely to be far more intense than the corresponding response to climate change.

Of course outrage is a social and cultural product, and not a brute fact. It would be possible for officials to heighten or to reduce outrage in either domain. In particular, those concerned about the risks associated with climate change might well be able to increase outrage by identifying the leading contributors to climate change and suggesting that with certain steps they might reduce the relevant risks.

Cultural and Social Influences

I have attempted to explain the divergent American reactions to terrorism and climate change by reference to individual cognition. But different groups with different cultural orientations focus on different sources of danger and on widely diverse worst cases. Consider a mundane example: "Many Germans believe that drinking water after eating cherries is deadly; they also believe that putting ice in soft drinks is unhealthy. The English, however, rather enjoy a cold drink of water after some cherries; and Americans love icy refreshments."[167] Other cultural variations are more dramatic. In some cultures, judgments about what causes risks, and what reduces risks, would seem extremely puzzling in others.[168]

Dan Kahan, Paul Slovic, and their coauthors have drawn attention to "cultural cognition"—to risk-related judgments that are a product of cultural orientations.[169] In their approach, human beings can be sorted into four groups: individualists, hierarchists, egalitarians, and solidarists.[170] Those who fall into the individualist camp tend to distrust government regulation and to believe in free markets; hence they are unlikely to be greatly concerned about climate change. The same is true of hierarchists, who favor the established social order and reject efforts to disrupt it; controls on climate change might well be seen as disruptive. By contrast, egalitarians are skeptical of businesses and other institutions that are thought to produce large-scale inequalities in society; egalitarians are sympathetic to environmental causes in general, and they are greatly concerned about climate change. The same is true of solidarists, who believe that human beings owe strong duties to one another—duties that environmental degradation violates.

Kahan, Slovic, and their coauthors claim to show that cultural cognition helps to explain public reactions to numerous risks, including those associated with climate change. Egalitarians and solidarists are significantly more concerned about climate change than are hierarchists and individualists. Indeed, Kahan, Slovic, and their coauthors find that cultural dispositions are a more accurate predictor of such judgments than party identification and demographic characteristics such as race, religion, gender, and wealth.

In the context of climate change, those who believe society has "become too soft and feminine" or government "interferes too much in our daily lives" are more likely to resist strong measures to combat climate change. Cultural differences might also be associated with different judgments about particular risk-reduction measures connected with terrorism. The Patriot Act, for example, likely splits people along lines that are cultural in the sense used by Kahan, Slovic, and their coauthors.

Some groups consider climate change to be a more serious threat than terrorism, and those groups appear to be identifiable along cultural lines. My own small-scale surveys at the University of Chicago and Yale Law Schools found that most respondents consider climate change the more serious problem, by a margin of 74 percent to 26 percent. Most Americans do not agree. The University of Chicago and Yale studies did not test for cultural dispositions, but we can say, with a lot of confidence, that compared with individualists and hierarchists, egalitarians and solidarists are likely to rank the risks of climate change as equivalent to or higher than those associated with terrorism.

But why, exactly, are individualists less concerned about climate change than are egalitarians? What connects "culture" to perceptions of risk? To make progress, we should try to specify the mechanisms by which culture contributes to judgments about hazards. A key point involves social influences. If people do not know whether climate change causes serious risks, they are likely to form their judgments on the basis of what they learn from those they know and trust. People who believe that climate change is a serious problem might simply be following the views of others. Social influences come in two forms: informational and reputational.[171] Suppose that trusted people believe that climate change is a serious problem and imposes significant risks. If trusted people believe this, other people have a reason to go along with them, because that belief supplies valuable information. Alternatively, people might silence themselves within certain groups for fear of alienating other group members. If dissenters in some groups argue publicly that the risk of terrorism has been overstated, or that climate change is not a serious problem, they will risk their reputations and possibly even their careers. When people are divided along certain lines, and when certain beliefs tend to "cluster," it is typically because of social influences. To the extent that beliefs about climate change are a product of cultural cognition, social influences are a large part of the explanation.

We might also want to explore attitudes toward terrorism and climate change as they operate across different nations. Perhaps something in American culture is responsible for the divergent reactions. But even if this is so, culture should not be treated as a black box. Domestic judgments in every nation are inevitably affected by perceptions of domestic consequences and in particular of domestic costs and benefits. We will see the point in the case of ozone-depleting chemicals and ratification of the Kyoto Protocol. Cross-national variations are subject to the same influences that affect individual behavior. Salient events can greatly increase fear in one nation but not others, and divergences in salience help to explain cross-national variations. Availability helps to explain such variations—though what is available is affected by, as well as a contributor to, cultural differences.

Worst Cases Over Time

The worst-case scenarios associated with terrorism are highly salient. American reactions are greatly affected by availability, probability neglect, and outrage. By contrast, the worst-case scenarios are dampened for climate change, because Americans believe that they have relatively little to lose from greenhouse gas emissions and that expensive regulation would mostly help people in other nations in the distant future. Partly for that reason, they have not been willing to spend a great deal to reduce the problem. The images associated with terrorism are concrete and easy to envision; the images associated with climate change are highly abstract.

Of course interest-group pressures, media attention, and the statements of public officials shape public perceptions and affect the likelihood of any regulatory response. In 2004, the White House released a fact sheet on the war on terror, starting with a quotation from President Bush: "We're still not safe . . . We are a Nation in danger."[172] By contrast, Prime Minister Tony Blair argued that there is "no bigger long-term question facing the global community" than the threat of climate change.[173] Statements of this kind undoubtedly have contributed to the greater public concern with climate change in the United Kingdom.

Because of the 9/11 attacks, and because serious efforts to control climate change would inevitably impose high costs on the United States, any American official will have limited ability to shift the public's level of concern. But the fear of terrorist attacks can certainly be heightened or diminished—and public officials could heighten the salience and hence the level of concern about the risks associated with climate change, and hence magnify the public demand for a regulatory response.

If the public's analysis of likely costs and benefits shifted, perhaps as a result of more vivid incidents of tangible harm, domestic controls on greenhouse gases and American participation in international agreements would be far more probable.[174] For the risks associated with climate change, availability is not simple to promote; but vivid images are possible to provide here as well. Single incidents and small shocks could make an extraordinary difference in terms of law and regulation.[175] With respect to terrorism, the attack of 9/11 was not exactly a small shock, but a single incident, on a single day, radically altered the associated risk perceptions of Americans—and greatly affected law as well.

To be sure, what is available to some may not be available to all, in part because of social influences, and in part because of individual, cultural, and national predispositions. It follows that some nations will find the bad outcomes associated with one or another risk to be "available" not only because of highly publicized events, but also because the relevant citizens are predisposed to focus on some risks rather than others. But even across national differences, public assessments can be altered by available incidents; if vivid incidents become salient, aggressive regulation is far more likely to be forthcoming.

CHAPTER TWO

A TALE OF
TWO PROTOCOLS

We can learn a great deal about potentially catastrophic risks by exploring the problem of ozone depletion, and the world's reaction to it. Climate change and stratospheric ozone depletion are so similar that many people are unable to distinguish between the two.[1] Consider some shared characteristics of the two problems.

(1) The threats from both ozone depletion and climate change have received public recognition as a result of relatively recent scientific work, theoretical and empirical. Ozone depletion was initially explored in a theoretical paper in 1974. One of the first papers about climate change was published much earlier, in 1896, but the current scientific consensus is a product of work done in the 1990s.[2]

(2) Both problems involve the effects of emissions from man-made technologies that come from diverse nations and that threaten to cause large-scale harm. Both problems come with disas-

trous worst-case scenarios, including exceedingly serious threats to human health.

(3) Because both ozone-depleting chemicals and greenhouse gases stay in the atmosphere for an extremely long time, the risks are difficult to reverse, even with immediate and aggressive action.

(4) No nation is able to eliminate these threats on its own. Indeed, no nation is even able to make significant progress on its own, certainly not in the long run. Because of the diversity of contributors, effective emission controls require international agreements.

(5) Both problems raise serious issues of international equity. Rich nations are the principal sources of ozone-depleting chemicals and greenhouse gases, and hence it is plausible to argue that corrective justice requires rich nations to pay poorer ones to reduce the underlying risks.

(6) Both problems raise serious issues of intergenerational equity. If neither problem is controlled, future generations are likely to face greater risks than the current generation, and a key question is how much to sacrifice in the present for the benefit of the future. The answer to this question is complicated by the fact that expenditures by the present, decreasing national wealth, may end up harming future generations, simply by ensuring that they too have less wealth on which to draw.

(7) The United States is a crucial actor in both domains, probably the most important in the world. The importance of the United States lies not only in its wealth and power; it also lies in the fact that the United States has been the most significant source of both ozone-depleting chemicals and greenhouse gases.

Notwithstanding these similarities, there is one obvious difference between the two problems: The first has been essentially solved, whereas very little progress has been made on the second.[3] An international agreement designed to control ozone-depleting chemicals was signed in Montreal in 1987 and ratified by 183 nations (including the United States, where ratification was unanimous in the Senate). As nations have complied with their obligations, global emissions of ozone-depleting chemicals have been reduced by over 95 percent, and atmospheric concentrations of these chemicals have been declining since 1994. By 2060, the ozone layer is expected to return to its natural state.

The Montreal Protocol thus stands as a spectacular success story in environmental protection. Its success owes a great deal to the actions not only of the United States government, which played an aggressive role in producing the protocol, but also to American companies, which stood in the forefront of technical innovation leading to substitutes for ozone-depleting chemicals.

With climate change, the situation is altogether different. To be sure, an international agreement, produced in Kyoto in 1997, did go into force in 2005, when Russia ratified it; the Kyoto Protocol has now been ratified by over 130 nations. But many countries are unlikely to comply with their obligations under the protocol, and the United States has firmly rejected the agreement, with unanimous bipartisan opposition to ratification. Partly as a result, worldwide emissions of greenhouse gases are projected to rise at a rapid rate in coming decades.

Why was the Montreal Protocol so much more successful than the Kyoto Protocol? I shall suggest here that both the success in Montreal and the mixed picture in Kyoto were driven largely by decisions of the United States, based on a domestic cost-benefit analysis. To the United States, the monetized benefits of the Montreal Protocol dwarfed the monetized costs, and hence the circumstances were extremely promising for American support and even enthusiasm for the agreement. As we will see, the United States had so much to lose from depletion of the ozone layer that it would have been worthwhile for the nation unilaterally to take the steps required by the Montreal Protocol. For the world as a whole, the argument for the Montreal Protocol was overwhelming.

But careful analysis and economic rationality were not the whole story: The nation's attention was also riveted by a vivid image, the ominous and growing "ozone hole" over Antarctica. Ordinary people could easily understand the idea that the earth was losing a kind of "protective shield," one that operated as a safeguard against skin cancer, a dreaded condition.

The Kyoto Protocol presented a radically different picture. Influential analyses suggested that the benefits of the protocol to the United States would be dwarfed by the costs. These analyses suggested that if the United States complied on its own, the nation would spend a great deal and gain relatively little. If all parties complied, the United States might still be a net loser. Because of the distinctive properties of the agreement, some analyses even suggested that it was unclear the world as a whole had more to gain than to lose from the Kyoto Protocol. For this reason, the circumstances were unpromising for a successful agreement, and they were especially bleak for American participation, regardless of which political party occupied the White House. An unfavorable cost-benefit ratio for the United States in particular, but also for the world, provides the central explanation for the mixed picture of the Kyoto Protocol.

These different assessments help to explain other anomalies as well. For example, they illuminate the pattern of almost universal compliance with the Montreal Protocol and the likelihood of widespread noncompliance with the Kyoto Protocol. They also help explain the fact that American companies strongly supported the Montreal Protocol while sharply opposing the Kyoto Protocol. They illuminate the behavior of European nations, above all the

United Kingdom, which were initially cautious in reacting to the problem of ozone depletion, on the ground that the scientific evidence was both theoretical and speculative. But European nations, and the United Kingdom in particular, have been quite aggressive in calling for action in response to the problem of climate change.

The United States is unlikely to ratify an international agreement to reduce greenhouse gases unless the perceived domestic costs of the relevant reductions decrease, the perceived domestic benefits increase, or both. Of course, moral commitments and behavioral factors may influence the ultimate judgment. If Americans become convinced that they are obliged to act to protect other nations or future generations from catastrophic outcomes, they might be willing to bear costs that would otherwise be unacceptable. If vivid incidents seem to demonstrate that the risk of climate change is real and serious, a response will be far more probable. But unless the costs of such a response decrease, or the perceived benefits increase, the United States will probably not take very costly action to reduce greenhouse gas emissions.

Without the participation of the United States, the success of any greenhouse gas agreement will be limited, because the United States accounts for such a high percentage of the world's emissions. There is another problem. China will be the largest emitter in the world as early as 2009, and its own cost-benefit assessment now parallels that of the United States. According to prominent analyses, stringent controls will impose extremely high domestic costs on China, in return for speculative or modest domestic benefits. If the United States does not participate in an international agreement, China is most unlikely to do so either; and China might well hold out even if the United States agrees to participate. These points have large implications for the content of a successful agreement.

Ozone Depletion

Chlorofluorocarbons (CFCs) were originally used as fluids in refrigerators, in part because they were far safer than the available alternatives, which were either flammable or dangerously toxic.[4] In addition to their numerous cooling applications, CFCs came to be used as propellants in aerosol spray cans. Widespread commercial and military uses for CFCs and related chemicals, prominently including halons, produced billions of dollars in revenues for their manufacturers.

The idea that CFCs posed a threat to the ozone layer was initially suggested in a stunning academic paper in 1974, written by Sherwood Rowland and Mario Molina.[5] According to their analysis, CFC molecules migrate slowly to the upper atmosphere, where ultraviolet radiation causes them to release chlorine atoms. These atoms could endanger the ozone layer, which protects the earth from sunlight. The potential consequences for human health were clear, for Rowland and Molina wrote only two years after the loss of ozone had been linked with skin cancer.[6] In 1971, it was prominently suggested that a 1 percent ozone loss would cause an additional 7,000 cases of skin cancer each year.[7] If Rowland and Molina were right, CFC emissions would create serious health risks.

In the years immediately following, depletion of the ozone layer received widespread attention in the United States, which accounted for nearly 50 percent of global CFC use. A great deal of theoretical and empirical work was done within the scientific community; the National Academy of Sciences and many other research institutions made contributions. Most findings supported the initial claims by Molina and Rowland.[8]

Meanwhile, the CFC industry attempted to conduct and publicize its own research, mounting an aggressive public relations campaign to discredit the association between CFCs and ozone deple-tion.[9] A senior executive at DuPont, the world's largest producer, testified before a Senate panel that the "chlorine-ozone hypothesis is at this time purely speculative with no concrete evidence . . . to support it."[10] At the very least, industry representatives suggested that no harm would come from each year's delay and that costly regulation should not be imposed until further research established that the risks were real.[11]

Consumers saw the problem differently. Because of intense media attention to the danger, American consumers swiftly cut their demand for aerosol sprays by more than half, thus dramati-cally depressing the market for these products.[12] The same public concern spurred domestic regulation. In 1977, Congress amended the Clean Air Act to permit the Environmental Protection Agency (EPA) to regulate ozone-depleting chemicals.[13] In 1978, EPA banned the use of CFCs as aerosol propellants in nonessential ap-plications and defined criteria for exemptions of "essential uses."[14] As a result of the ban, aerosol production in the United States plummeted by nearly 95 percent.[15] A significant reduction in America's contribution to ozone depletion was achieved quickly, and in a way that imposed exceedingly little cost.

Why did so many consumers respond? There are three answers. The first is that skin cancer is easy to envision, and an easily envi-sioned harm is especially likely to affect behavior. Second, people could easily imagine that a "protective shield" over the earth was in jeopardy, and this image was an energizing force. Third, a change in behavior was not especially burdensome to consumers. Aerosol spray cans were hardly essential to daily life, and a decision to sub-stitute some other product imposed no serious hardship.

Despite the flurry of domestic activity, no international agree-ment was in sight, and at first the effort to produce international cooperation seemed to be a clear failure. A central reason was the skepticism and opposition of the European Community (forerunner of the European Union), which firmly rejected regulatory measures of the sort taken by the United States.[16] In most European countries, the public was relatively indifferent to the ozone question, which had received little media attention.[17] Heavily influenced by private companies with an economic stake in the outcome, most European nations resorted to symbolic gestures such as voluntary emissions codes rather than regulatory restrictions. Industry arguments about the expense of such requirements, and the potential loss of tens of thousands of jobs, contributed heavily to the weak response in Europe.[18] The British government in particular was influenced by Imperial Chemical Industries, among the largest CFC producers in the world.[19] The export of CFCs played a large role in Britain's foreign exchange.

With the election of President Reagan in 1980, the American government became generally more skeptical about regulatory controls, and little happened from 1980 to 1982 to limit ozone-depleting emissions. In 1983, however, the United States asked the world to follow its own policies by banning uses of CFCs in aerosol propellants.[20] Significantly, the U.S. government did not ask for international action that would impose new domestic costs; it merely sought an agreement that would replicate its existing domestic restrictions, imposing regulatory burdens on others and thus conferring benefits on Americans at little or no additional expense. Nonetheless, industry organizations within the United States initially objected vigorously to the new position, contending that it gave undue credence to speculative science and fearing the rise of further controls on CFCs.[21] The government maintained its position despite these objections, but international negotiations were in stalemate through 1984.

In 1985, however, a new scientific analysis indicated that truly catastrophic harm was possible, stemming from a sudden collapse of ozone concentrations. The new scientific findings, and additional studies in 1987, showed that between 1957 and 1984 the total column of ozone over Antarctica had been depleted by 40 percent, and—even more dramatically—that a "hole" had formed in the ozone layer over Antarctica that was as large as the entire United States.[22] This vivid image captured the imagination of the public and turned the tide of American opinion in the direction of a total ban on CFCs. These studies also became a spur to international negotiations.[23] Because of this worst-case scenario, immediate action seemed critical. But still skeptical of the science and attuned to the costs, European leaders continued to reject an international agreement, contending that the United States was engaged in "scaremongering"[24] and that "Americans had been panicked into 'overhasty measures.'"[25]

Other careful scientific investigations made the threat increasingly difficult to ignore. A NASA/World Meteorological Association group provided an exceptionally detailed review of the evidence in 1986, concluding that continued growth in CFCs would produce large losses in the ozone layer.[26] In 1988, the Ozone Trends Panel, established by NASA, reiterated the basic finding that CFCs were the primary cause of the ozone "hole," and it offered a new analysis of a significant global trend.[27] These conclusions, generally taken as authoritative, helped pave the way for the Montreal Protocol.

The position of U.S. industry began to shift in 1986, apparently as a result of significant progress in producing safe substitutes for CFCs.[28] While still arguing that CFCs produced no imminent hazard, DuPont supported an international freeze on CFC emissions, seeing this step as a justified precautionary measure after the discovery of the Antarctic ozone "hole."[29] DuPont and other producers pledged to phase out production by an early date and also supported international controls. No doubt public relations was a factor here, as was the fact that the relevant products were no longer especially profitable. American producers had a comparative advantage over foreign producers in developing and marketing substitute products, and they came to see this as a new commercial opportunity.[30] The European Community even speculated that the Reagan administration's turnabout in 1983 was driven by the knowledge that American producers had secretly developed substitutes.[31]

Some U.S. officials in the executive branch agreed with industry that a freeze might be justified, but not emissions reductions. The view of Congress, however, was unambiguous. By a vote of 80–2, the Senate passed a resolution asking President Reagan to take aggressive action to protect the ozone layer, including an immediate freeze and the eventual elimination of ozone-depleting chemicals.[32]

What followed was a period of intense discussions within the Reagan administration. The Office of Management and Budget was skeptical of aggressive controls, while the Environmental Protection Agency was favorably disposed.[33] This internal disagreement was resolved after a careful cost-benefit analysis suggested that the costs of controls would be far lower than anticipated—and the benefits far higher. In the words of Richard Benedick, a high-level participant in the proceedings: "A major break . . . came in the form of a cost-benefit study from the President's Council of Economic Advisers. The analysis concluded that, despite the scientific and economic uncertainties, the monetary benefits of preventing future deaths from skin cancer far outweighed the costs of CFC controls as estimated either by industry or by EPA."[34] In particular, both EPA and the Council of Economic Advisers concluded that the ozone layer depletion would cause a "staggering" increase in the number of deaths from skin cancer—over five million by 2165.[35] The association between skin cancer and cherished leisure activities—such as lying on the beach, gardening, and other summertime activities—undoubtedly helped to spur a consensus that the problem needed to be aggressively addressed.

With the American position fixed, the stage was set for the negotiation of a new protocol. At an early point, the European Community, led above all by France, Italy, and the United Kingdom, urged caution and a strategy of "wait and learn."[36] Concerned about the economic position of Imperial Chemical Industries, the United Kingdom rejected aggressive action.[37] The United States took the lead in endorsing stringent additional controls; it was joined by several other nations, including Canada, New Zealand, Finland, and Norway. Those urging stringent controls placed particular emphasis on the problem of irreversibility. Because some CFCs last for a century or more, it was necessary to act immediately to avoid more expensive steps, and more destructive consequences, in the future.

Many months of discussions led to a decisive meeting in Montreal, starting on September 8, 1987, and including over 60 nations, more than half of them developing countries. The key provision in the protocol was not merely a freeze on CFCs but a dramatic 50 percent cut by 1998, accompanied by a freeze on the three major halons beginning in 1992. The 50 percent figure was a compromise between the American proposal for 95 percent reductions and the European suggestion of a mere freeze.

A knotty question involved the treatment of developing countries. While CFC consumption was modest in those countries, their domestic requirements were increasing, and a badly designed agreement could merely shift production and use of CFCs from wealthy nations to poorer ones, leaving the global problem largely unaffected. But developing nations reasonably contended that they should not be held to the same standards as wealthier nations, which were responsible for the problem in the first place. India and China in particular emphasized that nations with less than 25 percent of the world's population had produced over 90 percent of the world's CFCs.[38]

This claim was met by several steps, including both loosened restrictions on developing nations and financial assistance to them. Under Article 5 of the Montreal Protocol, developing countries are authorized to meet their "basic domestic needs" by increasing CFCs to a specified level for ten years, after which they would be subject to a 50 percent reduction for the next ten years. In addition, a funding mechanism was created by which substantial resources—initially $400 million—were transferred to poor countries. These provisions were criticized as unduly vague, essentially a way of deferring key questions; but they provided an initial framework, one that has worked exceedingly well. The Montreal Protocol imposes trade sanctions on those who do not comply, and these create a strong incentive for compliance.

Costs and Benefits of CFC Regulation

Why did the United States adopt such an aggressive posture with respect to ozone depletion? A large part of the answer is that cost-benefit analyses, by the Council of Economic Advisers and others, suggested that the United States had far more to gain than to lose by a well-designed agreement. The EPA's analysis projected that existing emissions would produce over 5 million skin cancer deaths by 2165, together with over 25 million cataract cases—figures that would be cut to 200,000 and 2 million, respectively, by a 50 percent CFC reduction (see Table 2). Of course, the underlying science did not allow uncontroversial estimates. What matters was the perception of domestic costs and benefits—and in the late 1980s, nearly every systematic analysis suggested that the Montreal Protocol was very much in the interest of the United States.

According to the EPA's numbers, the United States could even justify unilateral action, because the health benefits of eliminating CFCs in America alone would create huge gains for the American public. But if the world joined the Montreal Protocol, the benefits would be nearly tripled, preventing 245 million cancers, including more than 5 million cancer deaths, by 2165.[39] And the projected cost of the Montreal Protocol was relatively low—a mere $21 billion. Even this figure turned out to be too high, because of unforeseen technological innovation.[40]

One of the most noteworthy features of the ozone depletion problem is that over time, the United States was anticipated to be a decreasingly large contributor to that problem. In the short run, aggressive action by the United States alone was amply justified by the domestic cost-benefit calculus. In the long run, however, the

Table 2   Costs and benefits of Montreal Protocol to the United States (in billions of 1985 dollars).

	Montreal Protocol	Unilateral implementation of Montreal Protocol by the United States
Benefits	3,575	1,363
Costs	21	21
Net benefits	3,554	1,352

United States would do much better with global cooperation, especially from developing nations, which would be increasingly important sources of ozone-depleting chemicals. American enthusiasm for the Montreal Protocol can be understood only in this light. We have no full accounting of the costs and benefits of the Montreal Protocol for the world. But if we build on a 1997 study in Canada, we can generate a very rough approximation (see Table 3).[41] Many of these specific numbers depend on contentious assumptions, but the broader conclusion that the Montreal Protocol was an extraordinary bargain for the world as well as for the United States is largely undisputed today.[42]

After the Montreal Protocol, restrictions on ozone-depleting substances have been rapidly strengthened, to the point where a worldwide phaseout of fifteen different CFCs was accepted in London in 1990.[43] The European Community, by then convinced of the danger, sought a timetable for further reductions, leading to an agreement for total elimination of CFC use and production by

Table 3 Global benefits and costs of Montreal Protocol, 1987–2060.

Cases of skin cancer avoided	20,600,000
Cases of skin cancer deaths avoided	333,500
Cases of cataracts avoided	129,100,000
Monetized benefits (including damages to fisheries, agriculture, and materials; not including health benefits)	$459 billion
Monetized benefits of deaths averted	$333 billion
Monetized health benefits (nonfatal skin cancers and cataracts averted)	$339 billion
Monetized costs	$235 billion
Net benefits	>$900 billion

2000. Imperial Chemical Industries, an original source of British skepticism about regulatory controls, was playing a different role by this point, having come to appreciate the economic opportunities in shifting to substitute chemicals.[44]

When the European Community announced that it would phase out CFCs by 1997, the United States, not to be outdone, announced that it would achieve that goal by 1996. The accelerated action was spurred by evidence that the costs of the phaseout would be much lower than expected and that damage to the ozone layer was even greater than recently thought. Since that time, almost all nations have agreed to phase out CFCs. New damage to the ozone layer has essentially ceased, and the ozone "hole" is shrinking. In the environmental domain, the Montreal Protocol stands as the most stunning success story in the history of international cooperation.

Climate Change

Concern about greenhouse gases has arisen in the same general period as concern about ozone-depleting chemicals. For both problems, worst-case scenarios have played a large role in public debate. But many of the major actors in the ban on CFCs have reversed their positions on greenhouse gases. For ozone depletion, the United States first acted unilaterally and then sought international restrictions. For greenhouse gases, international action came first, and American domestic controls were exceedingly modest.

European nations were significant obstacles to international regulation of ozone-depleting chemicals, favoring an approach of "wait and learn." For climate change, they have been favorably disposed toward regulatory controls, with the United Kingdom taking the lead. The reversal of positions suggests that it is hopelessly inadequate to portray the United States as skeptical of global solutions to environmental problems, or to see the European Union as more committed to environmental goals. Nor is it adequate to portray the American position on greenhouse gases as entirely a function of Republican leadership. The difference depends instead on assessments of national interest, public opinion, and the role of powerful private actors.

Since the late 1980s, international organizations have shown a great deal of concern about climate change. In December 1988, a resolution of the United Nations General Assembly declared climate change to be a "common concern of mankind" and asked for a global response. In 1989, the European Community signaled that it would support an international agreement to deal with the problem. In 1992, more than 180 nations, including the United States, signed the Framework Convention on Climate Change during the Rio Conference on Environment and Development. In fact, the United States was the first industrialized nation to ratify the Framework Convention, which set the stage for everything that has happened since.

Unlike the Montreal Protocol, the Framework Convention lacked quantitative limits for emissions reductions. When the Convention was negotiated, the United States strongly resisted such limits, as the United Kingdom had done in the early stages of the debate over ozone-depleting chemicals. The Framework Convention generally limited itself to information-gathering requirements and vague aspirations, such as stabilization of emissions to prevent "dangerous interference" with global climate. The parties agreed to produce, at a later stage, a legal instrument that would establish quantitative limits for developing countries. The convention was ratified by the United States Senate in 1992 and entered into force two years later.

The Framework Convention started a new process, including meetings to be held annually. In 1995, the parties to the convention (including the United States, now led by President Clinton) met in Berlin and agreed to set emissions limits at specific periods and to agree to a protocol that would embody those limits. The Clinton administration appeared to support the "Berlin Mandate," which asked industrialized nations to accept restrictions on greenhouse gas emissions. But other national leaders were unenthusiastic about this commitment.

In 1997 the Senate unanimously adopted Resolution 98, which asked President Clinton not to agree to limits on greenhouse gas emissions if the agreement would injure the economic interests of the United States or if it failed to "mandate new specific scheduled commitments to limit or reduce greenhouse gas emissions for Developing Country Parties within the same compliance period."[45] Indeed, the Senate unanimously concluded that any "exemption for Developing Country Parties is inconsistent with the need for global action on climate change and is environmentally flawed." It added that it "strongly believed" that the proposals under consideration "could result in serious harm to the United States economy, including significant job loss, trade disadvantages, increased energy and consumer costs, or any combination thereof."

Senate Resolution 98—a bipartisan bill opposed by no Democratic member of the Senate—was exceedingly important, because the commitments it required from developing countries were highly unlikely to be made. In passing this resolution, the Senate essentially guaranteed that the United States would not ratify any agreement to reduce greenhouse gas emissions. By contrast, ten years earlier, during the Reagan administration, a near-unanimous Senate had voted in favor of aggressive action to protect the ozone layer, and in 1996 a unanimous Senate voted to support a more rapid phase-out of CFCs than was required by the Montreal Protocol and its amendments.

The Clinton administration took an equivocal approach to the Senate resolution and indeed to the Kyoto negotiations in general. In part because of the presence of Vice President Al Gore, the administration did favor some kind of international response.[46] Nonetheless, at times it spoke in support of voluntary measures rather than regulation, and it favored steps that would impose relatively little burden on the national economy.

During the Kyoto negotiations in December 1997, the United States supported relatively modest regulatory limits, arguing against reductions in emissions levels and instead for stabilizing current levels.[47] The restrictions supported by the United States were distinctly weaker than those sought by the European Union and Japan. In conformity with the Senate's resolution, American negotiators made serious efforts to persuade the major developing countries to agree to limit their emissions at some future date; they refused.

In fact, many of the American positions were rejected during the negotiations. Ultimately, most of the major developed nations, including the United States, agreed to the Kyoto Protocol, which set forth firm quantitative limits on greenhouse gas emissions. Specified reductions were limited to the "Annex 1" nations—those regulated by the protocol. The list was designed to ensure that, taken as a whole, the nations would show an aggregate reduction of 5 percent from their total levels of emissions in 1990—a reduction that must be met in the period between 2008 and 2012. For example, the United States was required to reduce 1990 emissions by 7 percent; Japan by 6 percent; the European Union by 8 percent. Some nations were permitted to increase emissions; these included Iceland, Norway, and Australia. Notably, the Kyoto Protocol did

not impose trade sanctions or other penalties on those who failed
to comply, as did the Montreal Protocol. Developing nations made
no commitments at all, though they were permitted to engage in
emissions trading with Annex 1 nations.

Why, exactly, were these particular emission reductions chosen?
The simplest answer is national self-interest, especially in the case of
developing nations, which agreed to no limits at all.[48] In 1996, India's greenhouse gas emissions exceeded Germany's; South Korea's
exceeded France's; next to the United States, China was the largest
emitter of greenhouse gases in the world—but none of these nations was restricted by the Kyoto Protocol. Russia was given a target emission rate of 100 percent of its 1990 emissions, but in 1997
its actual emissions were merely 70 percent of that amount, because
of economic difficulties that had significantly decreased energy use.
The trading system created by the Kyoto Protocol ensured a huge
economic boon to Russia, as everyone was aware.

Germany appeared to accept significant reductions—8 percent
of its 1990 levels, to be reached by 2012. But in fact, by 1997 its
own emissions were already 10 percent lower than in 1990. The reduction was a result of reunification with the former East Germany,
whose plummeting economy led to radical emissions decreases. For
the United Kingdom, the story is not altogether different. The target, a reduction of 8 percent, was less severe than it seemed, because
state subsidies of natural gas had already led, in 1997, to a level 5
percent below that of 1990. By far the biggest loser, in terms of the
actual costs of mandatory cuts, was the United States.

It should therefore be unsurprising that a strong bipartisan consensus in the Senate stood in opposition to ratification. Not one
member, Democratic or Republican, publicly supported the Kyoto
Protocol. Although Vice President Gore played a key role in the
negotiations, the Clinton administration promised Congress that it

would not adopt measures to implement the protocol before Senate ratification and that it would not seek ratification unless it had obtained "meaningful participation" from developing countries.[49] Indeed, the whole process had an air of unreality to it, because "everyone on both sides of the Atlantic already knew in 1997 that the U.S. could never join the protocol as drafted."[50]

The Bush administration exhibited no such ambivalence. In 2001, President Bush described the Kyoto Protocol as "fatally flawed" and "effectively dead," emphasizing the nonparticipation of developing countries. In a key letter, President Bush wrote, "I oppose the Kyoto Protocol because it exempts 80 percent of the world, including major population centers such as China and India, from compliance, and would cause serious harm to the U.S. economy." In fact, the United States attempted to persuade other nations, above all Japan and Russia, to reject the protocol as well.

The Kyoto Protocol went into effect in 2005, and the number of nations formally committed to it is impressive indeed. Of the original participants in the process that led to Kyoto, the United States and Australia are the only nonratifiers. In 2001, the Marrakech Accords led to further innovations, in which developing countries were made beneficiaries of funds to assist with technology transfer.[51] Although the level of the funds remains unspecified, donors led by the European Union pledged to grant $410 million annually.[52] To this extent, the Montreal Protocol and the Kyoto Protocol might appear to be roughly parallel. But the appearance is badly misleading. As we shall see, the world is most unlikely to come close to meeting the Kyoto targets.

Costs and Benefits of the Kyoto Targets

For the United States and the world, the benefits of the Montreal Protocol were projected to dwarf the costs. What are the relevant figures for the Kyoto Protocol? Because of the nature of the climate change problem, any answer will be highly disputable, and I shall devote some attention to the disputes here.[53] My goal is not to resolve these disagreements but to clarify the benefits and costs as they were perceived at the time. Of course members of the Senate do not base their decisions on formal cost-benefit analysis, and the role of such analysis within the executive branch is not constant. But the underlying figures, or at least a rough perception of their magnitude, undoubtedly affected domestic behavior.

Begin with costs to the United States. An early analysis in the Clinton administration found "modest" costs from the Kyoto Protocol, producing a mere 4–6 cent increase in the price of gasoline and an annual increase in the average family's energy bill of $70–$110 by 2010.[54] But these projections were disputed, even within the administration itself. A study by the Department of Energy projected a gasoline price increase ranging from $1.39 to $1.91 per gallon and a 20–86 percent increase in the price of electricity by 2010.[55] An industry-funded study done at the Wharton School projected costs far in excess of these estimates.[56] In addition to a 65 cent per gallon increase in the price of gasoline and a near-doubling of the price of energy and electricity, it predicted a loss of 2.4 million jobs and a drop of $300 billion in the nation's GDP. The average annual cost totaled $2,700 per household.[57]

In my view, these figures were wildly inflated, but they received a great deal of publicity. One of the most careful, objective, and influential analyses, published in 2000, comes from William Nordhaus and Joseph Boyer.[58] As they show, a great deal depends on the amount of emissions trading. If trading were freely available, the cost to American companies would be dramatically reduced, because they could avoid expensive emissions reduction requirements and rely instead on purchasing permits. Additional uncertainty about the numbers stems from the fact that technological innovation might drive down costs, as it did in the case of CFCs. The worst case for the Kyoto Protocol—a scenario involving no effective trading—would produce total costs of $852 billion for the United States, in present value. The best case—involving global trading—would cost the United States $91 billion. Nordhaus and Boyer suggest that the most likely figure is $325 billion, which assumes trading among the Annex 1 nations but no one else.

The costs for the world as a whole are projected to be lower— merely $217 billion in the case of Annex 1 trading, and $884 billion in the case of no trading.[59] The reason is that many nations, especially those in Eastern Europe, would receive a great deal of money from permit sales, and hence they would count as net winners quite apart from any environmental benefits they might reap. The mere granting of permits produces tens of billions of dollars in gains for both Russia and Europe—a total of $112 billion from Annex 1 trading. These billions of dollars in revenue amount to a kind of transfer, and whether they should count as a "benefit" from the Kyoto Protocol is a legitimate question. But even if such amounts are included, the worldwide costs of the protocol are in the hundreds of billions of dollars.

What would the United States and the world receive in return for these anticipated costs? Here too there is a great deal of uncertainty—even more so than on the cost side.[60] Let us begin with the anticipated costs of climate change in general, and then turn to the effect of the Kyoto Protocol. The two issues are quite different, and it is important to separate them. Even if the anticipated costs of climate change are high, a particular response might do little to reduce those costs and hence produce little in the way of benefits.

In its 2001 report, the Intergovernmental Panel on Climate Change projected an increase of between 1.4 and 5.8° Centigrade by 2001. In 2007, the International Panel narrowed the range of uncertainty, offering a range of best estimates, from various scenarios, of between 1.8° C and 4.0° C warming by 2100. It is obvious that an increase of 1.4° would cause far less damage than an increase of 5.8°.[61] But specialists greatly disagree about the likely harm, even assuming a particular increase in global mean temperatures.[62] If climate change is abrupt, the harm will be far higher than otherwise; abrupt climate change may lead to worldwide catastrophe.[63] The magnitude of the risk of catastrophe is disputed, and any such risk must be incorporated in the overall analysis.[64] How to incorporate a risk of catastrophe is also disputed (see Chapter 3). In addition, a great deal turns on the selection of the discount rate. Because many of the gains from emissions reductions will be experienced in the future, a low discount rate will obviously mean far higher benefits from risk reduction than a high discount rate (see Chapter 6).

According to Nordhaus and Boyer, the present worldwide cost of climate change is in the vicinity of $4 trillion.[65] To put that cost in perspective: The annual GDP of the United States is $13 trillion, suggesting a capital stock value of at least $100 trillion.[66] But $4 trillion is a great deal, and even that figure may be far too low if a low discount rate is used or if climate change is abrupt.[67] According to other estimates, climate change will reduce the GDP of developed nations by 1 or 2 percent and reduce the GDP of developing nations by 5 percent or more.[68] Still other estimates now suggest that the overall cost of climate change will be significantly higher—perhaps as high as 6 to 8 percent of the world's GDP, or even more.[69]

If the Kyoto Protocol could eliminate the total cost of climate change, few analysts doubt that it would be worthwhile. But according to Nordhaus and Boyer, the agreement would actually have a meager effect, reducing anticipated warming by a mere 0.03° C by 2100.[70] According to another estimate, the agreement would reduce anticipated warming by 1.2° C by 2300.[71] Climate change is a function of aggregate emissions of greenhouse gases, and the Kyoto Protocol would have only a small effect on aggregate emissions. There are three points here. First, emissions from China, India, and other developing countries—now substantial contributors to climate change, and anticipated to be even greater contributors in the near future—are not regulated by the agreement at all. Second, past emissions of greenhouse gases will continue to contribute to warming; even a substantial reduction in future emissions will not eliminate the problem. Third, the Kyoto Protocol requires parties not to make substantial cuts in emissions but merely to return to a point slightly below emissions levels in 1990—a point at which greenhouse emissions were already causing climate change.

What are the anticipated effects of climate change and the Kyoto Protocol for the United States? According to prominent projections, the United States is very unlikely to face the most serious damage from climate change.[72] Some estimates suggest that American agriculture will actually be a net winner as a result of global warming.[73] Other estimates suggest that Americans will be net losers, but not nearly to the extent of other nations, in part because the most serious adverse health effects are not anticipated and in part because the United States economy is relatively less dependent on agriculture.[74] In this light, we can offer a rough projection of the costs and benefits of the Kyoto Protocol for the United States alone—a projection designed not to offer anything like an accurate point estimate but to describe what prominent analysts suggested when the United States was making its key decisions (see Table 4).[75]

According to these numbers, the Kyoto Protocol is not a good bargain for the United States. The anticipated benefits of $12 billion are hardly trivial, but they are dwarfed by the anticipated costs of $325 billion. Significant unilateral action to comply with the

Table 4   Costs and benefits of Kyoto Protocol for the United States (in billions of 2000 dollars).

	Kyoto Protocol	Unilateral action to comply with Kyoto Protocol
Benefits	12	0
Costs	325	325
Net benefits	−313	−325

Kyoto Protocol might well produce no benefits at all. If the United States engaged in emissions reduction on its own, it would be taking extremely costly action for speculative benefits—or at least that is how prominent actors perceived the situation at the time.

This is not to say that unilateral action by the United States would have no rationale.[76] Perhaps such action could begin a much broader and more inclusive process, ultimately persuading other nations, including China and India, to reduce their emissions as well. Perhaps such action could spur technological innovation in a way that would have substantial long-term consequences for climate change—and do so at a cost lower than what is now anticipated. But for climate change, any such strategy would be a gamble, and based on the figures offered by prominent analysts, it would not be the simplest to defend in conventional cost-benefit terms.

The larger point is that for the United States, the perceived costs of the Kyoto Protocol were much higher than the costs of the Montreal Protocol (by some $313 billion), and the perceived benefits were much lower (by some $3,562 billion). The most prominent officials in the Senate and in the Bush administration may not have been aware of the specific figures, and may not have based their decisions on a formal cost-benefit calculation of any kind. But an intuitive grasp of the consequences of the Kyoto Protocol played a key role in their decision not to support it. In the

Senate, both Republicans and Democrats appeared to be aware that the protocol would impose significant costs and deliver relatively low benefits, because developing nations were not included. In the executive branch, this perception of low returns and high costs was widely held, even among those who believed that climate change was a significant problem.

Of course interest-group power, or moral commitments, may push nations away from the outcome suggested by expert projections of costs and benefits. Both interest groups and moral commitments have played a significant role in the American debate over climate change. But with respect to the Kyoto Protocol, the formal and informal assessments of domestic costs and benefits had large effects in discouraging ratification.

For the world as a whole, the benefit-cost ratio for the Kyoto Protocol is better, but not particularly good, and not nearly as good as those for the Montreal Protocol (see Table 5). To be sure, the relevant numbers must be taken with many grains of salt, depending as they do on contentious assumptions about the degree of emissions trading, about technological innovation, about discount rates, about the likelihood of abrupt or catastrophic warming, and about the valuation of life and health. With a lower discount rate, and

Table 5 Costs and benefits of Kyoto Protocol for the world (in billions of 2000 dollars).

	Kyoto Protocol
Benefits	96
Costs	338 or 217 (if $112 billion in permits for Eastern Europe are included as offsetting benefits)
Net benefits	−242 or −119

modest changes in underlying assumptions, the benefits of greenhouse gas reductions can grow dramatically.[77] Reasonable people might expect the costs to be significantly lower or offer a significantly higher estimate of the benefits.[78] Perhaps the Kyoto Protocol would have served, and might still serve, as a start toward a broader and more inclusive agreement. But in light of the numbers that confronted the United States at the time, the argument for ratification of the Kyoto Protocol, based on estimated benefits for the world as a whole, was certainly unclear—far more so than the argument for ratification of the Montreal Protocol.

We can now see why the United States was skeptical of the Kyoto Protocol. But why did so many nations express enthusiasm for it? Part of the answer involves an assessment of domestic costs and benefits—one that seemed favorable or at least not unfavorable for many of the signatories, and uniquely unfavorable for the United States. Whatever the global benefits may or may not have been, many individual nations, especially in Eastern Europe, had a lot more to gain than to lose from signing the protocol—including valuable emissions licenses that could be traded for cash. Some of the nations that appeared to make ambitious promises to reduce their emissions, such as Germany and the United Kingdom, in fact did no such thing. Domestic self-interest played a large role in producing the particular national targets in the treaty, and those targets were not terribly demanding.

Some nations, or their leaders, may have benefited from the signaling effect of participation, especially if they could simultaneously embarrass the United States. If national leaders in certain countries could show a strong commitment to meeting a global international challenge, many domestic constituents would be pleased and impressed, and it would be all the better if the apparently strong commitment did not impose significant domestic costs.

Perhaps some nations were truly acting as global altruists. Perhaps some had an unusually pessimistic (or accurate) account of the consequences of climate change, or believed that the Kyoto Protocol would initiate a set of agreements that, in the end, would do far more good than harm. And perhaps some nations, especially those with the most to lose, did not believe that the Kyoto Protocol would, in fact, prove to be binding. In this view, the agreement was "cheap talk"—a way to signal a commitment that would not operate as a commitment in practice. Let us consider some evidence in support of this view.

Despite ratification by all Annex 1 nations except the United States and Australia, several nations that signed the Kyoto Protocol are very far from their reductions targets. Compliance is not required until some time between 2008 and 2012 (with the precise date varying by country); it remains possible that the situation will be better when the actual due dates arrive.[79] But full compliance is unlikely. Many countries in the European Union are far short of their targets under the Kyoto Protocol (see Table 6). The current numbers, and the existing trends, suggest that several EU nations will fail to meet their obligations. By contrast, compliance with the Montreal Protocol has been essentially perfect.

The Annex 1 countries taken as a whole are not doing better than the European Union (see Table 7).[80] A number of countries show emissions increases comparable to or higher than those of the United States. These include Canada, New Zealand, Australia, Austria, Greece, Ireland, Portugal, Spain, and Italy. True, substantial reductions in greenhouse gas emissions have occurred in Bulgaria, Estonia, Latvia, the Czech Republic, Lithuania, Hungary, Poland, Russia, Ukraine, Iceland, Luxembourg, the United Kingdom, Sweden, and Germany. But most of these nations are in Central and Eastern Europe, which has suffered serious economic distress and hence substantially lower levels of energy use. The economic situation there led to an overall reduction in emissions of 37 percent in the relevant period.[81]

Because of the situation in Central and Eastern Europe, the good news is that from 1990 to 2003 greenhouse gas emissions from Annex 1 parties decreased by a total of 18.4 billion tons—an average percentage decrease of 5.9 percent, apparently in line with the Kyoto target of 5.2 percent.[82] But the averages are badly misleading, because Kyoto's distribution of targets among nations would produce far greater overall decreases than those that have

Table 6   Kyoto targets for the European Union.

Country	Target	Change in emissions between 1990 and 2003 (%)	Compliant with requirements between 2008 and 2012?
Austria	−13.00	16.50	No
Belgium	−7.50	1.30	No
Denmark	−21.00	6.80	No
Finland	0	21.50	No
France	0	−1.90	Yes
Germany	−21.00	−18.20	Almost
Greece	25.00	25.80	Almost
Ireland	13.00	25.60	No
Italy	−6.50	11.50	No
Luxembourg	−28.00	−16.10	No
Netherlands	−6.00	1.50	No
Portugal	27.00	36.70	No
Spain	15.00	41.70	No
Sweden	4.00	−2.30	Yes
United Kingdom	−12.50	−13.00	Yes

Table 7 Kyoto targets for Annex 1 countries.

Country	Target	% change in emissions between 1990 and 2003	Compliant with requirements betwee 2008 and 2012?
Bulgaria	−8	−50.00	Yes
Czech Republic	−8	−24.20	Yes
European Union	−8	−1.40	No
Estonia	−8	−50.80	Yes
Latvia	−8	−58.50	Yes
Liechtenstein	−8	5.30	No
Lithuania	−8	−66.20	Yes
Monaco	−8	30.00	No
Romania	−8	−46.10	Yes
Slovakia	−8	−28.30	Yes
Slovenia	−8	−1.90	No
Switzerland	−8	−0.40	No
United States	−7	13.34	No—refuses to rati
Canada	−6	24.20	No
Hungary	−6	−31.90	Yes
Japan	−6	12.80	No
Poland	−6	−34.40	Yes
Croatia	−5	−6.00	Yes
New Zealand	0	22.50	No
Russian Federation	0	−38.50	Yes
Ukraine	0	−46.20	Yes
Norway	1	9.30	No
Australia	8	23.30	No—refuses to rati
Iceland	10	−8.20	Yes

occurred thus far. The reason is that the decreases have occurred in nations with already low emissions rates, while the nations with high emissions rates (above all the United States) are generally increasing, not decreasing, their emissions.

By 2010, overall emissions from wealthy nations may grow by as much as 17 percent from 2000 levels—and thus be significantly higher than the Kyoto targets.[83] An important conclusion is that if the United States were to attempt to meet the target set by the Kyoto Protocol, it would have to impose exceedingly aggressive regulatory restrictions. In view of the possible increases of emissions in most wealthy nations, and because the economies of Eastern Europe are recovering, Kyoto's goals are unlikely to be met.

Lessons Learned

What lessons follow from an understanding of the extraordinary success of the Montreal Protocol and mixed picture for the Kyoto Protocol? Since we have only two data points here, we must be careful in drawing general conclusions.[84] But two lessons seem both important and indisputable.

The first is that public opinion in the United States greatly matters, at least if it is reflected in actual behavior. When ozone depletion received massive attention in the media, American consumers responded by greatly reducing their consumption of aerosol sprays containing CFCs. This action softened industry opposition to regulation, because product lines containing CFCs were no longer nearly as profitable. In addition, market pressures from consumers spurred technological innovation in developing CFC substitutes. In the environmental domain as elsewhere, markets themselves can be technology-forcing. At the same time, public opinion put a great deal of pressure on public officials, affecting the behavior of legislators and the White House alike.

In Europe, by contrast, those involved in CFC production and use felt little pressure from public opinion, certainly in the early stages. The absence of such pressure, combined with the efforts of well-organized private groups, helped to ensure that European nations would take a weak stand on the question of regulation, at least at the inception of negotiations. In later stages, public opinion and consumer behavior were radically transformed in the United Kingdom and in Europe, and the transformation had large effects on the approach of political leaders there as well.[85]

With respect to climate change, the attitude of the United States remains remarkably close to that of pre-Montreal Europe, urging regulators to "wait and learn"; to date, research and voluntary action rather than emission reduction mandates have been recommended by high-level officials. It is true that since 1990 the problem of climate change has received a great deal of media attention in the United States. But the public has yet to respond to that attention through consumer choices, and the best evidence suggests that most American citizens are not, in fact, alarmed about the risks associated with a warmer climate. American consumers and voters have put little pressure on either markets or officials to respond to the risk.

To be sure, public opinion on this topic is not fixed, and public officials do have room to maneuver.[86] If prominent politicians proclaimed that climate change poses serious risks, that those risks can be reduced without significant costs, and that morality requires the United States to protect future generations from those risks, more aggressive action might well be possible. California has taken significant steps to control greenhouse gases partly because its citizens want it to do so. Behavioral factors, and not a simple engagement with costs and benefits, can drive public opinion in new directions.

The second lesson is that international agreements addressing global environmental problems will be mostly ineffective without the participation of the United States, and the United States is likely to participate only if the domestic benefits are perceived to be at least in the general domain of the domestic costs. In international law generally, the latter point is hardly novel, though it is disputed in its strongest forms.[87] My modest point here is that for global environmental agreements to be effective, the United States must become persuaded that it will not lose much more than it will gain.

Of course the United States accounts for only about one-fifth of global greenhouse gas emissions—a stunning per capita figure, but one that is not high enough to derail international action if other nations are willing to go forward without the United States. If the world were able to make significant cuts in the other 80 percent of emissions, it could do a great deal about climate change. The problem is that if the United States stands to one side, coordinated, aggressive action on the part of other nations will almost certainly be impossible. China—anticipated to be the world's largest contributor to greenhouse gases by 2009—is most unlikely to make significant cuts in its emissions without the participation of the United States.

At Kyoto, China and India proved unwilling to commit to cuts even when the United States suggested that it would participate. Those nations, and other developing countries, will likely be reluctant to confer benefits on industrialized nations, including the United States, unless there is a degree of reciprocity and perhaps significant side payments as well (as in the Montreal Protocol). On the other hand, China may eventually find itself in something like the same position with respect to climate change as the United States occupied with respect to the ozone layer—gravely threatened by the very emissions from which it profits. If China perceives itself as seriously endangered by climate change, it might well be willing to scale back its emissions, because domestic self-interest might so require.[88] But that point raises another serious problem, as we shall see.

Contributors and Victims

An international accord would be easiest to obtain if those who contribute most to the problem of climate change also have the most to lose from warmer temperatures. If so, they would face a strong incentive to scale back their emissions. Something of this kind was true in the context of ozone-depleting chemicals; the largest contributor (the United States) was also at particular risk. Such an accord is harder to achieve if the major contributors have relatively little to lose.

Table 8 gives a responsible estimate of anticipated losses from climate change.[89] These particular figures must be taken with many grains of salt: They assume 2.5° C warming by 2100, but with a worst-case scenario, involving the temperature increase of 4° C or more, the damages would undoubtedly be much higher. Even on the assumption of 2.5° C warming, higher levels of damage are possible; the numbers here are hardly worst-case scenarios. But even if we make significant adjustments in the numbers, some nations are clearly much more vulnerable than others.[90] Russia stands to be a net gainer from global warming, with substantial benefits to agriculture. India is particularly vulnerable to health risks and agricultural losses, and nations in Africa stand to lose a great deal from

Table 8 Damages of a 2.5° C warming by 2100 as a percent of GDP.

India	4.93
Africa	3.91
OECD Europe	2.83
High income OPEC	1.95
Eastern Europe	0.71
Japan	0.50
United States	0.45
China	0.22
Russia	−0.6

climate-rated diseases. The large losses in GDP for India and Africa are therefore not merely monetary ones. They reflect massive increases in illnesses and premature deaths.

In light of these figures, we might expect that Russia would not be especially enthusiastic about controls of greenhouse gas emissions—except, perhaps, if an emissions trading system ensured that Russia would get a lot of money (as the Kyoto system in fact does). Like Russia, China is projected to benefit in agricultural production, and its health losses would be relatively modest, far below those expected in Africa and India. The United States faces limited threats to both agriculture and health. Because agriculture accounts for only about 2 percent of the American economy, climate change is unlikely to have a devastating economic effect even if American agriculture is harmed—and with certain projections, American agriculture might even benefit.[91] Higher temperatures will undoubtedly result in some increases in illnesses and deaths, but the United States is far less vulnerable than other nations.

We should therefore expect that the United States and China would be relatively less interested in reducing greenhouse gas emission; and as we have seen, their behavior is consistent with that prediction. The world's economy is interdependent, of course, and if many nations suffer serious adverse effects, the United States and China will be affected. And if warming rises well above 2.5° C, the United States and China will become vulnerable to catastrophic risks, like the rest of the world. But the central point is clear. The world's largest current contributor to climate change, the United States, ranks toward the bottom in terms of anticipated losses, and the largest contributor in the near future, China, ranks even lower. Perhaps unsurprisingly, citizens of China and the United States are less concerned about climate change than are citizens of Japan, France, Spain, India, Britain, and Germany.[92]

Now let us compare how much nations expect to lose from global warming with how much they stand to lose from *reductions* in greenhouse gas emissions. Table 9 offers a snapshot of global contributors in 2000 (limited to carbon dioxide, the leading greenhouse gas). According to these figures, the United States and China would be vulnerable to high burdens and costs if asked to reduce their emissions. Of course the picture would change if the United States or China developed a cheap way to reduce greenhouse gas emissions. But in the absence of such innovations, the leading emitters of greenhouse gases can expect to bear a significant burden if they make substantial cuts.

An important question, of course, involves trends over time. The major contributors in the past may not be the major contributors in the future. The existing data suggest that the largest contributors are likely to continue to qualify as such—but that important shifts, above all with emissions growth in China and India and emissions reductions in Russia and Germany, will also occur (see Table 10).

Table 9 Carbon dioxide contributors (%) as of 2000.

United States	20.6
China	14.7
European Union—25	14.0
Russia	5.7
India	5.6
Japan	3.9
Germany	3.0
Brazil	2.5
Canada	2.0
United Kingdom	1.9
Italy	1.6
South Korea	1.5
France	1.5
Mexico	1.5

Kevin Baumert et al., *Navigating the Numbers* 12 (2005).

With these trend lines, we can project changes by 2025. At that time, the developing world is expected to show an 84 percent increase in total emissions, accounting for 55 percent of the world's total.[93] In other words, poorer nations will be principal sources of the problem—a point that explains why the United States has been so skeptical about agreements that do not slow emissions growth in developing nations (see Table 11).[94]

But some nations, above all China and India, might reasonably object that their own contribution is smaller than the figures thus far suggest. In assessing relative contributions, we might be interested in *cumulative* emissions rather than annual emissions.[95] The overall stock might matter, not the current flow (see Table 12).

Table 10 Carbon dioxide emissions changes (%), 1990–2002.

China	49
United States	18
India	70
South Korea	97
Iran	93
Indonesia	97
Saudi Arabia	91
Brazil	57
Spain	44
Pakistan	60
Poland	−17
EU-25	−2
Germany	−13
Ukraine	−48
Russia	−23

Kevin Baumert et al., *Navigating the Numbers* 15 (2005).

Table 11 Relative contributions of annual carbon dioxide emissions by country/region (approximate % of worldwide emissions) over time.

	1990	2003	2010	2015	2020	2025	203
United States	23.4	22.8	21.0	20.0	19.4	18.9	18.
Europe	28.0	21.4	19.1	18.2	17.4	16.8	16.
China	10.6	14.1	19.3	20.8	22.2	23.3	24.
India	2.7	4.1	4.5	4.7	4.9	5.0	5.
Japan	4.8	4.8	4.0	3.6	3.3	3.0	2.
Africa	3.1	3.6	3.9	4.0	4.0	4.0	4.

Table 12 Cumulative CO$_2$ emissions (%), 1850–2002.

United States	29.3
EU-25	26.5
Russia	8.1
China	7.6
Germany	7.3
United Kingdom	6.3
Japan	4.1
France	2.9
India	2.2
Ukraine	2.2

Kevin Baumert et al., *Navigating the Numbers* 32 (2005).

Even if China's emissions rates pass those of the United States by 2009, it might well insist that it should not bear the same economic burden as a nation that has been responsible for a much larger percentage of aggregate emissions. Undoubtedly the purely domestic calculus—of costs and benefits—will play a significant role in any nation's decisions. But fairness judgments, attending to cumulative contributions, are unlikely to be irrelevant.

Nothing said here should be taken to suggest that the domestic cost-benefit analysis ought to be decisive in principle. In fact, it should not be. If one nation is imposing significant harms on citizens of another, it should not continue to do so even if, or because, a purely domestic analysis suggests that emissions reductions are not justified from the point of view of the nation that is imposing those harms. The problems of ozone depletion and climate change stem disproportionately from the actions of wealthy nations, whose citizens have disproportionately benefited. The emission of greenhouse gases could even be viewed as a kind of tort, producing damage for which emitters, and those who gained from their actions, ought to pay.[96] For example, energy and gasoline prices in the United States have been far lower than they would have been if those prices had included an amount attributable to the increased risks from climate change—risks that threaten to impose devastating harm on people in other countries.

Whether nations as such should be held responsible, and what such responsibility should specifically entail, are complicated questions. But in view of the fact that Americans have gained so much from activities that impose risks on citizens of other nations, it seems clear that they have a special obligation to mitigate the harm or to provide assistance to those who are likely to suffer. The assistance might take the form of financial or technological aid, making it easier to meet emissions targets, or monetary amounts designed to ease adaptation to hotter climates.

An additional moral issue stems from the fact that the citizens of Africa and India, the most vulnerable regions, are disproportionately poor. But the citizens of China, who stand to lose a great deal from significant restrictions on greenhouse gases, are also relatively poor, and the economic growth that is producing greenhouse gases is also contributing to significant reductions in their poverty. The issue of relative wealth and poverty should play a significant role in distributing the costs of emissions reductions.[97] If China is asked to make large reductions in a way that harms its own citizens, wealthy nations might well be asked to help; the extreme deprivation faced by citizens of Africa and India make it all the more important for past contributors and developed nations to offer assistance.

The moral issues raised by climate change are numerous, and they must be seriously engaged as part of both domestic discussions and international negotiations.[98] The Montreal Protocol holds out some hope here; judgments about moral responsibility and capacity to pay played a significant role in its various provisions. (It may not be irrelevant that the health risks of ozone depletion were faced mostly by light-skinned people, most vulnerable to skin cancer, whereas the most serious risks of climate change are faced by a group that prominently includes dark-skinned people, above all in Africa and India.) Incipient steps to help poor nations have been made in the context of climate change as well. But the evidence catalogued here raises doubts about the claim that, by themselves, moral obligations will provide enough motivation in the face of a palpably unfavorable cost-benefit analysis.

But let us return to simpler matters. With respect to the United States, the lesson of the Montreal Protocol can be captured in a single sentence: Where the domestic assessment strongly favors unilateral action, and where the same assessment suggests that a nation is likely to gain a great deal from an international agreement, that nation will favor such an agreement—unless, perhaps, well-organized private groups are able to persuade it not to do so. For the Kyoto Protocol, the lesson is equally simple: Where the domestic assessment suggests that unilateral action makes little sense, and where the same assessment suggests that a nation will lose a great deal from an international agreement, that nation is unlikely to favor such an agreement—unless, perhaps, the public is willing to demand that it do so. In light of these simple lessons, the two protocols present polar cases, and actually fairly easy ones.

Possible Worlds

The technocrats, both scientists and economists, were able to demonstrate that the Montreal Protocol was a terrific bargain for the United States, while the Kyoto Protocol presented a much less favorable picture. The overwhelming votes in the Senate reflected these assessments. But the overall judgments would have been far more difficult if the relevant numbers had been perceived as closer—if the scientific and economic judgments, working together, suggested that reasonable people could differ. Even if the United States was a modest net loser, perhaps moral considerations might have tipped, or might in the future tip, the national calculus in favor of an agreement to control climate change. If some method could be found to drive down costs and increase benefits, such a method would make the relevant agreement far more attractive not only to the United States but to the world as well—and hence increase the likelihood of compliance by nations that are now showing unfavorable trends.[99] I do not attempt to sketch the details of an ideal agreement here; much depends on difficult questions about the relationship between emissions reduction and adaptation, and about the right level of any emissions reductions.[100] But let us consider a few possibilities, starting with raising the benefits side of the ratio.[101]

A useful step would involve a clear distinction between stocks and flows.[102] To come to terms with past contributions, nations might participate in the creation of some kind of fund for climate change damages, with their participation reflecting their contributions to the total existing stock of emissions. India and China would not have to contribute much to such a fund, since so far they have not been the major emitters; the United States would be required to contribute a great deal. A step of this kind would be a sensible response to the fact that different nations have added dramatically different amounts to greenhouse gas concentrations.

A separate step would involve the response to existing flows. Perhaps a "polluters pay" principle could be made a part of an international agreement, so that nations would pay an amount to reflect their continuing contributions.[103] The resulting tax on green-house gas emissions might lead to reductions. It would be easy to impose something of this kind on domestic emitters, and an international agreement might provide a framework for the imposition of greenhouse taxes within nations as a whole. Alternatively, an understanding of past contributions and current emissions rates might be built into a structure closer to that of the Montreal Protocol, helping to serve as the foundation for both reductions requirements and economic transfers. The transfers might be designed to compensate for both past and future contributions to the problem. If high current contributors make significant cuts, perhaps their transfers need not be so large. If they continue to be high contributors, their transfers might be very high. If the goal is to ensure significant benefits to all participants, steps of this sort would be the place to start.

The overall benefits of greenhouse gas reductions could well turn out to be greater, domestically and for the world, than suggested by the most prominent analyses from several years ago—especially if the perceived damage from climate change increases.[104] If steps could be taken to reduce that damage, then the likelihood of a firm domestic response would of course increase.

On the cost side of the ratio, the first step would be to create an ambitious and reliable system for global emissions trading, which could make the cost-benefit ratio far more favorable for any agreement. The second step is to produce better targets and requirements, in a way that allows stringency to increase over time with new technological capacities.

In the case of "acid rain," the United States was able to reduce the cost of aggressive regulation by billions of dollars through an ambitious trading system.[105] For climate change, such a system would decrease the need for expensive regulation by allowing

American companies to "buy" American emissions credits from greenhouse gas producers in other nations. For the Kyoto Protocol, a system of global trading would reduce domestic costs from $325 billion to $91 billion, according to one projection, and reduce worldwide costs from $217 billion to $59 billion.[106] China would be far more likely to participate in an international agreement with an effective global emissions trading system. Perhaps China, India, and other poor nations could be subsidized with especially high allocations of trading rights, so as to come to terms with their relatively low past contributions, their general poverty, and their overall needs.

The emissions reductions targets in the Kyoto Protocol are both rigid and arbitrary. They start with an apparently random baseline year (1990) and ask nations to make apparently random percentage reductions from their emissions in that year.[107] But of course those targets were not truly random: Domestic self-interest, rather than sensible policy, produced these numbers. A better approach would include carbon taxes or emissions reduction requirements that grow over time as technology advances.[108] For ozone-depleting chemicals, as for lead, the United States followed a phase-down policy, one that allowed time for the development and marketing of adequate substitutes. No one is proposing the complete elimination of greenhouse gases; but tightening restrictions of emissions over time would make a great deal of sense.[109]

To achieve cost reductions, experiments in technology-forcing, designed to test whether the expense of emissions reductions have been inflated, also make sense. In 2006, California enacted a statute that would, by 2020, stabilize the state's emissions at 1990 levels—a step that calls for a 25 percent reduction from what 2020 emissions would have been under a "business as usual" approach. The enactment, by itself, will contribute close to nothing to reductions in global climate change by 2050, 2100, or any other date; and it will undoubtedly impose significant costs on the citizens of California. Why did California enact a program that would appear to produce no benefits while imposing real costs? The particular electoral dynamics of California undoubtedly played a role. Many Californians are greatly concerned about climate change, evidently for moral reasons, and the state's governor undoubtedly improved his prospects for reelection by showing his own commitment to the problem. Or perhaps the citizenry was motivated not only by moral considerations but also by an inaccurate perception of costs and benefits; perhaps the citizens, and some of the supportive officials, wrongly believed that California's action would by itself have a significant effect.

But here is another possibility: Perhaps Californians reasonably hoped that state action might spur additional reductions, both domestically and internationally, while also leading to technological changes that drive down the costs of emissions controls. Perhaps legislators and citizens believed that California's initiative would send an important signal to other states and even nations, in a way that will in fact produce large global benefits. If technology-forcing in California produces low-cost options, as in the case of ozone depletion, the likelihood of high benefits and reduced expenses will increase. Of course California is taking a gamble. But if low-cost substitutes do not emerge, the mandates in the statute could be relaxed—and hence it remains to be seen whether those mandates are as firm as they appear to be.

The California legislation provides an illuminating complication to the basic account in this chapter. In a sense, California was in the same position as was the United States with respect to the Kyoto Protocol, exploring an option that would apparently produce small benefits at significant cost. But California, unlike the country as a whole, willingly chose that option. Of course the political dynamics are quite different at the national level, at least for the present time. But perhaps those dynamics will change—especially if the California experiment proves to be successful.

Success and Failure

At first glance, the problems of ozone depletion and climate change seem exceedingly similar. In both contexts, nations appear to have a great deal to gain from cooperative action; technological innovation is highly desirable as a means of reducing the costs of regulation; intergenerational equity is a serious and complex issue; wealthy nations are responsible for the problem in the first place; and poor nations have a plausible claim to compensation, both for harm done and in return for their willingness to reduce emissions in the future.

Notwithstanding the similarities, the Montreal Protocol has proved a stunning success, and the Kyoto Protocol has largely failed. The contrasting outcomes are best explained by reference to the radically different approaches taken by the United States—by far the most significant contributor, per capita, to both ozone depletion and climate change. It is tempting to attribute those different approaches to the political convictions of the relevant administrations. But the Reagan administration, which pressed for the Montreal Protocol, was hardly known for its aggressive pursuit of environmental protection, and the Senate showed no interest in the Kyoto Protocol during the Clinton administration. The American posture, and hence the fate of the two protocols, was largely determined by perceived benefits and costs.

To the extent that the citizens of the United States have benefited from activities that inflict harms on other nations, those citizens are properly asked to help—through reducing their own emissions, through paying other nations to reduce theirs, and through payments to ease adaptation. But domestic self-interest will continue to be an important motivating force in international agreements on climate change. The task for the future is to devise an international agreement that resembles the Montreal Protocol in one critical respect: Its signatories, above all the United States and China, have reason to believe that they will gain more than they will lose.

CHAPTER THREE

CATASTROPHE

How should nations think about worst-case scenarios? If people's intuitions misfire, and if private and public decisions go badly wrong, can we devise a framework that might help? The Precautionary Principle, now used in many international documents, is often said to provide an answer.[1] Consider a few examples:

(1) The closing Ministerial Declaration from the United Nations Economic Conference for Europe in 1990 asserts, "Where there are threats of serious or irreversible damage, lack of full scientific certainty should not be used as a reason for postponing measures to prevent environmental degradation."[2]

(2) The 1992 Rio Declaration proclaims, "Where there are threats of serious or irreversible damage, lack of full scientific certainty shall not be used as a reason for postponing cost-effective measures to prevent environmental degradation."[3]

(3) The United Nations Framework Convention on Climate Change declares, "Where there are threats of serious or irreversible damage, lack of full scientific certainty should not be used as a reason for postponing [regulatory] measures, taking into account that

policies and measures to deal with climate change should be cost-effective so as to ensure global benefits at the lowest possible cost."[4]

(4) The Final Declaration of the First European "Seas At Risk" Conference states that if "the 'worst-case scenario' for a certain activity is serious enough then even a small amount of doubt as to the safety of that activity is sufficient to stop it taking place."[5]

Whatever the precise wording of the Precautionary Principle, worst-case scenarios, and the threat of catastrophic harm, lie at the heart of countless discussions about how to deal with hazards to safety, health, and the environment. For terrorism, hurricanes, war, ozone depletion, avian flu, and climate change, potential catastrophe plays a large role in private and public behavior. Many people urge a kind of One Percent Doctrine for all of these risks. They want to know: If there is a 1 percent risk that a military squadron will be destroyed in some battle, shouldn't we take extra steps to protect our soldiers? If there is a small chance of a devastating hurricane in a major city in the United States, shouldn't the government do a lot to protect its citizens? If we cannot exclude the possibility of a serious outbreak of the avian flu in Europe, shouldn't European governments be acting, right now, to eliminate that possibility?

If we focus on the risk of catastrophe, a distinctive version of the Precautionary Principle is possible: *When risks have catastrophic worst-case scenarios, it makes sense to take special measures to eliminate those risks, even when existing information does not enable regulators to make a reliable judgment about the probability that the worst-case scenarios will occur.* I shall call this the Catastrophic Harm Precautionary Principle.

This principle is at best a start, if only because it is lamentably vague. It does not define "special precautionary measures," and everything turns on exactly how special they are. Nor does the principle specify answers to three key issues: the threshold information that would trigger the principle; the role of costs; and how regulators should incorporate whatever information exists about the probability of catastrophe. We would not want to take infinitely burdensome steps to prevent worst-case scenarios, even when they are potentially catastrophic. After the attacks of 9/11, no one seriously suggested a one-year moratorium on all air travel within the United States, even though the Catastrophic Harm Precautionary Principle might seem to require that step. No one thinks we should respond to the risk of avian flu by banning international air travel. After the outbreak of AIDS, many people took precautions, but most of them did not cease sexual activity altogether.

My goal here is to explore various versions of the Catastrophic Harm Precautionary Principle, to show how they might be defended, and to qualify them. As a first approximation, we want to identify both the probability and the severity of worst-case scenarios; and we want to compare the expected value of precautions against their expected costs. Both expected value and expected costs should be measured in terms of well-being, not in terms of money. What matters is how lives are actually affected, not how much cash is gained or lost.

Of course, the idea of well-being is deeply contested, and so too is the idea of welfare (which I shall use as a synonym). Suppose that climate change is expected to result in significant numbers of extinctions and millions of deaths of animals. How exactly should that influence our assessment of the effects of climate change on well-being? To say the least, people disagree about how to answer that question. Or suppose that certain restrictions on greenhouse gases will result in a 1 percent loss in Gross Domestic Product, producing identifiable increases in unemployment and poverty. If we focus on welfare, is that 1 percent loss acceptable when the result is to reduce climate change by a specified amount? Some people would like to answer such questions by reference to the effects on human capabilities, understood in terms of what people are able to be and to do.[6] Those who endorse the "capabilities approach" contest many other understandings of well-being.

For present purposes, I shall use the idea of well-being (or welfare) without specifying its meaning; the idea should be taken as simply a placeholder for the best account. My hope is that for many problems, people who have different understandings of "well-being," or who are uncertain about the right understanding, can agree on the proper course of action notwithstanding their disagreements or their uncertainty. In this domain, as in so many others, we should be able to obtain *incompletely theorized agreements* on what to do—agreements on the right practice amidst disagreements or confusions about the specific theory that best justifies that practice.[7]

Whatever the right account of well-being, everyone should agree that if worst-case scenarios are exceedingly unlikely to come to fruition, then there are clear limits on how much we should do to eliminate them. Suppose that precautionary steps would impose huge burdens or that those very steps would subject millions of people to high probabilities of very-bad-case scenarios. If so, then doing everything we can to avoid the worst case is unlikely to be sensible. It is both necessary and possible, in short, to explore what is gained and what is lost by eliminating worst-case scenarios.

As we shall see, an analysis of the expected value of precautions makes sense, and is feasible, when probabilities can be assigned to the various outcomes, including those that qualify as catastrophic. Suppose, for example, that catastrophic harm is most unlikely to occur (say, below the threshold specified by any One Percent Doctrine) and that the cost of eliminating the relevant risk is very high (say, because it would significantly increase unemployment and poverty). In those circumstances, precautions may be more trouble than they are worth. An analysis of the expected value of precautions should be relevant even if margins of safety are appropriate and even if that analysis is not conclusive—and even if distributional considerations greatly matter, so that regulators should consider whether the harm is likely to be visited on the most vulnerable people or those least likely to be in a position to protect themselves.

The most modest approaches to catastrophic harm focus on both the probability and the magnitude of the harm, and appreciate the fact that the expected value of catastrophes is often much worse than we anticipate. Such approaches can provide a helpful response to some of the problems explored in Chapter 1. Less modest versions offer an extra layer of precaution—a form of regulatory insurance, designed to protect against the worst-case scenarios. The size of that extra layer depends on what we gain and what we lose from it—including other worst-case scenarios that the extra layer may itself create. For most problems, then, the Catastrophic Harm Precautionary Principle says, very simply, that both ordinary people and regulators should proceed by assessing the expected value of the options, including an appreciation of the distinctive harms associated with genuine catastrophes, and adding a margin of safety whose magnitude depends on its own expected value.

The question becomes far more difficult when we cannot assign probabilities to the various outcomes. Suppose, for example, that we have no idea how likely it is that climate change will produce catastrophic harm. My discussion of this problem is detailed and somewhat technical, but I shall suggest that even when we cannot assign probabilities, we can still identify a domain for a Catastrophic Harm Precautionary Principle, by attending to what is gained and what is lost by eliminating the most catastrophic outcome. If the worst-case scenario associated with one course of action is much worse than the worst-case scenario associated with a second course of action, and if we do not lose a great deal by following the second course of action, then the second course of action is the one to choose. The simplest lesson is this: Instead of ignoring worst-case scenarios, or automatically devoting extensive resources to their prevention, we should begin by asking exactly how bad they are, and how much is required to prevent them.

The Precautionary Principle

In the face of risks of serious harm, it has become common to invoke the Precautionary Principle.[8] Vice President Cheney's One Percent Doctrine is itself a precautionary principle; it insists that even if a serious terrorism-related harm is highly unlikely to come to fruition, we should take special steps to prevent it. And indeed, the United States has followed a kind of Precautionary Principle in the aftermath of the 9/11 attacks, responding to risks that were not likely to occur. The Iraq War was publicly defended by reference to the Precautionary Principle: Even if we could not be certain that Saddam Hussein had weapons of mass destruction, or would use them, the war might be justified as a way of eliminating the threat. (Why take chances with Saddam Hussein?) In order to understand what I shall have to say about worst-case scenarios, we have to back up a bit and explore the Precautionary Principle more generally.

Weak versions, strong versions   Unfortunately, the exploration is harder than it might seem, because what we are exploring is not clear. Twenty or more definitions of the principle have been offered, and they are not compatible with one another.[9] The most cautious and weak versions suggest, quite sensibly, that a lack of decisive evidence of harm should not be a ground for refusing to regulate. Consider the health risks associated with tobacco; decades ago, it made no sense for governments and individuals to treat the risk as zero merely because the evidence was uncertain. Controls might be justified even if it is impossible to establish a definite connection between, for example, low-level exposures to certain carcinogens and harmful effects on human health. The Ministerial Declaration of the Second International Conference on the Protection of the North Sea, held in London in 1987, sensibly suggests: "In order to protect the North Sea from possibly damaging effects of the most dangerous substances, a Precautionary Principle is necessary which may require action to control inputs of such substances even before a causal link has been established by absolutely clear scientific evidence."

The influential Wingspread Declaration, from a meeting of environmentalists in 1998, goes much further: "When an activity raises threats of harm to human health or the environment, precautionary measures should be taken even if some cause and effect relationships are not established scientifically. In this context the proponent of the activity, rather than the public, should bear the burden of proof."[10] Here the burden of proof is shifted to those who want to engage in risk-creating activity. In Europe, the Precautionary Principle is sometimes understood in a still stronger way, suggesting that regulators should build "a margin of safety into all decision making."[11] Another strong version suggests "that action should be taken to correct a problem as soon as there is evidence that harm may occur, not after the harm has already occurred."[12] The word "may" is the crucial one here, because it signals the need for corrective action even in the face of merely speculative evidence that a risk is serious.

The weak versions of the Precautionary Principle are unobjectionable and important. We do not walk in moderately dangerous areas at night; we exercise; we buy smoke detectors; we buckle our seatbelts; we might even avoid fatty foods (or carbohydrates). Every day, individuals and nations take steps to avoid hazards that are far from certain. We buy insurance, and much precautionary behavior is akin to the purchase of insurance. Sensible governments regulate risks that, in individual cases or even in the aggregate, have a well under 100 percent chance of coming to fruition. An individual might ignore a mortality risk of 1/500,000 in a given year, because that risk is pretty small, but if 100 million citizens face that risk, the expected number of deaths is 200, and the nation should take the problem seriously. For many risks, including those posed by pesticides and toxins, we do in fact regulate risks of 1/100,000, 1/200,000, even 1/500,000 or less.

To get a handle on the underlying issues, let us understand the Precautionary Principle in a strong way, to suggest that regulation is required in response to possible risks to health, safety, or the environment, even if the supporting evidence remains speculative and even if the economic costs of regulation are high. To avoid absurdity, the idea of "possible risk" must be understood to require a certain threshold of plausibility. No one thinks that regulators should respond if some human being, somewhere, urges that a risk is worth taking seriously. But under the Precautionary Principle in its stronger forms, the threshold burden is minimal, and once it is met, there is a presumption in favor of regulatory controls.

Paralysis and incoherence   The real problem with the Precautionary Principle, thus understood, is that it offers no guidance—not that it is wrong, but that it forbids all courses of action, including regulation.[13] Taken seriously, it is paralyzing, banning the very steps that it simultaneously requires. If you accepted the strong version, you would not be able to get through a single day, because every action, including inaction, would be forbidden by the principle by which you were attempting to live. You would be banned from going to work; you would be banned from staying at home; you would be banned from taking medications; you would be banned from neglecting to take medications. The same point holds for governments that try to follow the Precautionary Principle.

In some cases, serious precautions would actually run afoul of the Precautionary Principle. Consider the "drug lag," produced whenever the government takes a highly precautionary approach to the introduction of new medicines and drugs onto the market.[14] If a government insists on this approach, it will protect people against harms from inadequately tested drugs, in a way that fits well with the goal of precaution. But it will also prevent people from receiving potential benefits from those very drugs—and hence subject people to serious risks that they would not otherwise face. Is it "precautionary" to require extensive premarket testing, or to do the opposite? In 2006, 50,000 dogs were slaughtered in China, and the slaughter was defended as a precautionary step against the spread of rabies. But the slaughter itself caused a serious harm to many animals, and it inflicted psychological harms on many dog-owners, and even physical injuries on those whose pets were clubbed to death during walks. Is it so clear that the Precautionary Principle justified the slaughter? And even if the Precautionary Principle could be applied, was the slaughter really justified?

Or consider the case of DDT, often banned or regulated in the interest of reducing risks to birds and human beings.[15] The problem with such bans is that, in poor nations, they eliminate what appears to be the most effective way of combating malaria. For this reason, they significantly undermine public health. DDT may well be the best method for combating serious health risks in many countries. With respect to DDT, precautionary steps are both mandated and forbidden by the idea of precaution in its strong forms. To know what to do, we need to identify the probability and magnitude of the harms created and prevented by DDT—not to insist on precaution as such.

Similar issues are raised by the continuing debate over whether certain antidepressants impose a (small) risk of breast cancer.[16] A precautionary approach might seem to argue against the use of these drugs because of their carcinogenic potential. But the failure to use those antidepressants might well impose risks of its own, certainly psychological and possibly even physical (because psychological ailments are sometimes associated with physical ones as well). Or consider the decision by the Soviet Union to evacuate and relocate more than 270,000 people in response to the risk of adverse effects from the Chernobyl fallout. It is hardly clear that on balance this massive relocation project was justified on health grounds: "A comparison ought to have been made between the psychological and medical burdens of this measure (anxiety, psychosomatic diseases, depression and suicides) and the harm that may have been prevented."[17] More generally, a sensible government might want to ignore the small risks associated with low levels of radiation, on the ground that precautionary responses are likely to cause fear that outweighs any health benefits from those responses—and fear is not good for your health.[18]

The Precautionary Principle is often invoked in connection with genetic modification of food—a plausible concern in light of the multiple risks potentially created by that practice.[19] But many people believe that a failure to allow genetic modification of crops might well result in many deaths.[20] The reason is that genetic modification holds out the promise of producing food that is both cheaper and more nutritious—resulting, for example, in "golden rice," which might save many lives in developing countries.[21] My point is not that genetic modification will likely have those benefits or that the benefits of genetic modification necessarily outweigh the risks. The claim is only that if the Precautionary Principle is taken literally, it is offended by regulation as well as by non-regulation. If we are worried about worst-case scenarios, we might want to take special steps to regulate genetic modification of food; but such regulation has worst-case scenarios of its own.

As this example suggests, precautionary steps sometimes violate the Precautionary Principle because they give rise to *substitute risks*, in the form of hazards that materialize, or are increased, as a result of regulation. But the problem may be even larger than that. Some evidence suggests that any expensive regulation will have adverse effects on life and health.[22] An early study found that a statistical life is lost for every expenditure of $7 million;[23] a later study suggests that an expenditure of $15 million produces a loss of one life.[24] Another analysis finds that poor people are especially vulnerable to this effect—that a regulation that reduces wealth for the poorest 20 percent of the population will have twice as large a mortality effect as a regulation that reduces wealth for the wealthiest 20 percent.[25]

Both the phenomenon and the underlying mechanisms are greatly disputed, and I do not mean to endorse any particular account here or to suggest that an association between mortality and regulatory expenditures has been unambiguously demonstrated.[26] The only point is that many reasonable people believe this association is real. If so, then an expenditure of, say, $600 million to prevent an adverse health effect will lead to perhaps as many as sixty lives lost.

This point makes the Precautionary Principle hard to implement whenever regulation entails a significant cost. If this is so, the Precautionary Principle itself raises doubts about many precautions. If the principle argues against any action that carries a small risk of imposing significant harm, then regulators should be reluctant to require large expenditures to reduce risks, simply because those expenditures themselves carry risks. Here is the sense in which the Precautionary Principle is paralyzing: It stands as an obstacle to both regulation and nonregulation, and to everything in between.

Precautions and risk-taking everywhere It has become standard to say that some nations are more precautionary, and more concerned about worst-case scenarios, than are others. European countries, for example, are said to be more precautionary than the United States. If the argument thus far is correct, this conclusion is utterly implausible. First, it is implausible empirically. Some nations take strong precautions against some risks, but no nation takes precautions against every risk. As we have seen, the United States has followed a kind of Precautionary Principle with respect to ozone depletion, and certainly with respect to terrorism, but not for climate change or genetic modification of food. The United Kingdom was not particularly focused on the worst-case scenarios associated with ozone depletion; but it closely attends to those scenarios in the context of climate change. France is not precautionary with respect to nuclear power, and it followed no strong Precautionary Principle with respect to Saddam Hussein. But on many issues of health and safety, France takes aggressive precautionary measures. No nation is precautionary in general; costly precautions are inevitably taken against only those hazards that seem especially salient or insistent.[27] Comparing Europe to the United States, Jonathan Wiener and Michael Rogers have demonstrated this point in detail.[28]

But the larger objection is conceptual, not empirical. A nation can be precautionary with respect to some risks, and some worst-case scenarios, but not all of them. Taken in its strongest and crudest forms, the Precautionary Principle wrongly suggests that nations can and should adopt a general form of risk aversion. While precautions can be taken against particular hazards, they cannot be taken against every one.

It is tempting to defend the Precautionary Principle—certainly for health, safety, and the environment—on the ground that early warnings, offering only suggestive evidence of harm, often turn out to be correct.[29] I have emphasized that indisputable proof of harm should not be required to justify regulation; this is the sense in which the weak version of the principle is both unobjectionable and important. But the fact that suggestive evidence must be taken seriously does not make the strong version coherent. Suggestive evidence of harm can often be found on all sides of a question. And in any case, suggestive evidence of harm has often been found to be not an early warning ultimately worth heeding but instead a false alarm, producing unjustified fear and significant social losses of many kinds.[30]

Consider fears about fluoridated water in the 1950s, contaminated cranberries in 1959, MSG in Chinese restaurants in 1968, cyclamates in 1968, and mercury in tuna in 1970. None of these widely publicized "hazards" turned out to pose a serious threat to public health. According to an instructive effort to distinguish between prescient warnings and false ones, the "clearest hallmark of a true public warning during the period 1948–1971 was a reputable scientific news source. Warnings reaching the press from scientists operating in a conventional way at an orthodox scientific institution were true more than twice as often as those reaching the news from government officials or citizen advocates."[31] A reliable source is a reason to take a plea for precautions more seriously; but even such a source does not justify a general embrace of the strong version of the Precautionary Principle.

Cognition and precaution   If the argument thus far is correct, we need to ask why reasonable people endorse that principle. If precautions themselves create risks, and if no course of action lacks significant worst-case scenarios, it is puzzling why people believe that the Precautionary Principle offers real guidance. The simplest answer is that a weak version is doing the real work. The more interesting answer is that the principle seems to give guidance because people single out a subset of risks that are actually involved. In other words, those who invoke the principle wear blinders. But what kind of blinders do they wear, and what accounts for them? I suggest that two factors are crucial. The first, emphasized in Chapter 1, is availability; the second, which we have not yet encountered, involves loss aversion.

Availability helps to explain the operation of the Precautionary Principle for a simple reason: Sometimes a certain risk, said to call for precautions, is cognitively available, whereas other risks, including the risks associated with regulation itself, are not. For example, everyone knows that nuclear power is potentially dangerous; the associated risks, and the worst-case scenarios, are widely perceived in the culture, because of the Chernobyl disaster and popular films about nuclear catastrophes. By contrast, a relatively complex mental operation is involved in the judgment that restrictions on nuclear power might lead people to depend on less safe alternatives, such as fossil fuels. In many cases where the Precautionary Principle seems to offer guidance, the reason is that some of the relevant risks are available while others are barely visible.

In justifying the 2003 Iraq War on precautionary grounds, the Bush administration was highly alert to the risks associated with the regime of Saddam Hussein, but not so alert to the risks associated with the war and its aftermath. Bush's advisors seem to have focused his attention on the worst-case scenario associated with

Saddam Hussein, but on the best-case scenario associated with the war. Availability generally explains why the Precautionary Principle appears to give guidance when in fact risks and bad outcomes exist on all sides.

But there is another factor. Human beings tend to be *loss averse,* which means that a loss from the status quo is seen as more distressing than a gain is seen as desirable.[32] Loss aversion is not limited to human beings, by the way: pigeons, rats, and monkeys are especially averse to losses too. Because we dislike losses far more than we like corresponding gains, opportunity costs, in the form of forgone gains, often have a small impact on our decisions. When we anticipate a loss of what we already have, we often become genuinely afraid, in a way that greatly exceeds our feelings of pleasurable anticipation when we anticipate some addition to our current holdings.

The implication in the context of danger is clear: People will be closely attuned to the potential losses from any newly introduced risk, or from any aggravation of existing risks, but far less concerned about future gains they might never see if a current risk is reduced. Loss aversion often helps to explain what makes the Precautionary Principle operational. The status quo marks the baseline against which gains and losses are measured, and a loss from the status quo seems much more "bad" than a gain from the status quo seems good.

This is exactly what happens in the case of drug testing. Recall the emphasis, in the United States, on the risks of insufficient testing of medicines as compared with the risks of delaying the availability of those medicines. If there is a lot of testing, people may get sicker, and even die, simply because medicines are not made available. But if the risks of delay are off-screen, the Precautionary Principle will appear to give guidance notwithstanding the objections I have made. At the same time, the lost benefits sometimes present a devastating problem with the use of the Precautionary Principle. In the context of genetic modification of food, this is very much the situation; many people focus on the risks of genetic modification without also attending to the benefits that might be lost by regulation or prohibition. We can find the same problem when the Precautionary Principle is invoked to support bans on non-reproductive cloning. For many people, the possible harms of cloning register more strongly than the potential therapeutic benefits that would be made unattainable by a ban on the practice.

Of course, I do not mean to suggest that people will always take precautions against future losses. Tobacco smoking, obesity, sun exposure, and many other hazards to health lead to serious losses from the status quo and yet receive too little attention. The only point is that when people think that the Precautionary Principle gives guidance, it is sometimes because they fixate on losses from the status quo, and do not much think about the gains, and the reductions in risk, that an activity might eventually provide. The appeal of the Precautionary Principle, in the face of risks on all sides, presents many puzzles. Availability and loss aversion do not solve them, but they provide some helpful clues.

Distributional issues   Those who endorse the Precautionary Principle often do so on grounds of fairness, believing that the principle will assist the most vulnerable members of society.[33] But does the Precautionary Principle actually have that effect?

In the United States, the Clean Air Act takes a highly precautionary approach, requiring an "adequate margin of safety" and hence regulation in the face of scientific uncertainty.[34] In that sense, the Clean Air Act accepts the Precautionary Principle. At the same time, the Clean Air Act delivers especially large benefits to poor people and members of minority groups—larger benefits, on balance, than it gives to wealthy people.[35] In the international domain, aggressive action to combat climate change is likely to benefit poor countries, above all India and Africa, more than wealthy ones, which are less dependent on agriculture, more able to adapt, and less vulnerable to climate-related diseases such as malaria. These distributional effects of climate change are among the strongest points in favor of aggressive regulation of greenhouse gases.

But in many cases, the Precautionary Principle would have unfortunate distributional effects. Bans on DDT have already had bad effects in some poor countries, because of a rise in malaria.[36] Genetic modification of food might well be a similar example—according to some projections, the benefits are likely to be enjoyed most by poor people, not the wealthy.[37] And regulations in general have a disproportionately serious effect on poor people, simply because the price increases they entail are hardest for them to handle, and because regulation sometimes means fewer and less remunerative jobs.

Distributional issues should indeed be a central concern of any effort to prevent worst-case scenarios, but the Precautionary Principle is a crude, indirect, and sometimes perverse way of incorporating distributional concerns. The real question is whether more refined understandings of the principle can be developed. Let us turn, then, to that question.

Catastrophic Harm, Version 1: Expected Value

From the discussion in Chapter 1, a reasonable generalization is that when low-probability events occur, people become more fearful than they ought to be, but on average, people show less concern for such events than they should.[38] Overreaction and underreaction can produce serious difficulties. To see why, consider three stylized problems, creating three quite different sorts of risks.

- The first problem creates a 999,999 in a million chance that no one will die, and a 1 in a million chance that 200,000,000 people will die.
- The second problem creates a 50 percent chance that no one will die and a 50 percent chance that 400 people will die.
- The third problem creates a 100 percent chance that 200 people will die.

Suppose that government can eliminate all three problems at the same cost. If outcomes and probabilities are simply multiplied, the three problems are equivalent: the expected loss in each case is 200 lives. For the first problem—clearly a catastrophic worst-case outcome—we would have an extremely difficult time defending the view that no resources should be devoted to eliminating the underlying risk. Let us begin, then, with the most modest kind of Catastrophic Harm Precautionary Principle—one that favors precautionary steps based on an inquiry into expected value. The modest version might say: *Regulators should consider the expected value of catastrophic risks, even when the worst-case scenario is highly unlikely. Regulators should choose cost-effective measures to reduce those risks and should attempt to compare the expected value of the risk with the expected value of precautionary measures.* Under this approach, catastrophes are not receiving any particular attention. The central point is that they do not deserve, and should not receive, *less* attention than higher probability harms with equivalent expected value.

If the risk of an asteroid collision is tiny, and if asteroid collisions are not likely to cause serious harm, we should attempt to prevent asteroid collisions only if we can do so without making significant sacrifices. Many worst-case scenarios can be assessed in this way. Of course distributional considerations might also be taken into account. Even if the expected value of the harm is lower than the expected value of the precautions, we might take those precautions *if* the most vulnerable people would gain and the least vulnerable people would lose. (Perhaps distributional considerations should be made part of the inquiry into expected value.)

The One Percent Doctrine is easily understood in the light of the Catastrophic Harm Precautionary Principle that I have just sketched. If there is a 1 percent chance that Pakistani scientists are helping Al Qaeda obtain nuclear weapons, the expected value of the risk is very high; we should do a lot to eliminate a 1/100 risk that those determined to kill Americans will actually acquire nuclear weapons. (How much should be done to avoid a 1/100 risk that a major city will be destroyed?) Despite its modesty, this form of the Precautionary Principle has important uses. It prevents people from treating low-probability risks as if they were zero-probability events, and it forces people to consider and possibly even to imagine the consequences on all sides of the question, not only those that are cognitively available.

Of course, many real-world problems do not come with specified probabilities. Often we cannot say that a worst-case scenario has a 1/100,000 or a 1/1,000,000 chance of coming to fruition.[39] Sometimes we will have a range of probabilities, not a point estimate. When this is so, we can nonetheless speak of expected value, though with perhaps less confidence about the particular figure. Imagine, for example, a 50 percent chance that a risk is 1/10,000 and a 50 percent chance that it is 1/100,000, and that 1 million people are exposed to the risk. This means there is a 50 percent chance that the expected value is 100 lives and a 50 percent chance that it is 10 lives. The expected value of the risk, therefore, is 55 lives. But because there is a 50 percent chance that the expected value is 100 lives, we might want to take special precautions; whether we should do so depends on that expected cost of the precautions themselves. (Perhaps they also create mortality risks.) Or perhaps we know even less; perhaps the range is between a 20 percent and a 70 percent chance of 100 deaths, and a similar range for the possibility of 10 deaths. The simple point is that an inquiry into expected value can orient the inquiry, whether or not point estimates are possible. Often that inquiry will tell us what to do, even when the numbers can be reasonably disputed.

The principle I have sketched might well provide more protection than accords with ordinary intuitions and behavior. In order to obtain an understanding of those intuitions, I conducted an experiment with 176 law students, who were asked the following question:[40] *The government is considering two environmental problems. The first creates a 1 in 1 million risk of killing 200 million people, and a 999,999 in 1 million risk of killing zero people. The second creates a 1 in ten risk of killing 2,000 people, and a 9 in 10 risk of killing zero people. Do you think:*

(a)   the first problem has higher priority?

(b)   the second problem has higher priority?

(c)   the two problems have equal priority?

A strong plurality of 41 percent chose (b), whereas 36 percent chose (c) and only 22 percent chose (a). For low–probability risks of disaster, many people were willing to take their chances, preferring to address a higher probability risk with an equivalent expected value (in this case, 200 lives). Of course law students at particular institutions may not be representative of the population as a whole, but we might well expect the general population to show even *lower* concern for a low-probability, high-consequence risk. If so, calling attention to expected value would ensure that societies address, rather than ignore, potentially catastrophic harm.

To the extent that many people show little concern about climate change, part of the explanation lies in the fact that human beings often neglect low-probability, high-consequence risks, especially if the costs would be incurred immediately and if the benefits would not be realized until the distant future. A Catastrophic Harm Precautionary Principle, concerned with expected value, would supply a valuable correction to this tendency.

Catastrophic Harm, Version 2: The Social Amplification of Risk

A Catastrophic Harm Precautionary Principle, of the modest kind just sketched, raises several questions. The most obvious is whether a low-probability risk of catastrophe might not deserve *more* attention than higher-probability risks, even when the expected value appears to be equal. The reason is that the loss of 200 million people may be more than 1,000 times worse than the loss of 2,000 people. Pause over the real-world meaning of a loss of 200 million people in the United States. The nation would find it extremely hard to recover. Private and public institutions would be damaged for a long time, perhaps forever. What kind of government would emerge? What would its economy look like? Future generations would inevitably suffer. The effect of a catastrophe greatly outruns a simple multiplication of a certain number of lives lost. The overall "cost" of losing two-thirds of the American population is far more than 100,000 times the cost of losing 2,000 people.

The same point holds when the numbers are smaller. Following the collapse of a dam that left 120 people dead and 4,000 homeless in Buffalo Creek, Virginia, psychiatric researchers continued to find significant psychological and sociological changes two years after the disaster occurred. Survivors still suffered a loss of direction and energy, along with other disabling character changes.[41] One evaluator attributed this "Buffalo Creek Syndrome" specifically to "the loss of traditional bonds of kinship and neighborliness."[42]

Genuine catastrophes, involving tens of thousands or millions of deaths, would magnify that loss to an unimaginable degree. A detailed literature on the "social amplification of risk" explores the secondary social losses that greatly outrun the initial effects of given events.[43] The harm done by the attacks of 9/11, for instance, far exceeded the deaths on that day, horrendous as those were. One telling example: Many people switched, in the aftermath of the attack, to driving long distances rather than flying, and the switch produced almost as many highway deaths as the attacks themselves, simply because driving is more dangerous than flying.[44] The attacks had huge effects on other behaviors of individuals, businesses, and governments, resulting in costs of hundreds of billions of dollars, along with continuing fear, anxiety, and many thousands of additional deaths from the Afghanistan and Iraq wars.

We might therefore identify a second version of the Catastrophic Harm Precautionary Principle, also attuned to expected value but emphasizing some features of catastrophic risk that might otherwise be neglected: *Regulators should consider the expected value of catastrophic risks, even when the worst-case scenario is highly unlikely. In assessing expected value, regulators should consider the distinctive features of catastrophic harm, including the "social amplification" of such harm. Regulators should choose cost-effective measures to reduce those risks and should attempt to compare the expected value of the risk with the expected value of precautionary measures.*

Catastrophic Harm, Version 3: Precautions as Insurance

For some risks, people seek to create a margin of safety that operates as a kind of regulatory insurance. In deciding on our own behavior and the behavior of sensible governments, we might favor special precautions against worst-case scenarios. Perhaps it makes sense to "buy" extra insurance for catastrophic risks, on a principle of risk aversion. When low-probability risks of catastrophe are placed on-screen, so that people will not ignore them, many people are willing to pay much more to avoid those risks than the expected value would seem to warrant. Insurance companies make money for exactly that reason.

In fact, a well-known alternative to expected utility theory—called prospect theory—predicts that people will show risk aversion in circumstances of just this sort.[45] According to prospect theory, people prefer to protect themselves against a very small risk of a huge loss rather than a very high risk of a small loss, even if the expected value of the small loss is higher. Prospect theory suggests that, if the question is properly framed, people may be willing to devote special priority to a low-probability risk of catastrophe. The degree of the priority depends on two things: the degree of risk aversion, and what must be given up in order to obtain the margin of safety.[46] Many people are willing to spend a lot of money on insurance against worst-case scenarios—much more than the protection seems to be worth in terms of expected monetary value.

Is this a form of irrationality? The answer depends on what people are getting for their money and what they are losing. The costs of risk reduction always matter, and some insurance premiums prove far too expensive. But paying a special premium to avoid really bad outcomes is far from irrational. Consider this mundane example. Like many Americans, I am a member of the American

Automobile Association ("Triple A"). For $75 each year, my membership entitles me to various towing services in the event that my car breaks down. For many AAA members, including me, the membership fee is probably higher than its expected monetary value. In most calendar years many members, including me, do not call AAA at all. And if my car really did break down, I could probably find someone to tow it for less than I have paid in membership fees over time.

Still, being a member of AAA makes sense—at least once we think not in terms of money but in terms of well-being. If your car breaks down, you will probably become anxious and you might even be afraid; it's worth a lot to have a phone number that you can call for fast, reliable help. In fact, it's worth a lot to know in *advance* that you have that phone number in your wallet, in the event that a bad or worst-case scenario develops. Part of what people are buying with their AAA membership is assurance, before the fact, that they needn't much worry if their car breaks down. Perhaps they are (rationally) buying protection against their own (not entirely rational) fears. And in fact, people often take precautions in order to protect against fears and anxiety. AAA membership may not be a good deal, from a strictly monetary point of view. But in terms of people's sense of well-being, it makes a lot of sense.

This point has implications for insurance and for precautions in general. If John's $150,000 house were destroyed, he would be devastated emotionally and financially. It might well be worthwhile for him to spend $2,000 annually to ensure that he would be compensated for the financial loss, even if the expected monetary value of the loss does not justify that expenditure. John might want to know, in advance, that if his house is destroyed, he can rebuild his home—and put his life back together—quickly. And he might be willing to pay a lot for that peace of mind, even if the expected monetary value of the loss does not justify the cost of the premium. People want health insurance for a similar reason: if someone in the family gets sick, they do not want to spend time worrying about financial ruin—their energy would be better spent by attending to the sick family member. This everyday sense of security is valuable for its own sake, even if in most years a family's health insurance is not tapped and its cost outruns its expected value.

Moreover, the relationship between money and well-being is not direct; the last $10,000 in savings is worth a lot more, in welfare terms, than the first $10,000 of a significant amount of savings.[47] You might buy insurance, even if its expected economic cost exceeds its expected economic value, because you gain more than you lose in terms of welfare. For John, the difference between having, say, $120,000 each year or $118,000 each year may not much matter, because $2,000 on top of $118,000 is not such a big deal. But a sudden loss of $150,000 would be a very big deal if it happened. In terms of welfare, the loss of $2,000, subtracted from what he now has, is tolerable. Even if the expected monetary value of the loss of his house is only $1,990, because the loss is very unlikely, it is worth avoiding that loss, because money has a lot more value when you have less of it. John might willingly make an annual payment of $2,000 if that payment ensures that he will receive compensation for the loss of his house. To put it another way, people buy insurance for the simple reason that they value dollars less when they have a lot of dollars (as John has when paying his annual premium) and more when they have few dollars (as John would have if he lost his house).

Some degree of "pure" risk aversion helps to account for the willingness to buy insurance or to take precautions against worst-case scenarios. Suppose you are considering an operation. If you do not have it, you will lose a certain amount of well-being—let's call it ten units of well-being. With the operation, you have a 60 percent chance that you will not lose those ten units and a 40 percent chance that things will go wrong and you will lose twenty units of well-being. In terms of expected value, the operation makes a lot of sense. But well-being is not money, and you might not want to gamble on the loss of so much well-being, even though the odds favor a net gain. Eye surgery provides examples, even when the numbers are more favorable. You might decline surgery for nearsightedness or mild cataracts even though the expected value of surgery is far higher than that of the status quo. Why gamble on blindness when the current situation is not so bad?

Using the analogy to insurance, we might want to build a distinctive premium called *catastrophe aversion* into regulatory efforts to protect against catastrophic harm. This idea might be used as the basis for a third and more aggressive kind of Catastrophic Harm Precautionary Principle, embodying that premium: *Regulators should consider the expected value of catastrophic risks, even when the worst-case scenario is highly unlikely. In assessing expected value, regulators should consider the distinctive features of catastrophic harm, including the "social amplification" of such harm. Regulators should choose cost-effective measures to reduce those risks and should attempt to compare the expected value of the risk with the expected value of precautionary measures. Regulators should also consider creating a "margin of safety" for catastrophic risks, again with cost-effective measures; the extent of the margin of safety should be chosen with reference to what is lost and what is gained by creating it.*

Costs and tradeoffs   Suppose that eliminating the worst-case scenario would cost a great deal, or that doing so would introduce bad worst cases of its own. Under such circumstances, it is not at all clear that regulators should eliminate the worst-case scenario. If eliminating a catastrophic risk would itself be nearly catastrophic, perhaps the catastrophic risk should not be eliminated—at least if the worst-case scenario is most unlikely and if the nearly catastrophic risk from regulation would become inevitable.

The Catastrophic Harm Precautionary Principle might be further refined by paying close attention to the presence of risk–risk tradeoffs, or catastrophic risk–catastrophic risk tradeoffs, or risk–catastrophic risk tradeoffs. Catastrophic risk–catastrophic risk tradeoffs are among the most interesting. The war in Iraq was defended as a means of avoiding catastrophe, and it might even have been justified by reference to the Catastrophic Harm Precautionary Principle: If Saddam Hussein possessed weapons of mass destruction (and at the time there was certainly some chance that he did), the risk of a catastrophic nuclear or biological attack could not be completely dismissed. But a war to remove him from power itself created serious risks. The resulting risk tradeoffs called for an assessment of probability: What are the risks from war, and what is the likelihood of catastrophic harm from refusing to make war?

Some people believe that the risks arising from the war have themselves now reached catastrophic levels, and so we must compare catastrophic risks with catastrophic risks. Efforts to control emissions of greenhouse gases could easily be analyzed in similar terms. At the very least, they pose risk–catastrophic risk tradeoffs.

Our governing principle is getting long now, but better: *Regulators should consider the expected value of catastrophic risks, even when worst-case scenarios are highly unlikely. In assessing expected value, regulators should consider the distinctive features of catastrophic harm, including the "social amplification" of such harm. Regulators should choose cost-effective measures to reduce those risks and should attempt to compare the expected value of the risk with the expected value of precautionary measures.*

Regulators should also consider creating a "margin of safety" for cata-strophic risks, again with cost-effective measures; the extent of the margin of safety should be chosen with reference to what is gained and what is lost by creating it. In deciding on steps to reduce catastrophic risk, regulators should take into account the possibility that those steps will impose risks of their own, including catastrophic risks.

Timing   The risk of catastrophe can be immediate, as in the case of terrorist attacks; but sometimes a potential catastrophe poses no threat until the relatively distant future, as many people believe to be the case for climate change. Suppose that the burdens of precautions are incurred immediately, but the benefits will not be enjoyed until decades later. If so, people are likely to be skeptical about precautionary steps, even if they are ordinarily responsive to a serious risk of catastrophe.

Why is this? You would probably rather have $500 today than $500 in twenty years. Most people discount money that will not be available until the future. The appropriate discount rate for regulatory benefits raises many controversial questions, and I shall take them up in Chapter 6. But whatever rate we use, most people agree that future losses or gains should be valued at a lower figure than otherwise equivalent current losses or gains.

On the other hand, we can easily imagine situations in which people are giving far too little weight to future harms—discounting the costs too heavily. They might be treating those harms as ir-relevant, or nearly so, because of myopia, wishful thinking, or a simple failure of the imagination or of empathy with those who will be at risk.[48] A survey finds that with respect to water quality im-provements, people show pretty extreme time preferences—greatly favoring current improvements over much more beneficial improvements merely two years later.[49] The conclusion is that people give future benefits about half of their correct discounted value.[50] For these reasons, there is a particular need for a Catastrophic Harm Precautionary Principle when the risk will not materialize until the distant future.

The point can be fortified with an understanding of the likely political dynamics. Suppose that the costs of precautions will be incurred immediately, and that the benefits will not be enjoyed for many decades. If so, elected officials will have a strong incentive to delay. The reason is that they will face political retribution for imposing immediate costs and might well receive little or no political gain for delivering long-term benefits. We have seen that in the case of climate change, the temporal disparity between costs and benefits creates a strong incentive to delay, even if immediate precautions are justified, simply because those who are most likely to benefit do not vote.

This point provides an additional reason to endorse a Catastrophic Harm Precautionary Principle, one that attempts to overcome the danger that future risks will receive less attention than they deserve. As I have formulated it, the principle should automatically overcome that danger.

Catastrophic Harm, Version 4: Uncertainty versus Risk

In some contexts, risk-related problems involve hazards and worst-case scenarios of ascertainable probability; and ascertainable probability has been the assumption of the discussion thus far. Maybe we can say that the risk of death, from a certain activity, is 1/100,000, or at least that it ranges from 1/20,000 to 1/500,000, with an exposed population of, say, 10 million. We might be able to say that the risk of catastrophic harm from climate change is under 10 percent but above 1 percent. But as the economist Frank Knight has maintained, we can imagine circumstances in which analysts cannot specify even a range of probability.[51] Regulators—and ordinary people—may find themselves acting in a situation of *uncertainty* (where outcomes can be identified but no probabilities can be assigned), rather than in a situation of *risk* (where outcomes can be identified and probabilities assigned to various outcomes).[52] Even worse, regulators and ordinary people are sometimes acting under conditions of *ignorance:* They are unable to specify either the probability of bad outcomes or their nature—they do not even know the magnitude of the harms they face.[53]

When existing knowledge allows regulators to identify outcomes but does not permit them to assign probabilities to each, it might be rational to follow the Maximin Principle: *Choose the policy with the best worst-case outcome.*[54] (The term "maximin" is a shorthand for "maximizing the minimum.") In the environmental context, perhaps elaborate precautions can be justified by asking officials to identify the worst case among the various regulatory options ("If we do X, this bad thing may be the outcome; if we do Y, this less bad thing may be the outcome"), and select that option whose worst-case is least bad. Perhaps the Maximin Principle would lead to a fourth and exceptionally aggressive form of the Catastrophic Harm Precautionary Principle—one that would urge elaborate steps to combat terrorism, avian flu, and climate change.

In its simplest and crudest form, the principle might say: *Regulators should identify, and attempt to eliminate, the worst-case scenario.* This principle is vague as well as crude; it does not specify the option set within which regulators should act. Are they looking at all approaches to climate change, or to the environment as a whole, or to the various challenges that America faces, or to the various challenges faced by the world? But for purposes of getting the analysis off the ground, the principle provides a start.

Suppose that the resulting precautionary steps would impose various hardships, but that even the worst of these hardships are not nearly as bad as the worst outcomes associated with terrorism, avian flu, and climate change. If especially aggressive measures are justified to reduce the risks associated with these hazards, one reason is that they carry with them potentially catastrophic outcomes, and existing information does not allow us to assign probabilities to these worst-case scenarios. The same analysis might be applied to many problems, including nuclear energy, nanotechnology, AIDS, asteroid collisions, and genetic modification of food.

To understand the arguments for and against applying the Maximin Principle, we need to back up a bit. Does it *generally* make sense to eliminate the worst-case scenario? Let us begin by putting the issue of uncertainty to one side and exploring a numerical example that involves risk instead: *Which would you prefer?*

(1)   A 99.9 percent chance of gaining $2,000, and a 0.1 percent chance of losing $6, or

(2)   A 50 percent chance of gaining $5, and a 50 percent chance of losing $5.

Under the Maximin Principle, option two is preferable because option one has a worse worst case—but most of us would sensibly select option one, which has a far higher expected value. To choose two, you would have to show an extraordinary degree of risk aversion. And if you are tempted to choose two in any case (hard to imagine—is losing $6 really so awful?), it would be easy to devise an example in which almost no one would follow the Maximin Principle. Which would you choose: a 99.999 percent chance of winning $5 billion, and a 0.001 percent chance of losing

$5.25, or a 50 percent chance of gaining $5, and a 50 percent chance of losing $5?

Let us imagine an everyday illustration of the kinds of decisions in which the Maximin Principle might seem attractive: A reporter living in Los Angeles has been told that he can take one of two assignments. He can go to Iraq to cover American efforts to overcome violence and terrorism. Or he can go to Paris to cover anti-American sentiment in France. The Iraq assignment has, in his view, two polar outcomes: (1) He might have the most interesting and rewarding experience of his professional life, or (2) he might be killed. The Paris assignment has two polar outcomes as well: (1) He might have an interesting experience, one that is also a lot of fun, or (2) he might be lonely and homesick. Our reporter might be tempted to choose Paris, on the ground that the worst-case scenario for that choice (homesickness) is so much better than the worst-case scenario for Iraq (death). This way of thinking often influences many major life decisions (changing jobs, going to law school, having children, getting married) and also regulatory policy, where one or another approach has a worst-case scenario that is identifiably much worse.

But eliminating the worst case is not always a sensible principle for making decisions. Suppose that the reporter has a different choice: staying in Los Angeles or going to Paris. Suppose too that on personal and professional grounds, Paris is far better. There is, of course, a tiny chance that the plane might crash on the way to France. A plane crash is extremely unlikely, but it cannot be ruled out. If the reporter follows the Maximin Principle in this situation, he will stay in LA. But doing so seems absurd, even a form of madness. (One version of it actually has a name: agoraphobia.) Using an example of this kind, John Harsanyi contends that the Maximin Principle should be rejected because it produces irrationality: "If you took the maximin principle seriously you could not ever cross the street (after all, you might be hit by a car); you could never drive over a bridge (after all, it might collapse); you could never get married (after all, it might end in a disaster), etc. If anybody really acted in this way he would soon end up in a mental institution."[55]

Harsanyi's argument might also be invoked to contest the use of the Maximin Principle even in the choice between Iraq and Paris. Rather than simply identifying the worst-case scenario, the reporter might attempt to specify the likelihood of being killed in Iraq. Perhaps the likelihood is really quite small, notwithstanding the highly publicized deaths that do occur (especially salient when the victims are journalists). Perhaps the reporter should reject the fourth version of the Catastrophic Harm Precautionary Principle. Perhaps the Maximin Principle is just a way of neglecting the issue of probability and hence is senseless. We have seen that in some circumstances, probability neglect ensures that people will attend only to the worst-case scenario. But if probabilities can actually be assessed, and if that scenario is extremely unlikely to come to fruition, probability neglect is hard to defend, even for people who are exceptionally risk averse.

Suppose that the risk of death in Iraq turns out to be 1 in a million for our reporter, and that the choice of Iraq would be much better, personally and professionally, than the choice of Paris. We would need to know something about the reporter's situation, values, and tastes to understand how to resolve this problem, but certainly it would be more plausible for the reporter to choose Iraq, with its stipulated low risk, than to make the decision by obsessively fixating on the worst that might happen.

But something important is missing from Harsanyi's argument, and even from the reporter's analysis of the choice between Los Angeles and Paris: Risks, and equally bad worst-case scenarios, are on all sides. If the reporter stayed in Los Angeles, he might be killed in one way or another, and hence the use of the Maximin Principle does not by itself justify the decision to stay in the United States. Maybe an untimely death would be more likely in Los Angeles. And contrary to Harsanyi's argument, the Maximin Principle does not really mean that people should not cross streets, drive over bridges, and refuse to marry. The reason is that failing to do those things might produce other disasters—you could get killed because you *didn't* cross that street, drive over that bridge, or get married to that nice person. To implement the Maximin Principle, or a general injunction to take precautions, or even the fourth version of the Catastrophic Harm Precautionary Principle, we must identify all relevant risks, not just a subset.

Harsanyi neglects the possibility that precautions against one set of risks will create risks of their own. If we are not careful, a Catastrophic Harm Precautionary Principle that attempts to eliminate the worst cases might produce nightmarish or even catastrophic scenarios too. What I have said against the Precautionary Principle in general—that it neglects the full universe of risks, including the risks of precautions—might apply to more refined versions as well. Nonetheless, the more general objection to the Maximin Principle holds under circumstances of risk. If probabilities can be assigned to the various outcomes, we should not reject the course of action with the much higher expected value merely because it also comes with a very bad worst case. If your surgeon says to you: "If you have this operation, you have a 99.99 percent chance of being cured from your crippling back pain, and a 0.01 percent chance of being paralyzed," most people will, and should, have the surgery.

Of course, many people are risk averse, or averse to particular risks. Life is short, people are busy, and occasionally they are more reluctant to take risks than an analysis of expected value suggests.[56]

But *if* the realistically likely outcomes are so much better in Paris and the risks are very small, our reporter should stop obsessing about the worst case and get on that plane to France. When probabilities can be assigned, following the Maximin Principle seems to require infinite risk aversion, and for that reason it is simply foolish.

For regulatory policy, the implication is clear. A Catastrophic Harm Precautionary Principle makes sense if it emphasizes expected value; it even makes sense if it embodies risk aversion, in the form of a "margin of safety" against the worst risks. But simply identifying the worst-case scenario and attempting to eliminate it does not make sense. As stated, the fourth version of the Catastrophic Harm Precautionary Principle must be rejected. Still, the problem of uncertainty raises distinctive questions.

Catastrophic Harm, Version 5: Uncertainty and Precautions

I have suggested that the Maximin Principle—"Choose the policy with the best worst-case outcome"—has sometimes been recommended under circumstances of uncertainty rather than risk.[57] In a valuable paper on environmental policy, Stephen Gardiner invokes John Rawls's argument for the Maximin Principle, made in the context of distributive justice.[58] Rawls's claims are part of a general argument for his famous Difference Principle, which suggests that behind a "veil of ignorance"—that is, lacking knowledge of their own abilities, their characteristics, and their personal situation—people would choose to allow inequalities only to the extent that those inequalities operate to the advantage of the least well-off.

In Rawls's view, people would not choose to maximize average utility—understood as the average level of well-being across the population—by, for example, selecting a situation in which a strong majority of people end up in a very good position but some peo-

ple do very badly. Rawls contends that—behind the veil of ignorance—people would allow inequalities *only if* they are necessary to
help those at the bottom. Thus, for example, if the inequalities of a
capitalist society "raise the floor" by ensuring economic growth
that helps the most disadvantaged, they are justified. But if inequalities leave some people in desperate circumstances, they are unjust.
In a sense, Rawls can be taken to argue that, behind a veil of ignorance, people would pay a lot of attention to the worst-case scenario—and they would attempt to eliminate it.

Why does Rawls believe that people would choose the Difference Principle rather than maximizing average utility? Rawls argues that when "grave risks" are involved and when probabilities
cannot be assigned to the occurrence of those risks, the Maximin
Principle is the appropriate decision rule, at least if the chooser
"cares very little, if anything, for what he might gain above the
minimum stipend that he can, in fact, be sure of by following the
maximin rule."[59] Rawls contends, then, that the Maximin Principle
is justified (1) in the face of potentially catastrophic outcomes, (2)
where probabilities cannot be assigned, and (3) where the loss from
following this principle is a matter of relative indifference.[60] This,
then, is his argument for the Difference Principle: If choosers were
to select average utility, they might end up being the ones facing
catastrophe; perhaps they would be doomed to miserable and desperate lives. By stipulation, people cannot assign probabilities to the
various outcomes behind the veil of ignorance. In Rawls's view,
people are unlikely to care much about what they lose by abandon-
ing average utility in favor of the Difference Principle.

In the context of distributive justice, these claims have proved
highly controversial. Perhaps you would not choose to eliminate
the worst-case situation behind the veil of ignorance; perhaps you
would be willing to choose average utility, at least if the average is

high enough. Maybe you would be willing to take your chances on doing very badly. But as Gardiner has shown, Rawls's argument can be used as the basis for a "core" Precautionary Principle in the environmental setting—and indeed much more generally, covering terrorism, avian flu, hurricanes, and asteroid collisions too. When the three conditions are met, precautions—in the form of efforts to avoid the worst-case scenario—might be adopted. Here, then, is a fifth version of the Catastrophic Harm Precautionary Principle: *Regulators should eliminate the worst-case scenario, if it is potentiallycatastrophic, when probabilities cannot be assigned to the various outcomes and when the cost of eliminating the worst-case scenario is essentially zero.*

Gardiner adds, sensibly, that to justify such a principle, the threats that are potentially catastrophic must satisfy some minimal threshold of plausibility. If they can be dismissed as wholly unrealistic (space aliens might take over the earth if the Olympics are held as scheduled), then the threats should not be addressed. Gardiner believes that the problem of climate change can be usefully analyzed in these terms and that it presents a good case for the application of the Maximin Principle. In a similar vein, Jon Elster, speaking of nuclear power, contends that eliminating the worst-case scenario is the appropriate choice when it can be identified and when the best consequences from the alternatives are the same.[61] In fact, Elster appears to believe that aggressive restrictions on nuclear power are justified on this ground.

Might Vice President Cheney's One Percent Doctrine be understood in this light? The answer is no. If the chance is 1 percent, we are operating under risk, not uncertainty. But consider the Some Percent Doctrine, which might well capture Vice President Cheney's actual meaning: If there is some chance of serious harm, and we cannot assign a probability to it, then perhaps we should treat it as a certainty—at least if the outcome would be horrific, should the risk come to fruition.

Here, then, is the basic argument in favor of an especially strong form of the Catastrophic Harm Precautionary Principle—a principle that calls on regulators, under circumstances of uncertainty, to identify and eliminate the worst-case scenario. Taken seriously, this principle would have large consequences for regulatory policy, at least if conditions of uncertainty are common. But several objections can be raised, and ultimately I shall reject this strong form of the Catastrophic Harm Precautionary Principle, on the ground that it does not focus on two key questions: the difference between the worst-case scenario and the second-worst-case scenario, and what we lose, exactly, by taking precautions against the worst-case scenario.

Objection 1: the argument is trivial   An initial problem with Gardiner's argument is that it risks triviality, above all because of condition (3), requiring that people care little about what is lost when they follow the Maximin Principle. If individuals and societies can eliminate an uncertain danger of catastrophe for essentially no cost, then of course they should eliminate that danger! If you are asked to pay $1 to avoid a potentially catastrophic risk to which probabilities cannot be assigned (your death and the death of those you love), you will surely pay $1. And if two options have the same best-case scenario, and if the first has a far better worst-case scenario, people should of course choose the first option.

There is nothing wrong with this argument—in fact, it provides a valuable clarification. But the real world rarely presents problems in this form. Where policy and law are disputed, the elimination of uncertain dangers of catastrophe imposes both burdens and risks. In the context of terrorism, for example, efforts to eliminate the worst case—through the Iraq War, limits on personal privacy, restrictions on liberty—are hardly costless. They create risks and have bad worst cases of their own. We could easily imagine other efforts to eliminate the worst-case scenarios associated with terrorism: abridgments of free speech, racial and religious profiling, travel restrictions imposed on those of Arab descent, wars with millions of civilian casualties. Here too the Maximin approach, taken seriously in some quarters, would have exceedingly high costs.

In the cases of avian flu, asteroid collisions, and climate change, to say that regulators can or should care "very little, if anything," for what might be lost by eliminating the worst-case scenario is implausible. If nations followed the Maximin Principle for avian flu, they would kill a lot of birds, and they would also call for restrictions on international travel that would impose huge burdens and costs. If they followed this principle for asteroid collisions, they would be pouring immense resources into learning how to destroy or divert asteroids. If nations approached climate change by trying to eliminate the worst-case scenario, they would spend a great deal to reduce greenhouse gas emissions, and the result would almost certainly be higher prices for gasoline and energy and a rise in unemployment and poverty. Something similar can be said about genetic modification of food, because elimination of the worst-case scenario, through aggressive regulation, might well eliminate an inexpensive source of nutrition that would have exceptionally valuable effects on countless people who live under extreme deprivation.

The real question, then, is whether regulators should embrace the Maximin Principle in real-world cases where doing so imposes burdens and creates risks. If they should, it is because condition (3) is too stringent and should be abandoned; and this would require a revision of the corresponding Catastrophic Harm Precautionary Principle. Even if the costs of eliminating the worst-case scenario are significant, and even if regulators care a great deal about incurring those costs, the question is whether it makes sense to eliminate the worst-case scenario when nations face uncertain dangers of catastrophe. In the environmental context, some people have so claimed, resulting in a formulation that could be adapted to many problems:[62] *Regulators should eliminate the worst-case scenario if it is catastrophic and if probabilities cannot be assigned to the various outcomes; they should eliminate that scenario even if the burdens involved in doing so are quite high.* This admittedly vague formulation takes us directly to the next objection.

Objection 2: the Maximin Principle assumes infinite risk aversion   Rawls's arguments in favor of adopting the Maximin Principle for purposes of distributive justice were subject to scathing attacks from economists.[63] The central challenge was that the principle would be chosen only by those who demonstrated infinite risk aversion. To see this objection, let us return to Rawls's context: What kinds of distribution would people choose under a veil of ignorance, in which they knew nothing about their own capacities or prospects, or their own place in social life? Compare the following possibilities: *(1) In a population of one million people, everyone receives $10,000 in annual income. (2) In that same population, everyone receives $1,000,000 in annual income, but one person receives $1,000 in annual income.* If we don't know where we are likely to stand in this distribution, will we really choose (1), so as to eliminate the worst-case possibility? Or would we choose (2), on the ground that the expected outcome is so much better (for ourselves and almost everyone else), and the chance of the worst worst-case ($1,000) is tiny—only one in one million?

Rawls himself was speaking not of money but of an index of "primary goods," which included not only wealth and income but also civil liberties, health, and the social bases of self-respect. To be faithful to Rawls, the figures I have used—$10,000, $1,000,000, $1,000—would have to be converted into some kind of "primary goods index." But even if we are speaking of such an index, or some other account of welfare, sensible people are unlikely to choose option (1) and reject a situation in which they (and almost everyone else) would have a much better chance of a much better outcome.

In the words of one of Rawls's most influential critics, "Even though the stakes are great, people may well wish to trade a reduction in the assured floor against the provision of larger gains."[64] To adapt this objection to the regulatory context: Some degree of risk aversion with respect to catastrophic harms is plausible, and this point supports some modest forms of the Catastrophic Harm Precautionary Principle (the first three versions explored above). But even under circumstances of uncertainty—the argument goes—following the Maximin Principle demonstrates infinite risk aversion. Why should we be infinitely averse to the risks of asteroid collisions or avian flu or climate change, and use such an extraordinary level of resources to combat those risks, when we could use the same resources to avoid other much more likely risks, admittedly with less bad worst-case scenarios?

This challenge, though tempting, is wrong, because the Maximin Principle does not assume infinite risk aversion. Suppose that people are really operating in circumstances of genuine uncertainty, in which probabilities cannot plausibly be assigned to various outcomes. The objection that eliminating the worst-case scenario assumes infinite risk aversion depends on denying that uncertainty exists. If we are truly uncertain, no probabilities can be assigned; the idea of risk aversion makes sense only in the context of ascertainable probabilities. True, you would show infinite risk aversion if you were willing to do or spend anything to avoid a *tiny* chance of a terrible outcome. But it is not true that you would show infinite risk aversion if you were willing to spend anything to avoid an *uncertain* chance of a terrible outcome. To understand this distinction, we need to explore uncertainty directly.

Objection 3: uncertainty does not exist   Many social scientists have denied the existence of uncertainty. People make decisions all the time, even when they are not able to make probability judgments, and these very decisions suggest that people assign probabilities and do not operate under circumstances of uncertainty. Milton Friedman, for example, writes of the risk-uncertainty distinction that "I have not referred to this distinction because I do not believe it is valid. I follow L. J. Savage in his view of *personal probability,* which denies any valid distinction along these lines. We may treat people as if they assigned numerical probabilities to every conceivable event."[65]

Friedman and other skeptics are right to insist that people's choices suggest that they assign probabilities to events. Our decisions about whether to fly or drive, whether to walk in certain neighborhoods at night, and whether to take risky jobs can be understood as an implicit assignment of probabilities to bad or catastrophic events. Regulators themselves make decisions—including decisions about terrorism and climate change—from which subjective probabilities can be calculated. Perhaps by identifying the actual choices of the United States, France, Israel, Syria, North Korea, Iran, and Germany, we can infer the judgments of the relevant nations about the probability of, say, catastrophic terrorist attack, or catastrophic climate change, or catastrophic hurricanes.

But these points do not make for a good objection to Knight, who was concerned with objective probabilities rather than subjective choices.[66] Knight's claim was that people sometimes lack the knowledge that would permit them to make probability assignments at all—even if they try to do so. To see the point, consider here the fact that animals, no less than human beings, make choices from which subjective probabilities can be assigned. My dog, a Rhodesian Ridgeback named Perry, makes a number of decisions every day. From his decisions, we might be able to infer his judgments about the likelihood of, say, being killed in a car accident, or by a terrorist attack, or by another human being, or by a thunderstorm. From his behavior, carefully observed over the years, I would estimate his respective judgments as roughly 20 percent (car accident), 0 percent (terrorist attack), 10 percent (human being), and 99.9 percent (thunderstorm). But what should we make of these numbers? Do they suggest that Knightian uncertainty does not exist? The existence of subjective probability judgments from dogs, horses, and elephants does not mean that animals do not ever face genuine uncertainty—circumstances under which they are unable to assign probabilities to outcomes.

We can even imagine primitive societies, past or present, in which people act to ward off threats of various kinds but in which they are wholly unable to assign probabilities to those threats. Or suppose that the question is the likelihood that at least 100 million human beings will be alive in 10,000 years. For most people, equipped with the knowledge they have, no probability can sensibly be assigned. Perhaps uncertainty is not unlimited; the likelihood can reasonably be described as above 0 percent and below 100 percent. But beyond that point, little can be said.

Suppose that I present you with a urn containing 250 balls and ask you to pick one; if you pick a blue ball, you receive $1,000, but if you pick a green ball, you have to pay me $1,000. Suppose I refuse to disclose the proportion of blue and green balls in the urn—or suppose I don't know the proportion, because it has been determined by a computer. These examples suggest that it is wrong to deny the possible existence of uncertainty, signaled by the absence of objective probabilities.[67] Some nations, some of the time, operate like primitive societies, or like those asked about population sizes in 10,000 years, or like those befuddled by guessing games involving urns.

For Friedman and other skeptics, denying the existence of uncertainty presents an additional problem. When necessary, human beings certainly do assign subjective probabilities to future events, including catastrophic ones. But the assignment is a function of how the situation is described, and formally identical descriptions can produce radically different judgments. People are unlikely to give the same answer to the question, "What is the likelihood that 10 percent of people will suffer an adverse effect from a certain risk?" and to the question, "What is the likelihood that 90 percent of people will not suffer an adverse effect from a certain risk?" The merely semantic reframing affects probability judgments; and this is surely true for hazards involving terrorism, climate change, and avian flu, as well as more mundane hazards.[68] If this is so, it is hard to say that we can infer, from subjective estimates, anything like the objective judgments that would take us from uncertainty to risk.

We have already seen that subjective probability judgments are notoriously unreliable, because they are frequently based on rules of thumb and biases that lead to serious errors. Why should regulators believe that subjective estimates, subject as they are to framing, availability bias, and other problems, have any standing in the face of the objective difficulty or impossibility of making probability judgments? Suppose that regulators conclude that it is objectively impossible to assign a probability to the risk of catastrophic harm from climate change. Even if individuals and governments assign subjective probabilities, should their assignments have any bearing on what ought to be done?

Writing in 1937, John Maynard Keynes, often taken to be a critic of the idea of uncertainty, clearly saw the distinction between objective probabilities and actual behavior: "The sense in which I am using the term ['uncertain' knowledge] is that in which the prospect of a European war is uncertain . . . About these matters there is no scientific basis on which to form any calculable probability whatever. We simply do not know."[69] This is so even if, as Keynes immediately added, we act "exactly as we should if we had behind us a good Benthamite calculation of a series of prospective advantages and disadvantages, each multiplied by its appropriate probability, waiting to be summed."[70] Even if subjective expected utilities can be assigned on the basis of behavior, we cannot exclude the possibility that regulators (like everyone else) are operating in circumstances of genuine uncertainty.

Objection 4: uncertainty is too infrequent to be a genuine source of concern for purposes of policy and law   Perhaps regulatory problems, including those mentioned here, hardly ever involve genuine uncertainty. Perhaps regulators are usually able to assign probabilities to outcomes; and where they cannot, perhaps they can instead assign probabilities to probabilities (or where this proves impossible, probabilities to probabilities of probabilities). For example, we have a lot of information about the orbits of asteroids, and good reason to believe that the risk of a devastating collision is very small. In many cases, such as catastrophic terrorist attack, regulators might be able to specify a range of probabilities—say, above 0 percent but below 5 percent. Or they might be able to say that the probability that climate change presents a risk of catastrophe is, at most,

20 percent. Some scientists and economists believe that climate change is unlikely to create catastrophic harm, and that the real costs, human and economic, will be high but not intolerable. In their view, the worst-case scenarios can be responsibly described as improbable.

Perhaps we can agree that pure uncertainty is rare. Perhaps we can agree that, at worst, regulatory problems involve problems of "bounded uncertainty," in which we cannot specify probabilities within particular bands. Maybe the risk of a catastrophic outcome is above 1 percent and below 10 percent, but maybe within that band it is impossible to assign probabilities. A sensible approach, then, would be to ask planners to identify a wide range of possible scenarios and to select approaches that do well for most or all of them.[71] Of course, the pervasiveness of uncertainty depends on what is actually known, and in the case of climate change, people dispute what is actually known. Richard Posner believes that "no probabilities can be attached to the catastrophic global-warming scenarios, and without an estimate of probabilities an expected cost cannot be calculated."[72] A 1994 survey of experts showed an extraordinary range of estimated losses from climate change, varying from no economic loss to a 20 percent decrease in gross world product—a catastrophic decline in the world's well-being.[73]

Knowledge has certainly increased since 1994, and we have probably moved from uncertainty to risk, or at least from uncertainty to bounded or partial uncertainty.[74] Even if Posner is wrong, and even if uncertainty is rare, it cannot be ruled out of bounds; at least a degree of uncertainty, in which probabilities cannot be assigned within specified bands, is not so rare.

On maximin, rationality, and genuine uncertainty   Now turn to the most difficult question: What is the appropriate approach to genuine uncertainty? Is the Maximin Principle—choosing the policy with the best worst-case outcome—a rational strategy, or the right one, or is it silly? To get hold of these questions, let us offer another variation on the fourth version of the Catastrophic Harm Precautionary Principle: *When choosing among courses of action, regulators should have, as their highest priority, the elimination of the worst-case scenario under circumstances of uncertainty, at least if other things are roughly equal.* This formulation has the advantage of providing a clean test: the other-things-being-equal proviso ensures that regulators do not have to ask whether elimination of the worst-case scenario is particularly burdensome or costly. I will turn to that question in due course.

Actual decisions   The actual judgments that people make cannot tell us what we should do. But they are interesting and important in their own right, and they give some clues about the public demand for regulation (and thus are likely to shape government behavior).

People sometimes show a degree of *uncertainty aversion,* in the sense that they avoid gambles to which probabilities are not assigned. Some pioneering work was done by Daniel Ellsberg.[75] Assume that people are asked to choose among two lotteries, each involving an urn with 100 balls. All of the balls are either black or red. For the first lottery, the urn contains an equal number of black and red balls. For the second lottery, the urn contains an unknown proportion of black balls and red balls. People receive a specified amount of money for correctly guessing the color of balls randomly chosen from the urn. It turns out that most people prefer the first lottery to the second, and thus display aversion to uncertainty.

But their uncertainty aversion is limited. If people would receive a lot more money from a correct guess in the second lottery, they would probably choose the second lottery. So long as uncertainty aversion is not infinite, avoiding the worst case will not always be the preferred decision rule. In fact, most people will tolerate the worst-case scenario if the question is properly framed.

In an experiment that tests this proposition, I asked seventy-one University of Chicago law students the following question: *The government is considering two environmental problems. For the first, the government is able to estimate the probability that a bad outcome will occur. It believes that there is a 90 percent chance that 600 people will die (and the death of 600 people is the worst-case scenario). It also believes that there is a 10 percent chance that 400 people will die. For the second problem, the government cannot assign probabilities to the various outcomes; the worst-case scenario is that 700 people will die. Do you think:*

(1) *the first problem should receive higher priority?*

(2) *the second problem should receive higher priority?*

(3) *the two problems should receive equal priority?*

Sixty-three percent chose the first option, with the remainder equally divided between options two and three. Only 18.5 percent wanted to eliminate the worst-case scenario (option two). In light of this pattern of responses among law students, we can reasonably conjecture that the general population will show no consistent preference for an approach that eliminates the worst worst-case scenario under circumstances of uncertainty, when a different approach can eliminate a highly probable but somewhat less-bad scenario.

Suppose that people were asked to choose between two government programs. Program A would eliminate a hazard that creates a 99 percent chance that 100,000 people will die and a 1 percent chance that 99,500 people will die. Program B would eliminate a hazard that creates an uncertain chance that between 0 and 100,010 people will die. I am willing to predict, with a lot of confidence, that the vast majority of people will choose Program A—and hence reject the program that would eliminate the worst-case scenario.

Why is this? The Principle of Insufficient Reason says that when people lack much information about probabilities (say, they know the probability is somewhere between 1 percent to 40 percent), they will act as if each probability is equally likely.[76] Whether or not this principle should be accepted in general, we know that when people make actual decisions, they often use it.[77] Here is another experiment with a larger group of law students from two institutions (the University of Alabama and the University of Chicago):[78]

One thousand people are at risk from an environmental hazard. If regulators take approach A, a minimum of 400 people will die, and a maximum of 500 people will die; regulators are unable to assign probabilities to the various outcomes. If regulators take approach B, a minimum of 10 people will die, and a maximum of 600 people will die; regulators are unable to assign probabilities to the various outcomes. Which approach should regulators choose?

In this experiment, 85.5 percent of people chose approach B, even though it ran the risk of the worst-case scenario (600 deaths). Why did approach B seem better to so many people? Apparently they began by presuming at least roughly equal probabilities under circumstances of uncertainty and concluded that they would much rather go the route that has a much higher expected value, given that presumption.

People do not always focus on, and attempt to eliminate, the worst-case scenario. If that scenario is extremely vivid, and if it is drawn to people's attention, they might neglect the issue of probability and attempt to eliminate it (as we saw in Chapter 1). But under ordinary circumstances, they will choose to eliminate the worst-case scenario at all costs only when the Principle of Insufficient Reason, perhaps accompanied by a degree of risk aversion, suggests that they should.

Catastrophic Harm and Maximin: Two Questions

We could learn a lot more about people's actual judgments when faced with catastrophic risks. But these judgments cannot be used to resolve the question of how regulators or the rest of us should behave. The question of what ought to be done must therefore be separated from the question of how people actually choose. A great deal of work explores the former question, and certainly the Maximin Principle has not been ruled out as a candidate for rational choice under uncertainty.[79]

In deciding whether to choose a policy that eliminates the worst-case scenario, a great deal should turn on two simple questions: (1) How much worse is the worst-case scenario than the next-worst scenario, and the third-worst, and so forth? (2) What, exactly, is lost by taking steps to eliminate the worst-case scenario? These questions suggest a (happily) final version of the Catastrophic Harm Precautionary Principle:

In deciding whether to eliminate the worst-case scenario under circumstances of uncertainty, regulators should consider the losses imposed by eliminating that scenario, and the size of the difference between the worst-case scenario under one course of action and the worst-case scenario under alternative courses of action. If the worst-case scenario under one course of action is much worse than the worst-case scenario under another course of action, and if it is not extraordinarily burdensome to take the course of action that eliminates the worst-case scenario, regulators should take that course of action. But if the worst-case scenario un-

der one course of action is not much worse than the worst-case scenario under another course of action, and if it is extraordinarily burdensome to take the course of action that eliminates the worst-case scenario, regulators should not take that course of action.

As with most of the other formulations, this version is not a decision rule; it is too vague for that. But it provides the right place to start.

By emphasizing the relative badness of the worst-case scenario and the magnitude of the loss from trying to eliminate it, I am attempting to build on the Rawls/Gardiner suggestion that the Maximin Principle is the preferred rule when little is lost from following it. It is true that regulators sometimes lack the information that would enable them to answer key questions. But answers to those questions may well be possible even if regulators cannot assign probabilities to the various outcomes with any confidence.

To see the value of the inquiry I am proposing, suppose that you are choosing between two options. The first has a best-case outcome of 10 and a worst-case outcome of -5. The second has a best-case outcome of 15 and a worst-case outcome of -6. It is impossible to assign probabilities to the various outcomes. The Maximin Principle would favor the first option, to avoid the worse worst case (-6); but to justify that choice, we might want to know something about the *meaning* of the differences between 10 and 15 on the one hand and -5 and -6 on the other. If 15 is much better than 10, and if the difference between -5 and -6 is not huge, then we might well choose 15, -6. But if the difference between -5 and -6 greatly matters—if it is a matter of life and death, say—then eliminating the worst case is much more attractive.

Now let us turn these numbers into their policy equivalents. If the worst-case scenario is only slightly worse than the next-worst-case scenario, and if a nation loses a great deal by eliminating the worst-case scenario, the nation should probably refrain from eliminating the worst-case scenario. This kind of analysis would help regulators make progress on all of the questions of current concern, ranging from avian flu to terrorism to climate change.

A skeptic might object here that for this analysis to get off the ground, we must make at least an implicit assignment of probabilities to the various outcomes—in defiance of the underlying assumption, which is that we cannot assign such probabilities. Suppose that −6 is only a little bit worse than −5 and that 15 is indeed much better than 10. Even if so, we would indeed choose 10, −5 over 15, −6 *if* we thought that for the latter option, −6 was 99.99 percent likely, and that for the former, 10 was 99.99 percent likely. By stipulation, no assignment of probability is possible. As a result—the objection continues—we have not yet identified a way to choose between the two options. When we choose 15, −6 over 10, −5, on the dual assumptions that −6 and −5 are not terribly different, and that 15 is great while 10 is merely good, it must be because we are making implicit judgments about the relevant probabilities, to the effect that it is not overwhelmingly likely that if we choose 10, −5, we will end up with 10, or that if we choose 15, −6, we will end up with −6. And if this objection is right, then the final version of the Catastrophic Harm Precautionary Principle depends, at least in some loose sense, on the assignment of probabilities. If this is so, then my argument in favor of that version will not work, because it ultimately rests on some such assignment, which rejects the assumption of uncertainty.

So stated, the objection is indeed right as a formal matter. If we really are unable to assign probabilities, my suggested approach will fail. That approach depends, then, on some softened version of the Principle of Insufficient Reason. It does not necessarily depend on an *equal* assignment of probabilities to every point along the range. But it does rest on a judgment that under conditions of uncertainty—about where the probability falls between 0 percent and 100 percent—it is at least more likely that we will end up somewhere between 0 percent and 98 percent, or between 2 percent and 100 percent, than at 99 percent or at 100 percent. Perhaps people do, but should not, assign equal probabilities to various outcomes under circumstances of uncertainty; this is a disputed question.[80] Perhaps the assignment of equal probabilities is an unfounded (and desperate?) effort to transform problems of uncertainty into problems of risk. Perhaps the judgment that a hazard is more likely to be between 0 percent likely and 98 percent likely than 99 percent likely is simply fighting the assumption of uncertainty.

But even if this is so, the approach I am suggesting seems more reasonable, on pragmatic grounds, than any imaginable alternative. Most of the time, individuals and societies will not do well if they fixate on the worst-case scenario and attempt to eliminate it, when the next worst-case scenario is almost as bad and when the costs of eliminating the worst case are extremely high. If it is objected that the reference to what is most reasonable suggests that people are not really operating under genuine uncertainty, or do not believe that they are, then the only possible answer is this: The objection is correct, strictly speaking, but my suggested inquiry, captured in the final version of the Catastrophic Harm Precautionary Principle, will be more sensible, and more productive of good outcomes in the long run, than any other possibility.[81]

If this conclusion is at least plausible, then we can venture a rough analysis of whether to follow the Maximin Principle under conditions of uncertainty. Sometimes a rejection of that principle is indicated because the worst-case scenario is not much worse than the second worst-case scenario, and because a great deal is lost by taking steps to eliminate the worst-case scenario. But sometimes the worst case is the worst by far, and sometimes we lose relatively little by eliminating it. For this kind of analysis to work, of course, we must be able to produce cardinal rankings among the outcomes—that is, we must be able to rank them not merely in terms of their badness but also in terms of how much worse each is than the others. That approach will not work if cardinal rankings are not feasible—as might be the case if (for example) we cannot compare the catastrophic loss from climate change with the loss from huge expenditures on reductions of greenhouse gas emissions. Much of the time, however, cardinal rankings are possible.

To bring the whole analysis down to earth, imagine two polar situations with respect to climate change. First, suppose that the catastrophic dangers associated with climate change could be eliminated if every nation contributed $10 million to a special fund. On reasonable assumptions, that cost would be fully acceptable. Second, suppose that the catastrophic dangers associated with climate change could be eliminated only if every nation contributed enough resources to reduce standards of living by 30 percent worldwide, with a corresponding increase in global poverty. If climate change really does pose an uncertain danger of total catastrophe, the Maximin Principle argues in favor of this extraordinary reduction in worldwide standards of living.

But to incur burdens of this magnitude, we might want to insist that the danger of catastrophe rise above the minimal threshold—that there be demonstrable probability, and a not-so-low one, that the catastrophic risk will materialize. Call this a threshold requirement for extremely significant expenditures in response to a catastrophic risk under conditions of uncertainty. We might require a demonstration that the risk of catastrophe for climate change is over, say, 10 percent, or at least not below, say, 1 percent (back to the One Percent Doctrine). Of course, the extent of the catastrophe matters; if we are facing a 10 percent chance of the extinction of humanity, a 30 percent reduction in worldwide standards of living would certainly be worthwhile.

Imagine an individual or society lacking the information that would permit the assignment of probabilities to a *series* of hazards with catastrophic outcomes; suppose that the number of hazards is ten, or twenty, or a thousand. Suppose too that such an individual or society is able to assign probabilities (ranging from 1 percent to 98 percent) to an equivalent number of other hazards—with outcomes that range from bad to extremely bad but never catastrophic (with catastrophe being suitably defined). Suppose finally that every one of these hazards can be eliminated at a cost—a cost that is high but that does not, once incurred in individual cases, inflict harms that count as catastrophic.

The Maximin Principle suggests that our individual or society should spend a great deal to eliminate each of the ten, or twenty, or hundred potentially catastrophic hazards. But once that amount is spent on even one of those worst-case hazards, we might have nothing left to combat the extremely bad hazards, even those with a 98 percent chance of occurring. We can even imagine that a poorly informed individual or society would be condemned to real poverty and distress, or even worse, merely by virtue of following the Maximin Principle.

Suppose that, now or in the future, we have no way to assign probabilities to the threat of catastrophe associated with avian flu. Would it make sense to ban all international travel? To ban all travel from nations that have had at least one confirmed case? Measures of this kind have, in fact, been considered and proposed in high circles. But if the analysis here is right, supporting such measures without exploring the costs and burdens they would impose, and without knowing that the risk is above a certain level, is senseless.

Nothing here is meant to suggest that eliminating the worst-case scenario is forbidden, or even not required, by rationality.[82] My claim is, instead, that when one course of action leads to a worst-case scenario that is much worse than the worst-case scenario under an alternative course of action, and when eliminating that worst worst-case does not result in huge or extremely significant losses and burdens, then the Maximin Principle should be followed. The final version of the Catastrophic Harm Precautionary Principle turns out to be quite appealing.

Precautions against Catastrophe

To recapitulate a long and lamentably complicated discussion: The most modest version of the Catastrophic Harm Precautionary Principle insists that regulators should pay attention to expected value, even when catastrophe is most unlikely. A slightly less modest version adds that the expected value of a catastrophe is much higher than it might appear, because of significant and sometimes nonlinear increases in harm produced by the social amplification of risk. A more aggressive version asks for a degree of risk aversion, on the theory that people do, and sometimes should, purchase insurance against the worst kinds of harm. The degree of this margin of safety depends on what we gain and what we lose from it. I have also suggested that it sometimes makes sense to adopt a still more aggressive form of the Catastrophic Harm Precautionary Principle, one that follows the Maximin Principle by selecting the worst-case scenario and attempting to eliminate it.

But eliminating the worst-case scenario is not *generally* a sensible strategy. First, it is usually senseless under circumstances of risk, unless we assume an implausibly high degree of risk aversion. Second, regulators are rarely operating under circumstances of pure uncertainty; often rough probabilities can be ascribed to serious outcomes, and if not, at least rough probabilities can be ascribed to probabilities. But under circumstances of genuine uncertainty, when the worst-case scenario is exceptionally bad and when removal of that scenario does not inflict especially serious losses, it makes sense to eliminate the worst case.

Any Catastrophic Harm Precautionary Principle must be attentive to the full range of social risks, including the expected losses from the precautions themselves. It makes no sense to take steps to avert catastrophe if those very steps would create catastrophic risks of their own. If a preventive war designed to reduce the risks of terrorism from one source would increase those very risks from another source, then the Catastrophic Harm Precautionary Principle is indeterminate. Risk–risk tradeoffs are common; catastrophic risk–catastrophic risk tradeoffs are less so, but they are not difficult to find. And here as elsewhere, distributional considerations matter. The principle should be applied in a way that reduces extreme burdens on those least able to bear them.

One final note. Some of what I have said here might be understood to call for a form of cost-benefit analysis. But my emphasis has been on welfare, not on monetary equivalents. The core of the analysis focuses on what is lost and what is gained by precautions; and if we really want to know what is lost and what is gained, we will think about welfare, not about money. To be sure, I have not said much about how the notion of welfare should be specified; there is room for disagreement on that count. But we can often make a great deal of progress in deciding how to approach worst-case scenarios without resolving the most fundamental questions about the meaning of welfare. I shall turn to the question of cost-benefit analysis, and the role of monetary equivalents, in Chapter 5.

For the moment, we should explore another characteristic of worst cases: irreversibility.

CHAPTER FOUR

IRREVERSIBILITY

Most worst-case scenarios appear to have an element of irreversibility. Once a species is lost, it is lost forever. The special concern for endangered species stems from the permanence of their loss (outside of Jurassic Park). One of the most serious fears associated with genetically modified organisms is that they might lead to irreversible ecological harm. Because some greenhouse gases stay in the atmosphere for centuries, the problem of climate change may be irreversible, at least for all practical purposes.[1] Transgenic crops can impose irreversible losses too, because they can make pests more resistant to pesticides.[2] If we invest significant wealth in one source of energy and neglect others, we may be effectively stuck forever, or at least for a long time. One objection to capital punishment is that errors cannot be reversed.

In ordinary life, our judgments about worst-case scenarios have everything to do with irreversibility. Of course an action may be hard but not impossible to undo, and so there may be a continuum of cases, with different degrees of difficulty in reversing. A marriage can be reversed, but divorce is rarely easy; having a child is very close to irreversible; moving from New York to Paris is reversible, but moving back may be difficult. People often take steps to avoid courses of action that are burdensome rather than literally impossible to reverse.

In this light, we might identify an Irreversible Harm Precautionary Principle, applicable to a subset of risks.[3] As a rough first approximation, the principle says this: *Special steps should be taken to avoid irreversible harms, through precautions that go well beyond those that would be taken if irreversibility were not a problem.* The general attitude here is "act, then learn," as opposed to the tempting alternative of "wait and learn." In the case of climate change, some people believe that research should be our first line of defense. In their view, we should refuse to commit substantial resources to the problem until evidence of serious harm is unmistakably clear.[4] But even assuming that the evidence is not so clear, research without action allows greenhouse gas emissions to continue, which might produce risks that are irreversible, or at best difficult and expensive to reverse. For this reason, the best course of action might well be to take precautions now as a way of preserving flexibility for future generations. In the environmental context in general, this principle suggests that regulators should proceed with far more aggressive measures than would otherwise seem justified.[5]

But the problem is not limited to environmental protection. If cultural treasures are at risk, we might take special steps to preserve them too. The same is true, perhaps, in the context of terrorism, because terrorist attacks may well produce irreversible losses of many kinds.

The Value of Options, the Value of Uses

To see the relevance of irreversibility, let us begin with the monetary valuation of an environmental good, such as a pristine area.

Some people will be willing to pay to visit it on a regular basis, and they might be very upset at its loss. But others will be willing to pay to preserve it even if they will not use it. In fact, many citizens would be happy to give some money to save a pristine area, especially if animals can be found there. Hence, "existence value" is sometimes included in the valuation of environmental goods,[6] and indeed federal courts have insisted that agencies pay attention to that value in assessing damages to natural resources.[7] Taken as a group, citizens of most nations would be willing to pay a great deal to maintain the existence of a remote island and its ecosystem or to preserve an endangered species.

But some people are also willing to pay for the *option* to use an environmental amenity in the future, even if they are unsure whether they will exercise that option at any time.[8] Suppose that a pristine area has been proposed for development, and the worst-case scenario would involve irreversible damage. Many people would be willing to pay a significant amount for the option of deciding later to preserve the area rather than develop it. Under federal law, option value must also be considered in the assessment of damages to natural resources.[9] Many regulations pay attention to option value in the environmental context.[10] For many goods, people are willing to pay and to do a great deal in order to ensure that their options are preserved.

Here, then, is a simple sense in which irreversible harm causes a loss that should be considered, and one that must be included in measures of value. Whether or not we turn that value into some sort of monetary equivalent, it ought to matter. Some skeptics contend that it "is hard to imagine a price for an irreversible loss,"[11] but people certainly do identify prices for such losses, or at least for the risk of such losses.[12]

What is true for policy and law is true for ordinary life as well.

Suppose that you are not sure whether you want to attend a particular school or to take a particular job. Unable to make up your mind, you might be willing to do and (in a sense) pay a lot to keep your options open. People take steps to preserve their options all the time. Alert to the risk of a worst-case scenario, they take steps to protect themselves against its occurrence—not only by purchasing insurance but also by buying options. The practice is no less important if it is sometimes invisible and if we are sometimes not conscious of what we are doing.

The Basic Argument

The idea of option value, as used in the monetary valuation literature, is closely related to the use of the notion of options in the domains of law and policy. The simple claim is that when regulators are dealing with an irreversible loss, and when they are uncertain about the timing and likelihood of that loss, they should be willing to pay a sum—the option value—in order to maintain flexibility for the future. The option might not be exercised if it turns out that the loss is not a serious one. But if the option is purchased, regulators will be in a position to forestall that loss if it turns out to be large. The Irreversible Harm Precautionary Principle is based on the idea that regulators should be willing to buy an option to maintain their own flexibility. (I am using terms that suggest monetary payments, but the basic point holds even if we are skeptical about the use of monetary equivalents; "purchases" can take the form of precautionary steps that do not directly involve money.)

In the domain of finance, options take multiple forms.[13] An investor might be willing to purchase land that is known to have deposits of gold. Even if the cost of extraction is currently too high to justify mining, ownership of the land creates an option to mine if the market price for gold increases, the cost of mining decreases, or both.[14] A standard "call option" is the right but not the obligation to purchase an asset at or before a specific date at a specified price. (You might buy the right to purchase a share of stock in your favorite company at $50, six months from now.)

In another variation, people might seek the right to abandon a project at a fixed price, perhaps on the occurrence of a specified worst-case scenario. (You might agree to perform some service for someone but obtain the right not to perform in the event of bad weather, bad health, or some other contingency.) Alternatively, people might obtain the right to scale back a project, to expand it, or to extend its life. Options that recognize multiple sources of uncertainty, of the sort that can be found for many regulatory problems, are termed "rainbow options."

Option theory has countless applications outside the domain of investments. Many people would be willing to do, and possibly even spend, a great deal to preserve their option to have another child—even if they are not at all sure that they really want to have another child. Or consider narrow judicial rulings, of the sort celebrated by judicial minimalists, who want courts to make decisions that are focused on particular details and that leave many questions undecided.[15] Narrow rulings can be understood as a way of buying an option, or at least of paying a certain amount in return for future flexibility. Judges who leave things undecided and focus their rulings on the facts of particular cases are in a sense forcing themselves, and society as a whole, to purchase an option in return for flexibility in the resolution of subsequent related problems.

Whether that option is worthwhile depends on its price and the benefits that it provides. In the case of marriage, suppose that because of law or social norms, divorces are or become difficult to obtain, so that a decision to marry could not be readily reversed. If so, prospective spouses might be willing to do a lot to maintain their flexibility before marrying—a lot more than they would be willing to do if divorce were much easier.

An understanding of option value might explain the emphasis on irreversible losses in the National Environmental Policy Act (NEPA) and other environmental statutes. The central point of NEPA is to ensure that government officials give serious consideration to environmental factors before they take action that might threaten the environment. If the government is building a road through a wilderness area, or drilling in Alaska, or licensing a nuclear power plant, it must produce an environmental impact statement that lays out the environmental effects. The production of these statements can be burdensome and costly, but when irreversible losses are involved, the public, and those involved in making the ultimate decision, ought to know about them.

Option value is one of the supporting ideas behind the Irreversible Harm Precautionary Principle. In a classic essay by Kenneth Arrow and Anthony Fisher, the authors imagine that the question is whether to preserve a virgin redwood forest for wilderness recreation or to open it to clear-cut logging.[16] If the development option is chosen, the destruction of the forest is effectively irreversible. Arrow and Fisher assume the authorities cannot yet assess the costs or benefits of the proposed development. If development produces "some irreversible transformation of the environment, hence a loss in perpetuity of the benefits from preservation," then it is worth paying something to wait until the missing information is available. Their suggestion is that "the expected benefits of an irreversible decision should be adjusted to reflect the loss of options it entails."[17]

Fisher has generalized this argument to suggest that "where a decision problem is characterized by (1) uncertainty about future costs and benefits of the alternatives, (2) prospects for resolving or reducing the uncertainty with the passage of time, and (3) irreversibility of one or more of the alternatives, an extra value, an option value, properly attaches to the reversible alternative(s)."[18] If an irreversible harm is on one side and a reversible one on the other, an understanding of option value suggests that paying a premium to avoid the irreversible harm and preserve future flexibility is worthwhile.

Richard Posner has invoked a point of this sort as a justification for aggressive steps to combat climate change.[19] Posner acknowledges that the size of the threat of climate change is disputed, and hence it is tempting to wait to regulate until we have more information. But there is a serious problem with waiting, which is "the practically irreversible effect of greenhouse-gas emissions on the atmospheric concentration of those gases."[20] Thus, Posner reasons that "making shallower cuts [in emissions] now can be thought of as purchasing an option to enable global warming to be stopped or slowed at some future time at a lower cost."[21] This reduction in cost could result from lowering current emissions or simply from increasing the rate of technological innovations that make pollution reduction less costly in the future. Posner concludes that the option approach makes sense for other catastrophic risks as well, including those associated with genetically modified crops.

The general point here is that, as in the stock market, those involved in environmental protection are trying to project a stream of good and bad effects over time. The ability to project the stream of effects will improve, and hence much can be gained from being able to make the decision later rather than earlier. If better decisions can be made in the future, then putting the decision off to a later date has value. The key point is that uncertainty and irreversibility should lead to a sequential decision-making process. If better information will emerge, regulators might seek an approach that preserves greater flexibility.

Irreversibilities Everywhere

Unfortunately, the idea of irreversibility is highly ambiguous. Let us consider three possible interpretations. Under the first, an effect is irreversible when restoration to the status quo is impossible or at best extremely difficult, at least on a relevant timescale. For example, the "decision not to preserve a rich reservoir of biodiversity such as the 60 million-year-old Korup forest in Nigeria is irreversible. The alteration or destruction of a unique asset of this type has an awesome finality."[22] If this is the appropriate interpretation of irreversibility, then it is an aspect of seriousness. A second interpretation, standard in the economic literature on options, sees irreversibility in terms of sunk costs. A final interpretation emphasizes the problem of incommensurability: Some goods, such as pristine areas, may not be commensurable with other goods, such as money. The three interpretations lead to different understandings of the Irreversible Harm Precautionary Principle.

Irreversibility and seriousness   Under the first interpretation, no clear line separates the reversible from the irreversible. We have a continuum, not a dichotomy. The question is not whether some effect can be reversed, but instead at what cost. Note that areas that have been developed, or otherwise harmed, can often be returned to their original state, even if at considerable expense. Even lost forests can be restored. But sometimes the cost is prohibitive, and sometimes restoration is literally impossible.

At first glance, this point does not create a serious problem for the Irreversible Harm Precautionary Principle. The extent of the precaution should depend on the size of the bad effect and the cost and burden involved in reversing it. If climate change cannot be reversed at all, we should take more precautions than we would if it can be reversed only at great expense, monetary or otherwise. And if it can be reversed only at great expense, we would take more precautions than we would if reversal were easy.

But there is a more severe conceptual difficulty, which is that whether a particular act is "irreversible" depends on how it is characterized. Any death, of any living creature, is irreversible, and what is true for living creatures is true for rocks and refrigerators too; if these are destroyed, they are destroyed forever. And because time is linear, every decision is, in an intelligible sense, irreversible. If I play tennis at 11 a.m. today, that decision cannot be reversed, and what might have been done at that time will have been permanently lost. If government builds a new highway in upstate New York in May, that particular decision will be irreversible; nothing else will be done with that land in May, even though the highway can be later replaced or eliminated. This is the sense in which "irreversibility" depends on how the underlying act is characterized. If we characterize it narrowly as being and doing precisely what it is and does, any act is irreversible by definition.

Environmentalists who are concerned about irreversibility have something far more particular in mind. They mean something like a large-scale alteration in environmental conditions—one that imposes permanent, or nearly permanent, changes in those conditions. But irreversibility in this sense is not a sufficient reason for a highly precautionary approach. At a minimum, the irreversible change has to be for the worse, and it must also rise to a certain level of magnitude. A truly minuscule change in the global temperature, even if permanent, would not justify expensive precautions if it is benign or if it imposes little in the way of harm. A loss of a wisdom tooth is irreversible, but not a reason for particular precautions on behalf of wisdom teeth. A loss of an extremely small forest, with no wildlife, hardly justifies a special principle, even if that loss cannot be reversed. But loss of a large forest, with a lot of wildlife, is a very different matter.

At first glance, then, irreversibility matters only because of its connection with the magnitude of the harm; irreversibility operates as a kind of amplifier. In law, an illuminating comparison might be made with the idea that courts will refuse to issue a preliminary injunction unless the plaintiff can show the likelihood of an "irreparable harm" if the injunction is not granted. Irreparability is not a sufficient condition for granting the injunction; the harm must be large as well as irreparable. And if irreversibility in environmental protection is to be analyzed in the same way, then an Irreversible Harm Precautionary Principle is really part of a Catastrophic Harm Precautionary Principle, or at least a Significant Harm Precautionary Principle.

If so, the Irreversible Harm Precautionary Principle is important and must be taken into account; but it is not especially distinctive. The principle is also vulnerable, some of the time, to the same objections that apply to the Precautionary Principle as a whole. Significant and even irreversible harms may well be on all sides of risk-related problems, and a focus on one set of risks will give rise to others—perhaps environmental risks as well.

Irreversibility and sunk costs   Analysts of real options understand the idea of irreversibility in a different and technical way.[23] Irreversible investments are sunk costs—those that cannot be recovered. Examples include expenditures on advertising and marketing, or capital investments designed to improve the performance of a factory. Even the purchase of motor vehicles, computers, and office equipment is not fully reversible, because the purchase cost is usually a lot higher than resale value. Examples of reversible investments include the opening of bank accounts and the purchase of bonds. The problem with an investment that is irreversible is that those who make it relinquish "the possibility of waiting for new information that might affect the desirability or timing of the expenditure, and this lost option value is an opportunity cost that must be included as part of the investment."[24]

Everyone agrees that we should characterize as irreversible harms those environmental effects that are both serious and extremely expensive and time-consuming to reverse. This is the understanding that leads Posner and others to argue for the purchase of an "option" to slow down climate change at a lower rate in the future. Immediate adoption of a policy produces a "sunk benefit." But this argument ignores an important point: Irreversibility, in this sense, might well lie on all sides. Recall that regulation that reduces one (irreversible) environmental risk might well increase another such risk. Efforts to reduce climate change and other dangers associated with fossil fuel use, for example, may lead to increased dependence on nuclear energy, as has been urged by many observers. In China, nuclear energy has been actively defended as a way of combating climate change.[25]

As with the Precautionary Principle in general, so with the Irreversible Harm Precautionary Principle in particular: Measures that the principle requires on grounds of safety and health might well be prohibited on exactly those grounds. And if steps are taken to reduce greenhouse gas emissions, capital costs will be incurred, and they cannot be recouped. Sunk costs are a familiar feature of environmental regulation, in the form of mandates that require technological change. We may well be dealing, then, with irreversibilities, not irreversibility.

This point much complicates the application of the Irreversible Harm Precautionary Principle. As Fisher writes for climate change,

"It is not clear whether the conditions of the problem imply that investment in control ought to be slowed or reduced, while waiting for information needed to make a better decision, or that investment should come sooner to preserve the option to protect ourselves from impacts that may be revealed in the future as serious or even catastrophic."[26] Some observers have concluded, unlike Posner, that the existence of uncertainty and irreversibility argue for *less,* not more, in a way of investments in reducing greenhouse gas emissions. Those investments may themselves turn out to be irreversible. Everything depends on the likelihood and magnitude of the losses on all sides.

Posner's analysis does not use the idea of options in the technical sense. He emphasizes the cumulative effect of emissions on atmospheric concentrations of carbon dioxide. Because of that cumulative effect, a steady or even declining rate of emissions will still cause concentrations to increase. He notes that it may be much harder and more expensive to slow climate change in the future than in the present—a point that comes close to the technical understanding of irreversibility in the economic literature. But a gap in Posner's analysis is his neglect of the irreversible losses associated with greenhouse gas reductions.

I am not saying, and do not believe, that "wait and learn" is an adequate answer to the problem of climate change. That approach makes sense only if we lose very little when we defer investments while waiting to obtain more information about the benefits. But if a great deal is likely to be lost by deferring such investments, then the judgment should be reversed. And we have good reason to believe that the irreversible losses associated with climate change do indeed justify the irreversible losses associated with greater investments in emissions reductions, worldwide. My conclusion is that if irreversibility is defined in terms of sunk costs, it provides a distinctive understanding of the Irreversible Harm Precautionary Principle, in a way that helps to explain what makes worst cases worst.

Irreversibility and incommensurability   When people say that the loss of a pristine area, or of a species, is irreversible, they do not merely mean that the loss is grave and that it takes a lot to provide adequate compensation. They mean that what is lost is incommensurable—that it is qualitatively distinctive, and that when we lose it, we lose something unique.

The central claim here is that human goods are diverse and that we do violence to our considered judgments about them when we line them up along a single metric.[27] People do not value an endangered species in the same way that they value money. A beach, a friendship, and a child are distinguishable from specified monetary sums. If we see beaches, friendships, and children as equivalent to one another, or as equal to some amount of money, we will have an odd and even unrecognizable understanding of all three of these goods. Of course people are willing to make tradeoffs among qualitatively diverse goods, and they do so all the time. We will pay a certain amount, and no more, to be able to visit the beach, or to help preserve it in a pristine state; we will not pay an infinite sum to see our friends, or even to maintain our friendships; we will take some precautions, but not others, to protect our children.

The emphasis on incommensurability is not meant to deny that tradeoffs are made. The point is only that the relevant goods are not the same. When we say a loss is irreversible, we might mean that it is qualitatively distinctive and not fungible with other human goods. Many of those who are concerned about irreversible harms intend to stress this point.

This claim is both true and important, and it helps to explain what is meant by irreversibility. When worst-case scenarios arise, it is often because of the uniqueness of what is lost. But the need for tradeoffs remains important. A single person is incommensurable with money, and with other things that matter, but we do not attempt to drive risks of death down to zero. The claim about irreversibility does not mean that we should devote an infinite amount, or any particular amount, to prevent an incommensurable loss. What is gained by an understanding of incommensurability is a more vivid appreciation of why certain losses cannot be dismissed as mere "costs."

An Irreversible Harm Precautionary Principle, used in private decisions or democratic arenas, might be implemented with a recognition of the qualitative distinctness of many losses—especially when those losses affect future generations. Here too, however, precautionary steps may themselves impose incommensurable losses, not merely monetary ones. Environmental protection of one sort may create environmental problems of another sort. If the diverse nature of social goods is to play a part in the implementation of an Irreversible Harm Precautionary Principle, it must attend to the fact that diverse goods may be found on all sides.

Qualifications and Conclusions

The arguments for an Irreversible Harm Precautionary Principle, along with an understanding of its limitations, are now in place. We lack any kind of algorithm for implementing that principle. But we should be able to say that when a harm is irreversible in the sense that restoration is very costly or impossible, special precautions may be justified; that it often makes sense to "buy" an option to preserve future flexibility; and that the loss of cherished and qualitatively distinctive goods deserves particular attention. But there are three important qualifications, involving the idea of optimal delay, distributional considerations, and what I shall call precommitment value.

Optimal delay   Future Americans will almost certainly have and know more than current Americans; the same is true for France, Germany, China, the United Kingdom, India, South Africa, Canada, and numerous other nations. The history of the human race offers powerful evidence here. Most generations are richer and more informed than those that preceded them. To be sure, many people are worried that future generations are likely to be poorer in light of apparently serious threats, including environmental degradation, risks of war, population increases, and much more. But such worries have not been vindicated in the past, and it would be surprising if they were vindicated in the future.

As a result, future generations will probably be in a far better position, and possibly an unimaginably better position, to handle environmental problems that materialize in their time.[28] According to the economist Thomas Schelling, the nearly inevitable increase in wealth over time means that it "makes no sense to make current generations 'pay' for the problems of future generations."[29] Why should the relatively poor present transfer its limited resources to benefit the future, which is likely to be relatively rich? There is another problem. If we make expensive investments in precautions now—such as greenhouse gas reduction—we might diminish available resources for future generations, leaving them with less wealth to control the damage that actually occurs.[30]

The argument for "wait and learn" is strengthened by these points. And I shall have a fair bit to say about optimal delay and future generations in Chapter 6. But any such argument must also take account of the incontrovertible fact that waiting threatens to diminish the flexibility of future decisionmakers, perhaps severely.[31] In the case of endangered species, for example, the loss is permanent, and we must therefore be careful about delaying precautionary measures designed to ensure their continued existence.

Irreversibilities, distribution, and the least well-off   At first glance, an Irreversible Harm Precautionary Principle might seem to be especially beneficial to disadvantaged people.[32] In the context of climate change, aggressive precautions are projected to give far more to poor countries than to rich ones, partly because rich nations are so much less dependent on agriculture. But sometimes precautions in the name of irreversible harm can hurt the world's most vulnerable populations. For example, some of the risks associated with genetic engineering are irreversible, but the benefits of genetic engineering are likely to be felt most in poor nations. Even in the case of climate change, poor countries, including India and China, cannot easily afford aggressive regulation of greenhouse gas emissions; they will be better off in the short run, and possibly in the long run too, if they are allowed to continue to emit greenhouse gases (at least if other nations reduce their own).

In short, an analysis of distributional goals must be undertaken separately from an analysis of irreversibility. Sometimes we will hurt the least well-off, rather than help them, if we buy an option to preserve our own flexibility. The cost of the option might be paid mostly by those who can least afford it.

Precommitment value   In some domains, future flexibility is undesirable, and individual and societies are willing to pay a great deal to eliminate it. The tale of Ulysses and the Sirens is perhaps the most familiar example, and the idea of precommitment has many applications.[33] A constitution can itself be seen as a precommitment device by which we relinquish our flexibility in order to be governed by firm rules. Consider the Cold War, in which many people thought that the United States would do best if it committed itself to taking certain courses of action in the event of an attack (especially a nuclear attack); a precommitment can create deterrence.

In the environmental context, regulators might be willing to pay for precommitment strategies that will operate as a constraint on any number of problems, including interest-group power, myopia, weakness of will, and cognitive biases. The conventional Precautionary Principle, which places a thumb on the scales in favor of environmental protection, might be explained in these terms.[34] Perhaps the principle can be understood not as an effort to preserve flexibility, which can be bad, but as an effort to ensure a commitment to a course of action that will protect the environment.

The difficulty is now a familiar refrain: Any precommitment strategy may give rise to problems, including environmental problems, for which a precommitment strategy might also be justified. It is nonetheless important to see that option value is sometimes accompanied by precommitment value, for which some regulators might be willing to spend a great deal.

Environmental Injunctions

In many settings, paying for an option to avoid a risk of irreversible losses may make sense, depending on the size and nature of the loss if it is irreversible. If irreversible losses are on all sides, then we must assess their likelihood and magnitude before deciding on a course of action. Because environmental expenditures are typically sunk costs, an emphasis on irreversibility will sometimes argue in favor

of delaying, rather than accelerating, environmental protection—
depending on the magnitude and likelihood of the relevant effects.
An understanding of these issues helps to untangle some long-
standing disputes about the issuance of preliminary injunctions in
environmental cases. For many years, some courts of appeals held
that when environmental harm was alleged, federal courts should
adopt a presumption of irreparable damage and indeed a presumption in favor of injunctive relief.[35] In NEPA cases, if the agency had
failed to prepare an adequate environmental impact statement, the
result was a likely injunction: "Irreparable damage is presumed
when an agency fails to evaluate thoroughly the environmental impact of a proposed action."[36]

But what is the basis for the presumption of irreparable harm?
And what follows from it? Does it follow, for example, that the
United States Navy must be enjoined from conducting weapons-
training operations before it has obtained a permit to discharge
ordnance into the sea? The underlying issues are somewhat technical, but because they have great practical importance and bear directly on the real-world understanding of any Irreversible Harm
Precautionary Principle, injunctions warrant exploration here.

In response to the question about ordnance, the Supreme Court
said no.[37] Rejecting the suggestion that environmental violations
should give rise to automatic injunctions, the Court said that an injunction is an equitable remedy, subject to traditional balancing.
The Court said that it would "not lightly assume that Congress has
intended to depart from established principles" that allow lower
courts to exercise their discretion. In a later case, involving the
Alaska Native Claims Settlement Act, the Court underlined the
point and expressly rejected the presumption of irreparable harm
in environmental cases.[38] Nonetheless, the Court stressed that environmental problems raise distinct issues, because "environmental

injury, by its nature, can seldom be adequately remedied by money damages and is often permanent or at least of long duration, *i.e.,* irreparable." If an environmental injury is likely, "the balance of harms will usually favor the issuance of an injunction to protect the environment."

When courts of appeals endorse a presumption in favor of injunctive relief, they might be understood as adopting a version of the Irreversible Harm Precautionary Principle, and assuming that environmental harm is irreversible in one or another sense. Perhaps environmental losses are qualitatively distinctive; perhaps it is very hard to restore the status quo. This interpretation helps to explain the simplest exception to the lower courts' presumption in favor of injunctive relief cases, in which "irreparable harm *to the environment* would result if such relief were granted."[39] For example, courts were reluctant to grant an injunction against the use of a logging road if the injunction would prevent the removal of diseased trees that were threatening to spread infection through national forests.

Here, then, is a clear recognition of the existence of irreversibilities, or irreversibility-irreversibility tradeoffs. And when the Supreme Court rejected the presumption, it did so in favor of traditional equitable balancing—recognizing that serious harms, and perhaps irreversible harms, are on all sides. But even in doing so, the Court endorsed a kind of Irreversible Harm Precautionary Principle through its explicit recognition that environmental injury "is often permanent or at least of long duration."

What still remains undecided, after the Court's decisions in the 1980s, is the appropriate judicial posture in the face of violations of NEPA.[40] The Court's rejection of a presumption in favor of preliminary injunctions might well be taken to suggest that courts should rarely issue such injunctions in NEPA cases—especially, perhaps, in light of the fact that NEPA is a purely procedural statute, one that imposes information-gathering duties on agencies without requiring them to take that information into account in deciding what to do.[41] If courts cannot forbid agencies to act as they choose after producing an adequate environmental impact statement, injunctions might seem an odd remedy in the NEPA setting. But in the most elaborate discussion of the question, then-Circuit Judge Stephen Breyer suggested that injunctions are often appropriate in NEPA cases.[42] Breyer's discussion endorses an appropriately constrained Irreversible Harm Precautionary Principle, specially adapted to the NEPA setting.

Judge Breyer argued that NEPA is meant to prevent a particular kind of injury, one that should play a central role in the decision whether to grant an injunction. The purpose of NEPA is to ensure that officials take environmental considerations into account *before* they embark on a course of action: "When a decision to which NEPA obligations attach is made without the informed environmental consideration that NEPA requires, the harm that NEPA intends to prevent has been suffered." That harm is the increased risk of irreparable damage to the environment that arises "when governmental decision makers make up their minds without having before them an analysis (with prior public comment) of the likely effects of their decision upon the environment."

Irreversibility is central here, for it is a simple human fact that officials are less likely to shut down a nearly completed project than one that has just been started. The relevant harm "may well have to do with the psychology of decision makers, and perhaps a more deeply rooted human psychological instinct not to tear down projects once they are built." Judge Breyer's point, then, is that in deciding whether to issue a preliminary injunction, courts must take account of human psychology, and the potentially irreparable nature of the risk to the environment if the project is not stopped in a timely way.

None of this means that in NEPA cases, preliminary injunctions should issue as a matter of course; that view would endorse the Irreversible Harm Precautionary Principle in its crudest form. Sometimes injunctions will themselves impose serious harm, and sometimes the risk to the environment is trivial. But it makes sense to consider the risk that an inadequately informed decision to proceed will alter the status quo—ensuring that once an environmental impact statement is produced, it will be too late to have a meaningful effect on the outcome. If delay is not exceedingly costly, and if the risk of environmental harm is serious, injunctive relief is appropriate for NEPA violations. An understanding of the problem of irreversibility helps to explain why. In fact, Breyer's analysis, and his emphasis on the underlying psychology, is hardly restricted to the NEPA context; it might well be used by planners of many different kinds.

Irreversible and Catastrophic

Since worst-case scenarios are irreversible by their nature, we should be able to combine a concern about catastrophe with a focus on irreversible harm, in a way that generates an Irreversible and Catastrophic Harm Precautionary Principle. Suppose that by adopting precautions today, regulators can maintain flexibility to prevent a problem that is not only irreversible but potentially catastrophic as well. Suppose too that the likelihood of catastrophe can be specified at least within a certain range. If so, regulators might build on the discussion in Chapter 3 to assess expected value, including social amplification, to create a suitable margin of safety, and to include an analysis of the appropriate amount to protect against irreversible losses. An analysis of this kind might be done formally where all the variables can be specified. In ordinary life, and for some questions of law and policy, an informal analysis is good enough, or the best that can be expected. Sensible people make informal analyses all the time, in considering how much to do to protect against the worst-case scenarios associated with travel, illness, surgery, finances, and much more.

An Irreversible and Catastrophic Harm Precautionary Principle might also be used when the probability of the worst case cannot be specified with much confidence, or even when we are in the domain of uncertainty rather than risk. We might be willing to pay a great deal to maintain flexibility under these circumstances. Of course, significant expenditures can reduce flexibility, too; many problems involve not irreversibility but irreversibilities. Some of the most important irreversibilities are environmental in character, and this is one reason that special precautions are sometimes justified in the environmental domain.

Considerations of this kind provide the strongest basis for aggressive measures to combat climate change. The natural objections would either point to the irreversible costs of maintaining flexibility or question the probability that catastrophe will actually occur. The appropriate conclusion rests on an assessment of the empirical questions—but in my view, an appreciation of irreversibility and catastrophe offers a convincing ground for a sustained effort to reduce greenhouse gases. Exactly how sustained? Everything depends on what is gained and what is lost by those efforts. I will have more to say about this question. For the moment, let us turn to an issue that I have not yet explored—the issue of money.

CHAPTER FIVE

MONEY

In the United States, cost-benefit analysis is in the ascendancy. For over twenty years, American presidents have required agencies to perform CBA for major regulations; indeed, they have told agencies to regulate only if the benefits of regulation justify its costs.[1] Congress has also shown considerable interest in CBA, most prominently in the Safe Drinking Water Act, which asks agencies to produce quantitative assessments of both costs and benefits. For their part, federal courts have adopted a series of principles that promote CBA—saying that if Congress has not been clear, agencies may consider costs, take account of the substitute risks introduced by regulation, and exempt trivial risks from governmental control.

In its enthusiasm for cost-benefit analysis, the United States provides a sharp contrast to Europe, which has shown intense interest in the Precautionary Principle. CBA and the Precautionary Principle can lead in radically different directions. For example, many Europeans argue that the consequences of genetic modification are uncertain, that real harm is possible, and hence that stringent regulation is readily justified. By contrast, many Americans respond that the likely benefits of genetic modification are far greater than the likely harms and that stringent regulation is therefore unsupportable. With respect to climate change, many European leaders have argued in favor of precautions, even extremely expensive ones, simply to reduce the risk of catastrophe. But in the United States, a highly precautionary approach to climate change has had little appeal to national leaders, even those in the Democratic Party. Of course, the European posture on that topic is complex, not simple; but it is fair to say that with respect to climate change, precautionary thinking has had less appeal in the United States than elsewhere.

The tension between CBA and the Precautionary Principle raises serious questions about risk regulation. To engage in any kind of formal cost-benefit analysis, regulators must make difficult and often speculative judgments about the likely effects of alternative regulatory strategies; they must also turn those effects into monetary equivalents. How should we monetize the worst-case scenarios associated with climate change? For regulators, the easiest task is often the identification of costs, but even here they encounter formidable empirical problems. The monetary expense of regulations of different levels of stringency is difficult to project—especially because regulation often spurs technological innovation, greatly reducing the cost of risk reduction. In the context of ozone-depleting chemicals, the costs turned out to be far lower than anticipated, confounding early efforts at CBA. Interest groups have a stake in saying that regulation will be very costly and in emphasizing the worst cases associated with regulatory controls—perhaps including big increases in energy prices and big decreases in employment. Despite the claims of American industry, many people believe that aggressive regulation of greenhouse gases would have surprisingly low costs. Perhaps we can eliminate worst-case scenarios, much of the time, with lower economic burdens than we anticipate.

The identification of benefits presents even harder empirical problems—and knotty normative and conceptual ones as well. In the case of environmental harm, agencies must begin by estimating, in nonmonetary terms, the savings that are likely to result from regulation, including reductions in mortality and morbidity, along with improvements in visibility, recreation, aesthetics, animal welfare, property values, and more. These estimates are the foundation for the analysis on which agency decisions must largely depend. When science leaves room for doubt, as it often does, agencies typically specify a range of possibilities, representing low-end estimates and high-end estimates in addition to the best "point" estimate. Agencies might, for example, project that a certain regulation will save as many as eighty lives each year and as few as zero, with a preferred estimate of twenty-five.[2] These numbers inevitably involve a lot of guesswork. Often the worst-case scenario will be much worse than the best point estimate, and scientists will disagree about whether or not the worst-case scenario is sufficiently likely to deserve serious attention. In that event, how should regulators proceed?

After specifying the likely benefits, CBA requires agencies to engage in multiple acts of conversion, assigning monetary values to human lives, human morbidity, and a range of harms to the environment. Typically, American agencies assign such values on the basis of private "willingness to pay" (WTP). For example, the Environmental Protection Agency values a human life at about $6.1 million, a figure that comes from real-world markets. In the workplace and for consumer goods, additional safety has a price; market evidence is investigated to identify that price. The $6.1 million figure, known as the value of a statistical life (VSL), is a product of many studies of actual risks in the workplace, the housing market, and the market for consumer goods, attempting to determine how much workers and others are paid to assume mortality hazards. Suppose that people are paid $600, on average, to eliminate risks of 1/10,000; suppose, for example, that workers who face risks of that magnitude generally receive $600 in additional wages each year. If so, the VSL would be said to be $6 million.

Where market evidence is unavailable, agencies often produce monetary valuations on the basis of contingent valuation surveys, which ask people how much they are willing to pay to produce certain desirable outcomes—to save coral reefs or endangered species, to eliminate a risk of chronic bronchitis or curable lung cancer, and much more. I recently asked University of Chicago law students how much they would be willing to pay to eliminate a cancer risk of 1 in 100,000 from arsenic in drinking water. The median answer was $50, producing a VSL of $5 million—fairly close to the EPA's $6.1 million figure. Drawing on market evidence and contingent valuation studies, the EPA has valued a case of chronic bronchitis at $260,000, an emergency hospital visit for asthma at $9,000, hospital admission for pneumonia at $13,400, a lost workday at $83, and a specified decrease in visibility at $14.[3]

All of these figures are contestable. The $6.1 million VSL was chosen not because some authoritative study demonstrates that it is correct, but because it is the mean figure of a number of studies. But why should regulators use the mean figure? Some studies suggest that the figure is in the vicinity of $14 million.[4] For particular risks, such as those involving cancer, some people have suggested that the right figure is twice that.[5] If we are focusing on worst-case scenarios, perhaps we should accept the higher number, which would dramatically increase our estimates of the benefits from regulation.

For a proposed arsenic regulation, for example, the total benefits might fall at around $23 million (assuming, not implausibly, that eleven lives would be saved, and "discounting" those lives on the ground that they would be saved in the future) or instead at around $3.4 billion (assuming, not implausibly, that 112 lives would be saved and using high-end estimates of a VSL).[6] To say the least, a range of $23 million to $3.4 billion leaves regulators with a lot of discretion—especially if the costs of the regulation are in the vicinity of $200 million. In order for CBA to be workable, regulators need to have a relatively restricted range of possibilities.

Once a cost-benefit analysis is produced, what should be done with it? The most ambitious answer is that agencies should adopt regulations only when the likely benefits exceed the likely costs—and that if several possible regulations meet this test, agencies should select the one that "maximizes net benefits." On this approach, CBA provides the rule of decision, one by which regulators should be bound. But two obvious problems arise here. The first is that people's willingness to pay may not capture the benefits, to them, of the protection they seek. Poor people may be willing to pay very little for a risk reduction from which they would gain a great deal—for the simple reason that money is more valuable when you have little of it. The second problem is distributional. We need to know who, exactly, is paying the costs and receiving the benefits. If wealthy people are paying, we might want to go forward with the regulation even if the cost-benefit analysis suggests that we should not.

A more cautious response would be that agencies should generally require benefits to exceed costs, and should also seek to maximize net benefits, but that they need not do so. In this view, the outcome of the CBA provides a presumption but no more. The presumption could be rebutted by showing that the particular situation justifies a departure from the result indicated by CBA—as, plausibly, in cases in which poor people would stand to gain a great deal.[7] Or the presumption could be rebutted by the decision to create a margin of safety to shield against the worst-case scenarios (see Chapter 3). A still more cautious approach would be that in deciding what to do, regulators should consider the outcome of CBA simply as relevant information—to be considered alongside other relevant information. There are important differences between those who would make CBA determinative and those who would merely make it relevant. But even on the most cautious understandings of the role of CBA, government's choices would be significantly affected by the translation of benefits into monetary equivalents.

To say the least, it is highly controversial to claim that people's protection against risks to life and health is properly measured by their willingness to pay to avoid worst-case scenarios. Thus far, I have been focusing on what people have to gain and to lose from eliminating such scenarios; WTP is at best a proxy for what matters. It is at least equally controversial to use WTP as the basis for policies protecting endangered species, nature, and wildlife. But as we have seen, the Precautionary Principle raises serious problems of its own. How much precaution is the right level of precaution? Are costs relevant to the answer? We have seen that taking precautions against all risks, rather than a subset, is not possible, even in principle. If all risks cannot be reduced at once, how should regulators set priorities?

In this chapter, I approach these questions through a discussion of three illuminating and influential books that offer radically different approaches to regulatory protection, money, and the proper treatment of worst-case scenarios. Frank Ackerman and Lisa Heinzerling believe that CBA is a hopelessly crude tool, one that buries indefensible judgments of morality and politics.[8] Drawing on the war on terrorism, they argue for the Precautionary Principle instead—and they want government to focus in particular on worst-case scenarios and on irreversibility. By contrast, Adam Burgess uses the controversy over cell phones to suggest that the Precautionary Principle capitulates to, and even promotes, baseless public fears.[9] Objecting to what he sees as excessive fear of new technologies, Burgess argues for careful attention to scientific evidence and for regulation only when the risk is real. Focusing directly on worst-case scenarios, Richard Posner argues for CBA and economic analysis in a context in which it seems least promising: catastrophic risk.[10] He contends that climate change, asteroid collisions, terrorism, and other potentially catastrophic problems cannot sensibly be approached without a disciplined effort to quantify and monetize both costs and benefits. But where Ackerman and Heinzerling see CBA as an excuse for regulatory inaction, Posner invokes CBA on behalf of aggressive controls on greenhouse gases and other sources of potentially serious danger. Indeed, his central goal is to draw private and public attention to catastrophic risks that are exceedingly unlikely to come to fruition.

Building on the arguments made by Burgess and Posner, I shall mount a qualified defense of CBA here. Without some sense of both costs and benefits—both nonmonetized and monetized—regulators will be making a stab in the dark. We have seen that human beings have a great deal of difficulty in assessing risks, making them prone to both overreaction and neglect. CBA does not supply definite answers, and as I have said, it is only a proxy for what matters; but it can help to establish which risks are serious and which are not.

But building on the arguments made by Ackerman and Heinzerling, I shall explore some serious problems with CBA. As we have seen, regulators cannot always assign probabilities to bad outcomes, and when probabilities cannot be assigned, the standard form of CBA cannot get off the ground. In addition, willingness to pay is sometimes an inappropriate basis for regulatory policy. Human beings are citizens, not merely consumers, and their consumption choices, as measured by WTP, might be trumped by their reflective judgments as citizens. In any case, willingness to pay is dependent on *ability* to pay; when the poorest members of societies stand to gain from regulatory protection, they should be protected even if their poverty ensures that their WTP is low. This point helps to illuminate the controversial question whether and in what sense people in poor nations are "worth less" than people in rich nations.

Monetization and Its Discontents

Insisting that human deaths are not mere "costs," Ackerman and Heinzerling contend that CBA is morally obtuse. They argue that a well-functioning democracy should respect the informed judgments of citizens, rather than aggregating private consumption choices. Ackerman and Heinzerling much prefer the Precautionary Principle, which, in their view, is "a more holistic analysis" that argues for regulation in the face of scientific uncertainty and that is "committed to fairness within and beyond this generation."[11]

Ackerman and Heinzerling are aware that many people have turned to CBA because of widely publicized studies that purport to show a high level of arbitrariness in modern regulation.[12] According to such studies, regulations in the United States are wildly inconsistent. (Undoubtedly the same basic picture could be found elsewhere.) Sometimes the United States spends $100,000 or less to save a human life. Sometimes it spends tens of millions.

Cost-benefit supporters ask: Shouldn't nations be devoting their resources to serious health problems rather than trivial ones? If a nation can spend ten million dollars to save one thousand lives, shouldn't it do that, rather than wasting the money on a similarly priced program that saves only one or two people? We have seen that human beings make many errors in assessing risks, using rules of thumb and demonstrating biases that make them exaggerate some dangers and underestimate others. These errors seem to be replicated in existing policies; CBA might be defended as a promising corrective to blunders in citizens' perceptions of risk. In these ways, interest in CBA has been fueled less by contentious claims of value than by the pragmatic suggestion that it can assist in more intelligent priority-setting, not least in dealing with low-probability, high-impact events.[13]

Ackerman and Heinzerling believe that the attack on the current system is based on misleading studies, burying controversial and indeed implausible judgments of value. True, some regulations do not prevent many deaths, but they do prevent serious (nonfatal) harms to human health and also harms to ecosystems. The resulting benefits should not be disparaged. More fundamentally, Ackerman and Heinzerling argue that the key studies find low benefits partly because they greatly "discount" future gains to life and health. Everyone agrees that a dollar today is worth more than a dollar in twenty years; economists use a standard discount rate (often 3 percent to 7 percent annually) to convert future dollars into current equivalents. In calculating the benefits of regulation, they use the same discount rate for lives saved and illnesses averted. Ackerman and Heinzerling contend that this approach wrongly shrinks the value of regulations that will save people in the future. One of their central claims, then, is that the standard discount rate should not be applied to future savings in terms of life and health. (I explore this claim in detail in Chapter 6.)

Suppose that their arguments are right—that once economic values are properly assigned to environmental gains, few existing regulations will be condemned as requiring huge investments for trivial benefits. Regulators still might want to use cost-benefit analysis to improve current and future decisions. Ackerman and Heinzerling complain that to do this, they will have to produce a dollar value for a human life—and any such effort will be arbitrary, offensive, or worse. They reject the view that WTP, based largely on workplace studies, produces information that agencies should use. In their view, workers often have little knowledge about the risks they face, and hence they cannot be charged with consciously trading hazards against dollars. Even when workers are informed, they may have few options and hence little choice. If they accept a job with significant hazards for a low premium, it is not because they are genuinely free to choose.

Some anomalies in the empirical literature are highly relevant here. Nonunionized workers have sometimes been found to receive little or nothing for the reduction of statistical risks—and African-Americans have been found to receive much less than white people do.[14] Does it follow that regulators should treat the lives of nonunionized workers, or African-Americans, as worth especially little? Ackerman and Heinzerling add that the key studies ask only how much individuals care about risks to themselves. They ignore the fact that many of us value the lives of others too. I might be willing to pay only $60 to eliminate a 1/100,000 risk that I face, but I might be willing to pay much more than that to eliminate that risk from my child's life, and substantial amounts to help reduce the risks of my friends. Altruism is ignored in the current calculations.

Ackerman and Heinzerling also contend that statistically equivalent risks should not be treated the same, because people's valuations of mortality risks, and of worst-case scenarios, depend not only on the probability of harm but also on their nature and their context. About 3,000 people died from the terrorist attacks of 9/11—a much smaller number than die each year from suicide (30,500), motor vehicle accidents (43,500), and emphysema (17,500). Ackerman and Heinzerling approve of the fact that the reaction of the United States to the 9/11 attacks was not based on simple numerical comparisons; a kind of precautionary thinking played a major role. Drawing on work by psychologist Paul Slovic, Ackerman and Heinzerling emphasize that the risk judgments of ordinary people diverge from the risk judgments of experts—not because ordinary people are stupid or confused, but because they have a different normative framework for evaluating risks. While experts focus on the number of deaths at stake, most people are especially averse to risks that are unfamiliar, uncontrollable, involuntary, irreversible, inequitably distributed, man-made, or catastrophic.[15] Diverse valuations of diverse risks should play a role in regulatory policy.

For example, most of us are not greatly troubled by the cancer risks associated with x-rays, partly because those risks are voluntarily incurred. The risks of terrorism and even pesticides and air pollution are more alarming because individuals cannot easily control those risks. And when a risk is faced by an identifiable community—as, for example, when landfills with toxic chemicals are located in largely poor areas—the public is especially likely to object to what it will perceive as unfairness.[16] Ackerman and Heinzerling want to honor this objection. Hence, they complain that cost-benefit analysis disregards important qualitative differences among quantitatively identical risks. It also tends to ignore, and often to reinforce, patterns of social inequality, above all because it pays no attention to a key question, which is distributional: Who receives the benefits and who incurs the costs? For both domestic and international environmental issues, Ackerman and Heinzerling emphasize the importance of fairness. If environmental threats mostly burden poor people, regulators should take that point into account, whatever the cost-benefit ratio.

It is possible, of course, that when people make distinctions among statistically identical risks, they are making some kind of cognitive error. Perhaps the availability of an image or a recent experience is leading them to show serious concern about some risks and diminished concern about others. But for most of us, qualitative considerations do matter. If a risk is unfamiliar or involuntarily incurred, it may produce a serious public reaction, even if the numbers of lives at stake are not especially high and even when the public has a reasonable grasp of the statistical risk.

Ackerman and Heinzerling are also concerned about how cost-benefit analysts value nature. How much will human beings pay to save an animal or a member of an endangered species? Economists have tried to answer the question by actually asking people. For example, one study finds that the average American family is willing to pay $70 per year to protect the spotted owl, $6 to protect the striped shriner (an endangered fish), and as much as $115 per year to protect major parks against impairment of visibility from air pollution. Ackerman and Heinzerling ridicule these numbers, complaining that any precise monetary value fails to provide useful information. Bans on whaling, for example, are rooted in a widely shared ethical judgment, not in cost-benefit analysis. A democracy should base its decisions about the protection of nature on such ethical judgments, rather than by aggregating people's willingness to pay.

Ackerman and Heinzerling offer a final objection to CBA: the rights of future generations. Economists generally apply a discount rate to future gains and losses. With a 7 percent discount rate, $1,000 in twenty years is worth only $260 today. Cost-benefit analysts within the federal government have long applied the usual discount rate for money (in some periods, 7 percent) to the benefits of safety and health regulation, so that prevention of 1,000 fatal cancers in 2025 is equivalent to the prevention of 260 fatal cancers in 2005. Ackerman and Heinzerling respond that lives are not like money; they cannot be placed in a bank for the accumulation of interest. A discount rate of 7 percent radically shrinks the value of reductions in risk for those born, say, one hundred years from now. But current generations owe obligations to the future and should not discount measures that protect people not yet born.

Invoking the Precautionary Principle, Ackerman and Heinzerling argue that nations are obliged to take action against serious threats even before a scientific consensus emerges. Above all, and in a way that has close links to the discussion in Chapter 3, they want regulators to make regulatory decisions by attending to the worst-case scenario. If the worst case is extremely bad, aggressive regulation is desirable even if it might result in wasted money. When a nation spends too much on regulatory protection, it loses limited resources; but waste is far better than catastrophe. Hence, their "preference is to tilt toward overinvestment in protecting ourselves and our descendents."[17]

Ackerman and Heinzerling urge that this approach was taken in the context of military spending during the Cold War, arguing that the nation rightly prepared for worst-case scenarios. They see protection against terrorism in similar terms. Ackerman and Heinzerling want to treat health and environmental risks in the same way, with close attention to the worst that might happen.

Pointless Precautions?

Ackerman and Heinzerling do not focus in detail on any particular regulatory issue. By contrast, Burgess explores the idea of "precaution" with close reference to a single controversy: the health risks associated with cellular phones. Burgess does not explicitly discuss cost-benefit analysis, but he is highly skeptical of the Precautionary Principle, which, in his view, leads regulators to capitulate to baseless public fear. With respect to risk, Burgess insists that some risks are serious and others are not, and that science is the best way to tell the difference.

Many people are worried about the worst-case scenarios associated with cell phone use—including, perhaps, significant increases in rates of various illnesses and diseases. (He does not explore the genuine risks associated with cell phone use while driving—an important issue that I will not discuss here.) Burgess contends that notwithstanding countless efforts, no reputable study has demonstrated significant health risks as a result of emissions from cell phones or cell phone towers.[18] To date, much of the so-called evidence comes from anecdotes of the sort provided by cell phone opponent Debbie Collins, who contended that her daughter's health had greatly improved after she was removed from a school near a cell phone tower. Rejecting expert opinion, Collins stated: "She's a different child now—it's all the proof I need to convince me there is a link between those wretched masts and the health of children."[19] Another mother said, "I needed no more proof than that. This term he started at a new school and I can already see the change in him. His memory has improved and his headaches have gone."[20] Burgess is concerned that a precautionary approach, founded on statements of this kind, will both aggravate fear and impose burdens and costs for no good reason.

That approach had its origins in a media campaign. In the early 1990s, a number of newspaper stories in the United Kingdom contended, on the basis of little evidence, that mobile phones and base stations were producing harmful health effects. Apparently influenced by these stories, the European Commission in Brussels began an official inquiry in 1995, ultimately funding future research and concluding that adverse effects could not be ruled out. Public fears intensified in 1996 after the issue received attention in a consumer health program on the BBC and a widely read news story in the *Sunday Times* featuring the headline, "Mobile phones cook your brain." In 1997, alarmist reports grew in the media, suggesting that cell phones could produce illness and premature mortality (and also reduce sex drive). These reports helped to spur citizen action. By 1999, local political campaigns against cell phone towers became prominent, and they received favorable coverage in local and regional newspapers, which further energized public concern.

These campaigns significantly affected both private and public institutions. Evidently fearful of worst-case scenarios, the London Metropolitan Police Service told its officers to limit cell phones as a precautionary measure. Harrods banned cell phones from its premises. Speaking in explicitly precautionary terms, entrepreneur Richard Branson recommended the use of safety devices for his employees. Local governing councils across the United Kingdom attempted to ban or restrict mobile towers, particularly those near schools. At the national level, the minister for public health legitimated public fears, insisting that in such a context, "it is very important that" officials "work very hard to keep ahead of public anxiety."[21] In Burgess's account, precautionary responses by official institutions helped to fuel that very anxiety. Thus, it "is only through being taken seriously by state bodies that the allegations about hypothetical risks have been able to command authority and acquire momentum beyond the immediate reactions of some individuals."[22]

Burgess also makes some interesting and somewhat puzzling remarks about cross-cultural comparisons. In the United Kingdom, public focus on cell phone risks was intense; similar concerns were voiced in Australia, Italy, and South Africa. In Italy, the environment minister established a "green hotline" asking people to state their complaints about the "abusive" siting of cell phone towers. The Australian government funded a large-scale research project on potential adverse health effects. But in the United States, the brief burst of concern in the early 1990s rapidly dissipated, to the point where it is hard to find any serious private or public concern about health risks. And in Finland, no discernible public fear has arisen at all, even though Finland has the highest percentage of cell phone users in the world. (The fact that Nokia is Finland's biggest company is highly relevant here—a point, bearing on both worst-case thinking and cost-benefit analysis, to which I will return.)

Burgess thinks that the cell phone controversy is merely one example of the misuse of precautionary thinking in domains in which scientific evidence fails to support people's fears. For example, he challenges European skepticism about genetically modified food, describing it as "alarm"; and he mounts a broader attack on what he sees as the unhelpful belief that interference with nature is wrong. He is therefore troubled by a wide climate of sensitivity to small risks, especially those that are novel and associated with technological innovation. Precautionary thinking, he believes, helps to create a culture of fear.

The Costs and Benefits of Catastrophes

Judge Richard Posner is one of the founders of the economic analysis of law, and he should be expected to be enthusiastic about cost-benefit analysis. What makes Posner's discussion noteworthy is its focus on the application of that kind of analysis to the largest risks of all—those that might threaten the survival of the human race. Posner covers worst-case scenarios for an extraordinarily wide range of hazards, including genetically modified crops, robotics, and nanotechnology, but he focuses in particular on four: asteroid collisions, particle accelerators, climate change, and bioterrorism. Posner believes that none of these risks can be dismissed, and he thinks that CBA should be applied to each of them.

Consider, for example, the dangers associated with very powerful particle accelerators, which offer a truly extraordinary worst-case scenario. It is extremely unlikely, but evidently not impossible, that such accelerators will produce a highly compressed object called a "strangelet," which has the ability to convert whatever it encounters into a new form of matter. Posner quotes Sir Martin Rees, professor of physics at the University of Cambridge, who writes, "A hypothetical strangelet disaster could transform the entire planet Earth into an inert hyperdense sphere about one hundred meters across."[23] Posner accepts the widely held view that a strangelet disaster is exceedingly improbable, but he insists that it cannot be ruled out. As a result, he thinks that nations should be willing at least to ask whether the benefits of very powerful particle accelerators justify incurring the risk. On that question, he is quite doubtful.

Or consider Posner's treatment of climate change. Posner believes that the associated risks should be taken seriously, above all because of the possibility of truly catastrophic harm. He acknowledges that a leading economic expert on climate change, William Nordhaus, estimates its total cost at $4 trillion—a high figure, to be sure, but hardly astronomical, and one that allows cost-benefit analysis to get off the ground.[24] The United States has an annual GDP of $13 trillion, and as Posner points out, $4 trillion represents present value, which might be compared with the present economic value of the United States, roughly $100 trillion. Nordhaus produces his $4 trillion figure essentially through the methods that Ackerman and Heinzerling deplore—using willingness to pay and discounting the future. With different assumptions, the relevant figure might be far higher.[25]

Posner is concerned not with the objections made by Ackerman and Heinzerling, which he implicitly rejects, but with the possibility that Nordhaus's estimate greatly understates the problem, above all because of the dangers of abrupt warming, which would be especially destructive. Thus, Posner thinks that existing models do not rule out the possibility of (for example) very rapid changes in both temperature and sea levels, the evolution and migration of deadly pests, and even a runaway greenhouse effect produced by melting tundras, which would release large quantities of additional greenhouse gases. One worst-case scenario is "snowball earth": a world covered with a layer of ice several kilometers thick, as a result of massive increases in cloud cover that prevent sunlight from reaching the ground. Sounding very much like Ackerman and Heinzerling, Posner seeks to draw attention to the worst that might happen.

Many scientists and economists, including Nordhaus, believe that climate change is not likely to create catastrophic harm, and that the real costs, human and economic, will be high but not intolerable. In their view, the worst-case scenarios can be responsibly described as improbable. Posner disagrees. He believes that "no probabilities can be attached to the catastrophic global-warming scenarios, and without an estimate of probabilities an expected cost cannot be calculated."[26] Returning to the terms of decision theory, Posner contends that climate change presents a situation of uncertainty rather than risk. In this way, climate change differs from other potentially catastrophic risks that Posner explores, such as the strangelet disaster, which everyone characterizes as exceedingly unlikely.

In general, Posner does not claim that responses to catastrophic risks should be chosen solely by reference to cost-benefit analysis. But he proposes that CBA is indispensable and that it would be foolish to assess or to adopt responses without exploring both costs and benefits. While favoring CBA, Posner rejects the Precautionary Principle on the ground that it is too vague. He contends that once this principle becomes sensibly tempered, it turns into a form of CBA with risk aversion—a form of CBA which creates a margin of safety to protect against those dangers that produce special concern (see Chapter 3).

Posner concedes that any effort to apply CBA to catastrophic risks requires a great deal of guesswork. Consider the new and very powerful particle accelerator, Brookhaven's Relativistic Heavy Ion Collider. Posner is concerned about the extremely remote possibility that the Brookhaven Collider will destroy the earth; he wants to evaluate the proposal by reference to CBA. He notes that no effort has been made to monetize its benefits, but he ventures a "wild guess" that they amount to $250 million per year. (It is extremely hard to produce a figure, monetized or nonmonetized, to capture the benefits of basic research; for this reason Posner's guess is indeed wild.) With that amount, the collider would have a net present value of $400 million: $21.1 billion in benefits, assuming a 3 percent discount rate, over a projected ten-year span, minus the accelerator's construction and operating costs, which are $1.1 billion.

But what is the monetized value of the human race? To answer that apparently absurd question, Posner needs to estimate both the probability of extinction and its monetized cost if it comes to fruition. For probability, he ventures a figure of one in ten million—a figure that he also deems "arbitrary," though it is in line with several estimates by expert risk assessors. For monetized cost, based on a willingness to pay to reduce statistical risks and a 3 percent discount rate, he values the loss of the human race at $600 trillion(!). To produce this number, Posner values an individual life at only $50,000, based on an assumption of a very low WTP for tiny risks. He emphasizes that this is a quite conservative assumption and that it would be reasonable to choose higher values. Doing the arithmetic, Posner believes that the net benefits of the Brookhaven Collider are negative: −$100 million. Thus, he concludes that the collider should not be built.

Posner acknowledges that "global warming is the poster child for the limitations of cost-benefit analysis."[27] But even here, he thinks that progress can be made by attempting to be as quantitative as possible. We have seen that many economists, armed with cost-benefit analysis, oppose the Kyoto Protocol, arguing that its monetized costs probably would exceed its monetized benefits (recall that the protocol would do relatively little about the problem of climate change). Posner thinks this analysis is badly incomplete, because it ignores the possibility that government regulation will force technological innovation, thus producing dramatic decreases in greenhouse gas emissions; and dramatic decreases are necessary to reduce the risk of catastrophe. Posner is particularly interested in the potentially desirable effects of significant taxes on carbon emissions. Such taxes would create economic incentives to develop clean fuels and better methods of carbon sequestration. Posner acknowledges that in view of existing uncertainty and the high costs of emissions controls, it is tempting simply to wait for more scientific information. A problem with this approach is irreversibility (see Chapter 4). Posner does not offer a formal cost-benefit analysis for various approaches to the climate change problem. The reason is that his fundamental concern is abrupt warming, to which he believes that no probability can be assigned. In contrast to his quantitative analysis of particle accelerators, his analysis of climate change does not offer many numbers. His major argument is that making emissions cuts now would give us the flexibility to reduce warming in the future if that is what we need to do. He thus argues in favor of aggressive taxes on greenhouse gas emissions, above all to reduce the possibility of catastrophic risk and to eliminate truly horrendous worst-case scenarios.

Problems with Precautions

Ackerman and Heinzerling argue in favor of the Precautionary Principle. Burgess rejects it as leading to nonsensical outcomes. Posner believes that it must be converted into a form of CBA, one that embodies an aversion to those risks that deserve particular concern. At first glance, it is tempting to say, with Burgess, that the idea of precaution will lead to excessive controls on small or nonexistent risks. But we have seen that the most serious problem lies elsewhere. Risks are often on all sides of social situations, and risk reduction itself produces risks. Here is the sense in which the Precautionary Principle is paralyzing.

Like many other critics of CBA, Ackerman and Heinzerling do not sufficiently appreciate this point. They neglect the possibility that expensive regulation, focused on the elimination of worst-case scenarios, will actually hurt real people—and have worst-case scenarios of its own. Consider their seemingly offhand remark about protection against workplace hazards: The "costs of the regulation would probably be borne by the employers who would be required to maintain safer workplaces."[28] But the costs of regulation are often borne not only by "employers" but also by consumers, whose prices increase, and by workers, who might find fewer and less remunerative jobs and who are themselves consumers. When government imposes large costs on "polluters," consumers and workers are likely to pay part of the bill. And if prices increase, some risks will increase as well.

To be sure, some environmental regulations do increase employment and decrease prices. But as a general rule, we have no reason to believe that regulatory imposition of high costs will benefit workers and consumers; the opposite is far more likely to be true. And if we are focusing on worst-case scenarios, we must be alert to the possibility that costly regulations will create serious problems, including significant increases in unemployment and poverty.

In the context of cell phones, an emphasis on the burdens and costs of precautions helps illuminate a quite remarkable fact, one to which Burgess gives too little attention: Notwithstanding the popularity of precautionary thinking, and the apparent intensity of public fears about bad scenarios, those fears did not, in fact, produce large-scale controls on either phones or towers. Burgess offers no explanation of why such controls did not materialize, but his brief discussion of Finland provides a valuable clue. Is it really a paradox, or an irony, that fears of cell phones, and attention to worst-case scenarios, were especially weak in a nation that has the largest percentage of cell phone users in the world? Hardly. The Finnish economy is heavily dependent on Nokia and thus the cell phone industry; people in Finland do not want the Finnish economy to collapse. And if most citizens depend on cell phones, they are far less likely to accept sensationalistic claims of risk, simply because they have so much to lose from regulation. Imagine, for example, the likely public reaction to a current suggestion by an American politician that cell phones should be banned because they pose a cancer risk.

If the benefits of cell phone use are evident to all or most, then people will demand a great deal of evidence that the harm is real. Indeed, people will be strongly motivated to discount worst-case scenarios, and to consider them to be unrealistic and alarmist, when they are aware that imposing restrictions would be costly and burdensome. In short, the very idea of precautions, and the focus on worst-case scenarios, loses some of its appeal when people are aware that precautions impose costs and even risks of their own. When people are aware of that fact, some kind of balancing, involving both costs and benefits, is likely to emerge.

In a brief but highly illuminating discussion of another environmental issue, Burgess strongly supports the general point. He refers to a mining town in Colorado whose citizens were deemed, by the Environmental Protection Agency, to be at risk from toxic contamination. The town's citizens, already suffering from serious economic decline, responded not with fear, and much less with enthusiasm for a precautionary approach, but by demonizing the EPA, which it regarded as "the devil incarnate. Grimly they recounted how government bureaucrats had invaded their town uninvited, threatening residents with the prospect of condemned property, involuntary relocation, and unwelcome new legal requirements . . . And all, they claimed, over a hazard 'that doesn't exist.'"[29]

Whether or not the citizens of the mining town were right to deny the hazard, they were strongly motivated to do so, because its existence would produce large and palpable burdens. Far from succumbing to panic, the citizens were well aware of how much they had to lose from aggressive regulation; hence, they sought to dismiss real evidence of harm. Precautions and precautionary thinking, even against worst-case scenarios, seem far less attractive when people believe that precautions would produce significant burdens and risks.

Burgess does not draw attention to one of the remarkable lessons of his story, which is that the cell phone scare did not produce aggressive regulation not only because the evidence of harm was weak but also and more fundamentally because a growing number of people use cell phones and would be inconvenienced, or far worse, by such measures. Many users, for example, have come to rely on cell phones for obtaining help in emergency situations. In the context of genetically modified food, by contrast, the costs of regulation are not highly visible, at least not to Europeans. When both costs and benefits are on the public viewscreen, people become intuitive cost-benefit analysts, and they tend to be cautious about precautions—unless the evidence in their favor is perceived to be strong. This point brings us directly to the questions raised by CBA.

Costs and Benefits

Posner is enthusiastic about CBA, which Ackerman and Heinzerling deplore. To come to terms with their disagreement, it is important to explore how risks are turned into monetary equivalents. Under current practice, the economic values come mostly from real-world markets, producing evidence of compensation levels for actual risks. In basing CBA on calculations of this kind, regulators are not, in fact, producing a "value of a statistical life." In fact, they are not "valuing life" at all. They are not saying that the average American would pay $6.1 million to avoid death, or that a human life is, in some deep or metaphysical sense, worth that amount. Instead, they are generating numbers that reflect the market value of statistical risks. Typically officials are dealing with low-level risks, on the order of 1/100,000, and when they "value a life" at $6 million, they are really saying that the evidence suggests that people must be paid $60 to be subject to a risk of that magnitude—and that government will build on that evidence in making regulatory decisions.

Some people think that this practice is a form of madness. But there are two possible reasons why regulators in a democratic society might care about market valuations of statistical risks, and both are connected with individual choice. The first involves well-being. The second involves autonomy.

Let us imagine a highly artificial society in which every person faces multiple risks of 1/100,000, and every person is both adequately informed and willing to pay no more and no less than $60 to eliminate each of those risks. Imagine too that the cost of eliminating these 1/100,000 risks is widely variable, ranging from close to zero to hundreds of millions of dollars. Imagine finally (and this is an important assumption, which I shall question in due course) that *the cost of eliminating any risk is borne entirely by those who would benefit from eliminating that risk.* Under that assumption, regulation imposes the equivalent of a fee; for example, people's water bills will entirely reflect the costs of a policy that eliminates a 1/100,000 risk of getting cancer from arsenic in drinking water. If the per-person cost is $100, each water bill will be increased by exactly $100. On this assumption, regulation operates by asking people to pay for the benefits they receive.

At first glance, use of willingness to pay, under the assumptions I have given, is easy to defend. Why should people be forced to pay an amount for regulation that exceeds their willingness to pay? People are making their own judgments about how much to spend to avoid various risks—and those judgments should be respected.

To be sure, we might believe that a measure of redistribution is appropriate—that private sources, or government, should provide people with protection for free (that is, without cost to those who are benefited). But as a practical matter, regulation need not, and often does not, amount to a subsidy to those who benefit from it. When regulation is imposed, people have to pay for what they get. After the enactment of workers' compensation regulation, non-unionized workers faced a dollar-for-dollar wage reduction—corresponding almost perfectly to the expected value of the benefits they received.[30] For drinking water regulation, something similar is involved. When the government eliminates carcinogenic substances from the water supply, water companies do not bear the cost; it is passed on to consumers in the form of higher water bills. Often people neglect the fact that when government provides protection against worst-case scenarios, workers and consumers have to pay, rather than some abstraction called "industry" or "companies."

Those who are particularly interested in increasing human welfare will insist on the relevance of willingness to pay under the assumptions I have outlined.[31] If people are willing to pay $60, but no more, to eliminate a risk of 1/100,000, then we have some reason to think that their welfare is increased by asking them to pay up to that amount—and that their welfare is decreased by asking them to pay more. People's budgets face many demands, and if we refuse to spend more than $60 on a 1/100,000 risk, it may be because we would like to use our money for health care, food, shelter, recreation, education, or any number of other goods. Why should we be forced to devote our money to worst-case scenarios of any particular sort?

For purposes of evaluating this argument, it does not matter if the existing distribution of income is unjust or if poor people are, in an intelligible sense, coerced to run certain risks. The remedy for unjust distributions, and for that form of coercion, is hardly to require people to buy regulatory benefits on terms that they find unacceptable. Suppose that people are willing to pay only $60 to eliminate a 1/100,000 risk because they are not rich—and that if they had double their current wealth, they would be willing to pay $120. Even if this is so, government does them no favors by forcing them to pay the amount that they would pay if they had more money.

If we reject the argument from welfare, we might nonetheless accept willingness to pay on grounds of personal autonomy.[32] People should be sovereign over their own lives. This principle means that government should respect personal choices about how to use limited resources (again, so long as those choices are adequately informed). When people decline to pay more than $60 to eliminate a 1/100,000 risk, it is because they would prefer to spend the money in a way that seems to them more desirable. If regulators reject people's actual judgments, then they are insulting their dignity. The use of willingness to pay therefore can claim a simultaneous defense from accounts based on welfare and accounts based on autonomy.

When the assumptions just outlined are met, we have what might be described as easy cases for the use of the WTP criterion. In Chapter 4, we saw that money and health are in a way incommensurable—our reflective judgments do not permit us to line up dollars and risks along a single metric. But to see the easy cases as such, we do not need to make controversial arguments about commensurability or to make contested philosophical arguments. The underlying claim is a simple pragmatic one, to the effect that people are willing to trade money against decreases in statistical risks. If people actually make those trades, then government might well build on their practices in designing policies.

Objections

Several possible objections can be made to this line of argument. Some of these involve rights; others involve wrongs. Some of the most interesting involve the distinction between consumers and citizens, bounded rationality and limited information, and the problem of adaptive preferences.

Rights   In one view, people have a general right not to be subjected to risks of a certain magnitude, and the use of WTP will violate that right. Imagine, for example, that poor people live in a place where they face a 1/20 annual risk of dying from water pollution; it makes sense to say that the government should reduce that risk even if people are willing to pay only $1 to eliminate it (because they are poor) and even if the per-person cost is $5.

If people are facing a high risk of death and lack the money to eliminate that risk, it may well be correct to say that their rights are being violated. The only complication here is that in both practice and principle, rights are resource-dependent. What rights people are legitimately able to claim against their government is a product of the amount of available resources, and hence people's legitimate arguments for protection are inevitably affected by the level of resources in their society. But let us simply stipulate here that risks above a certain level should count as violations of people's rights—and that WTP does not much matter in those circumstances.

As an abstract claim about people's rights, this objection is entirely reasonable. Without entering into difficult philosophical territory about the foundations and nature of rights, we should be able to agree that something has gone badly wrong if people are exposed to serious risks and if their low WTP—a product of their poverty—prevents them from doing anything in response. Things are even worse if government uses their low WTP, and hence their poverty, to justify inaction in the face of those risks. Similarly, those who are subject to the risks of climate change might be able to claim that their rights are being violated, especially if they live in poor countries and are victims of greenhouse gas emissions from wealthy nations. It would be ludicrous to suggest that WTP is determinative of the appropriate use of government subsidies; a redistributive policy hardly tracks people's WTP. Would it make sense to say that government will give poor people a check for $100 only if they are willing to pay $100 for that check?

In many cases of risk regulation, however, rights violations are not involved; we are speaking here of highly improbable worst-case scenarios. If people are subject to a 1/500,000 risk of mortality as a result of their job, or from some kind of medical procedure, it is hard to say that their rights have been violated. If patients are willing to undertake surgery when they face a 1/100,000 chance that things will go badly wrong, their rights have not been violated. Even if rights can be involved when people are subject to small risks, people should be permitted to waive those rights at an agreeable price—at least on the assumptions that I am making. The proper response to an apparent rights violation is not to force people to buy protection that they do not want and cannot afford, but to provide a subsidy that will give them the benefit for free or enable them to receive the benefit at what is, for them, an acceptable price. But regulation—and this is the key point—often does no such thing; and in what I am calling the easy cases, the question is one of regulation under the stated assumptions. So long as that is the question, use of WTP does not violate anyone's rights.

Wrongs   A different objection would emphasize that those subject to risks might be able to complain of wrongdoing on the part of those who have created those risks. When a company subjects citizens of a town to a serious danger, and does so maliciously or without the slightest concern for their welfare, a wrong has been committed, even if the citizens are not willing to pay much to mitigate it. If a wrongdoer is threatening people with intentional harm, the threat should end; we do not ask how much potential victims are willing to pay the wrongdoer to make it end.

In fact, the crime of extortion is specifically designed to punish those who say: "Unless you pay me, I will hurt you." By definition, the appropriate level of wrongdoing—terrorism, assault, rape, murder—is zero. In some circumstances, wrongdoers should be punished, even jailed, and WTP is entirely beside the point. But we can go further. Perhaps those who cause harm, including companies endangering the environment, should be liable to those they injure even if they have not been malicious, reckless, or even negligent—and even if they are also producing social benefits. Perhaps well-functioning legal systems make those who are responsible pay for the injuries they inflict.

Intentional wrongdoers are held accountable through the payment of damages, even if the WTP of the affected population is low. Within tort theory, there is an active debate about whether liability should be imposed on actors who have not been negligent but have nonetheless inflicted harm. Strict liability (liability regardless of fault) can be supported by reference to a range of theoretical positions.[33]

But this point should not be read for more than it is worth. Cost-benefit analysis plays a legitimate role even in deciding on the appropriate response to wrongdoers—not excluding terrorists. True, we do not ask people to pay terrorists enough to make them stop. But the government does weigh the costs of risk reduction against its benefits, and in assessing both costs and benefits, willingness to pay matters. After the attacks of 9/11, the government did not eliminate air travel in the United States; the reason is that the benefits would not justify the costs. Governments legitimately consult their citizens in order to decide how much to pay for risk reduction measures. Even if wrongs are involved, it would be odd to say that people have a right to be required to pay more for risk reduction than they are willing to pay, at least if they are adequately informed.

In any case, much of risk reduction involves not wrongdoers but activities that involve a large set of social benefits and social costs—driving automobiles, building highways, providing energy, using heat and refrigerators. When those who engage in those activities are wrongdoers, they should be asked to change—but any such mandate must depend on its overall effects, and we cannot assess those effects without knowing about both costs and benefits. We can now see that the domain of the easy cases does not involve wrongdoers; it involves regulation that asks people to alter their behavior while also forcing those who benefit to pay for the alteration. For many worst-case scenarios, the easy case captures reality.

Citizens vs. consumers   An independent objection would stress that people are citizens, not merely consumers. On this view, regulatory choices should be made not after aggregating WTP but after citizens have deliberated with one another about their preferences and values. The argument against forced exchanges treats people as consumers; it envisions their decisions about safety as the same as their decisions about all other commodities. On this approach, purchases of protection against risks are being seen as equivalent to purchases of sneakers, cereals, and soaps. But in some contexts, this approach is badly misconceived. The American constitutional system is a deliberative democracy, not a maximization machine, and many social judgments should be made by citizens engaged in deliberative discussion with one another rather than by aggregating the individual choices of consumers.[34]

In the context of racial and sex discrimination, for example, sensible societies do not aggregate people's WTP. The level of permissible discrimination is not set by using market evidence to see how much people would be willing to pay to discriminate (or to be free from discrimination). Even if discriminators would be willing to pay a lot to avoid associating with members of unpopular groups, discrimination is banned. Nor is the protection of endangered species chosen on the basis of aggregated WTP. Whether and when to protect members of endangered species is a moral question to be resolved through democratic discussion, not through exercises in consumer sovereignty. In some contexts, use of WTP would wrongly see people as consumers purchasing products, rather than as citizens deliberating about values. Speaking in this vein, Amartya Sen emphasizes that "discussions and exchange, and even political arguments, contribute to the formation and revision of values."[35] He urges that in the particular context of environmental protection, solutions require us "to go beyond looking only for the best reflection of existing individual preferences, or the most acceptable procedures for choices based on those preferences."[36]

Sen's claims identify some serious limitations on the use of willingness to pay. But such objections should not be read as a wholesale attack on standard cost-benefit analysis. In trading off safety and health and in handling worst-case scenarios in our own private lives, our values and preferences are not frozen. Much of the time, our choices are a product of reflection and deliberation, even if we are simply acting as consumers. In deciding how much to do to avoid crime, motor vehicle accidents, and cancer, we think and reflect with others. It is true that moral questions are not to be resolved by aggregating private willingness to pay. Some preferences, even though backed by WTP, are morally off-limits, and policy should not take account of them. The preference for racial discrimination is an example. In addition, many people are unwilling to pay a great deal for goods that have strong moral justifications. Animal welfare is an example. The value of animals, and their freedom from cruelty and suffering, is not adequately captured by asking how much people are willing to pay to protect them. When people's WTP is morally questionable, the market model is inapplicable and WTP tells us very little.

But what about the easy cases? Do these arguments suggest that government should override individual choices about how much to spend to eliminate low-level risks, even when those choices are adequately informed? For environmental protection generally, it is indeed important to go beyond "the best reflection of existing individual preferences." But this point does not establish that people should be required to pay (for example) $100 to eliminate mortality risks of 1/100,000 when they are willing to pay only $75.

Inadequate information and bounded rationality   As I have stressed throughout, people have a difficult time in dealing with low-probability events. If people are not aware of what they could gain by regulation, their WTP might be too low. Maybe the availability heuristic will lead them to underestimate the risk—if people cannot recall a case in which some activity produced illness or death, they might conclude that the risk is trivial even if it is not. Or perhaps availability, along with probability neglect, will lead people to exaggerate risks, producing a willingness to pay that is wildly inflated in light of reality. Or perhaps people are unrealistically optimistic. Perhaps they edit out risks below a certain threshold, even though they should not. And if people are unable to understand the meaning of ideas like "1 in 50,000," or to respond rationally to such ideas, then there are serious problems with relying on WTP.

People's willingness to pay may also reflect excessive discounting of future health benefits. If workers are ignoring their own futures, or applying an implausibly high discount rate, then a good argument can be made for setting aside their WTP. In the context of climate change, the risk of catastrophe may seem too far in the future to raise sufficient concern. Certainly this is true for less dramatic risks that people face in their daily lives. Young smokers, for example, give too little attention to the long-term health harms caused by smoking. Those who choose a poor diet and get little exercise almost certainly fail to consider the long-term effects of their behavior. Self-control problems are an important part of bounded rationality. If a low willingness to pay reflects a failure to give adequate attention to the future, then we have good reason not to use WTP.

When WTP is a result of inadequate information or bounded rationality, appropriate adjustments should be made to WTP, and the VSL that emerges from WTP must be corrected. This is an important point—incorrect figures need to be fixed. Those who make this (correct) claim are challenging the optimistic assumption about human rationality that underlies the use of WTP in the easy cases. But they are not challenging the basic theory, because they acknowledge that our choices, at least once corrected, are the right foundation for policy.

Adaptive preferences   A related objection would emphasize that people adapt to limitations in existing opportunities, including social deprivation, and their preferences may reflect those adaptations.[37] Perhaps people show a low WTP for certain goods, including health improvements, simply because they have adjusted to certain "bads," including health risks. Perhaps people reduce cognitive dissonance by concluding that risks are lower than they actually are.[38] When people's preferences are a product of deprivation and injustice, we may not want to respect the preferences themselves. To generalize the objection, perhaps people suffer from a problem of "miswanting"; they want things that do not promote their well-being, and they do not want things that would promote their well-being.[39]

When this is so, use of WTP loses much of its underlying justification; people's decisions do not actually promote their welfare.[40] Moreover, individual autonomy, properly understood, may not require respect for all of people's decisions; some of them may be nonautonomous because they are a product of bad circumstances over which people have no control. Properly understood, the idea of autonomy requires not merely respect for whatever preferences people happen to have but also an insistence on social conditions that allow preferences to be developed in a way that does not reflect coercion or injustice.

In the case of some risks and worst-case scenarios, the relevant preferences are indeed nonautonomous. Many women face a risk of male violence under circumstances in which they believe that little can be done, and hence they adapt—treating the worst-case scenario fatalistically. If government can be confident that people are not willing to pay for goods that would greatly benefit them, government should probably abandon WTP.

In some contexts, this is a powerful objection. But most of the time, the objection has more theoretical than practical interest. Typically we are speaking of steps that would reduce low-level mortality risks (say, 1/100,000). We have no reason to believe that the use of informed WTP (say, $100) is a product of adaptive preferences. When such a reason exists, the judgment about the easy cases must be revised.

Individuation   Ackerman and Heinzerling reject the view that we can extrapolate, from workplace studies, a single figure for the value of statistical risks. They note that people care not only about the magnitude of the risk (is it 1/10,000 or 1/100,000?) but also about its nature and context. People may be willing to pay more to avoid the risk of death from cancer than to avoid a statistically equivalent risk of sudden, unanticipated death from an automobile accident. They might pay more to avoid the risk of death from air pollution or drinking water than they would pay to avoid a statistically equivalent risk of death from a workplace accident.

This objection is reasonable, but it is most sensibly taken as an argument for a more refined version of CBA, one that insists on variations among statistically equivalent risks.[41] A single number is genuinely obtuse; in fact, it is inconsistent with the very theory that gives rise to the use of WTP in the first place. If WTP is relevant because its use promotes welfare, autonomy, or both, then regulators should consult actual WTP, which varies across risks, rather than a single or unitary WTP, which grows only out of one set of risks and which cannot plausibly be applied to every risk of a given statistical magnitude. The real question is not whether to have more differentiated values for qualitatively identical risks, but how to find reliable evidence on which to base those values. Economists are starting to fill the relevant gaps in a way that supports the suggestion that a single WTP is far too crude.[42] This objection can be seen as an important and essentially friendly amendment to the governing theory, not as a reason to reject it.

In the easy cases, the argument for use of WTP emerges as

bowed but not broken. Sensible societies are interested in both welfare and freedom; when those who benefit from risk reduction must also pay for it, people's informed judgments should be respected. Important qualifications, even in the domain of the easy cases, must be addressed, but they do not refute the basic argument.

Harder Cases

The assumptions behind the easy cases are obviously artificial. Most important, people do not always pay all of the cost of the risk-reduction benefits they receive. When worst-case scenarios are eliminated, sometimes people pay only a little of the cost—or maybe even nothing at all. Sometimes regulators have a lot of control over whether and how much people must pay for those benefits. Perhaps regulators can take steps to ensure that potential victims pay little or nothing—or that much of the underlying payment comes from those who impose the relevant risks.

When this is so, the analysis is much more complicated. In the context of air pollution regulation, for example, poor people, and members of minority communities, have been net gainers; they do not have to pay for all of what they get.[43] It follows that a cost-benefit analysis based on people's WTP might not produce an adequate account of the welfare effects of air pollution regulation. Such regulation might be a good idea if we focus on overall well-being; maybe people, taken as a whole, are gaining more than they lose, even if the economic costs appear higher than the economic benefits. And even if overall welfare is not increased, the distributional gains are important to consider. We might approve of a regulation that makes poor people live safer and healthier lives, even if wealthy people have to pay significant sums to achieve those gains.

Suppose that the beneficiaries of a proposed drinking water regulation are willing to pay only $80 to eliminate a risk of 1/50,000 in drinking water; that the per-person cost of eliminating a 1/50,000 risk is $100; but that for every dollar of that cost, the beneficiaries pay only 70 cents. Suppose that the remaining 30 cents will be paid by water companies themselves, in the form of reduced profits, or by employees of the water companies, in the form of reduced wages. In this example, the costs of the regulation exceed the benefits; it is inefficient. If CBA provides the rule of decision, the fact that the monetized costs exceed the monetized benefits is decisive against the regulation.

But in principle, the analysis here is far harder than in the easy cases. After all, the beneficiaries of the regulation are being helped a lot. On what assumption must the WTP numbers control the decision? The assumption must be that economic efficiency is the goal of government, at least in the context of regulation—that in order to know what to do, we should aggregate the monetized benefits and monetized costs of regulation and act if and only if the benefits exceed the costs. When using the WTP numbers, government is acting as a maximization machine, aggregating all benefits and costs as measured by the WTP criterion. But for two reasons, this is a preposterous understanding of what government should be doing.

The first is that WTP is measuring gains and losses in monetary terms rather than in welfare terms. Those who gain in the harder cases may well be gaining more in terms of welfare than the losers lose; WTP does not answer that question. In the example just given, overall welfare might be increased, not diminished. Or imagine that a reduction in greenhouse gases greatly diminishes risks faced by people in developing nations, above all in Africa. Imagine too that such people are unable and hence unwilling to pay a great deal for the protection that they obtain. Imagine finally that the cost of the regulation is borne by people in wealthy nations, above all the United States and Europe, and that this cost is higher than the monetized benefits to people in developing countries. Even under these assumptions, the regulation might well produce large overall welfare gains. If people in developing countries are able to have much longer and healthier lives, they might well be gaining far more than people lose in the United States and Europe—even if their energy bills are higher, their automobile use is more expensive, and their wages and employment are reduced.

The second problem is distributional. Suppose that in terms of overall welfare, the regulation in question is not desirable; it makes aggregate welfare lower rather than higher. But suppose too that those who stand to benefit are poorer and more disadvantaged than those who stand to lose. If, for example, those who are willing to pay $80 are disproportionately poor, and those who pay the remainder are disproportionately wealthy, the regulation might be justified despite the aggregate welfare loss. We might well care most about those at the bottom and seek to improve their prospects, even if those at the top lose more than those at the bottom gain.

A standard response here that if redistribution is what we want, then we should act not through regulation but through the tax system, which is a more efficient way of transferring resources to those who need help.[44] The standard response is probably right; the tax system is the simplest, most effective, and best way to redistribute resources. But suppose that redistribution is not going to happen through the tax system. After all, no tax system redistributes resources across nations. If so, then regulation in the harder cases cannot be ruled off-limits despite its inefficiency. To be sure, the fact that a regulation is helpful to the most disadvantaged is not decisive in its favor. If it is trivially helpful and inflicts huge costs on everyone else, little can be said for it. But everything depends on the magnitude of the relevant effects. A program that produces large gains for the least well-off, by eliminating worst-case scenarios that really threaten them, would seem to be justified even if it imposes, in terms of WTP, slightly higher costs than benefits on balance.

The simple conclusion is that the argument for using WTP is most plausible in cases where the beneficiaries of regulation pay all or most of its cost. In such cases, WTP is reasonably used so long as people are adequately informed and not suffering from some kind of cognitive deficiency. The analysis must be different when the beneficiaries of regulation are paying only a small fraction of its costs. In such cases, the regulation can perhaps be justified as a redistributive measure or on welfare grounds. To know whether it can be so justified, we need to go beyond CBA and to identify the winners and losers. The key point is that distinguishing between the easy cases and the harder ones is crucial in order to appreciate both the uses and the limits of CBA.

Even in the hard cases, cost-benefit analysis provides relevant information, and it should not be abandoned. If the monetized benefits of regulation are lower than the monetized costs, regulators should be aware of that fact, even if it is not decisive. Within any particular nation, monetized costs and benefits can be exceedingly helpful, even in the hard cases. If China learns that it would cost $100 million to reduce exposure to a certain air pollutant, and that the monetized benefits would be $15 million, it should take those figures into account. Of course it needs to know what, in particular, these figures *mean*. Would the $100 million be felt in lower wages, more poverty, and worse health? Does the $15 million benefit mean that lives will be longer and healthier? Qualitative as well as quantitative accounts are exceedingly important.

And of course the beneficiaries of regulation might be rich, and those who must pay for it might be poor. Suppose, for example, that China becomes the principal source of greenhouse gases, and that people in wealthy nations in Europe would be the major beneficiaries of emissions reductions. By hypothesis, reductions would hurt people who are relatively disadvantaged, and help people who are relatively advantaged. We can easily imagine cases in which both CBA and distributional considerations raise doubts about regulations that attempt to eliminate worst-case scenarios.

Global Risk Regulation and Cross-National Valuations

The analysis thus far has significant implications for global risk regulation and cross-cultural variations in willingness to pay and in the value of a statistical life. People in poor nations will show a lower WTP and hence a lower VSL than people in wealthy nations. And in fact, studies find a VSL as low as $200,000 for Taiwan, $500,000 for South Korea, and $1.2 million for India—but $19 million for Australia (see Table 13).[45]

Because poor people have less money than rich people, it follows that the monetary value of risks should greatly diverge from one nation to another. Building on evidence of this kind, some assessments of the effects of climate change find far higher monetized costs from deaths of people in rich countries than from deaths of people in poor countries.[46] In its Second Report in 1995, the Intergovernmental Panel on Climate Change calculated that a life in an industrialized country was worth $1.5 million, whereas a life in a developing country was worth only $150,000. Not surprisingly, these assessments have been highly controversial; John Broome, for example, notes that under this approach, an American life is worth ten or twenty Indian lives, a judgment that he deems "absurd."[47]

As a result, some analysts, including the Intergovernmental Panel, have opted for a worldwide VSL of $1 million. But this choice

Table 13 Value of a statistical life (VSL) across nations.

Nation and year of study	VSL (in year 2000 US$)
Taiwan (1997)	0.2–0.9 million
South Korea (1993)	0.8 million
India (1996/97)	1.2–1.5 million
Hong Kong (1998)	1.7 million
Canada (1989)	3.9–4.7 million
Switzerland (2001)	6.3–8.6 million
Japan (1991)	9.7 million
Australia (1997)	11.3–19.1 million
United Kingdom (2000)	19.9 million

seems quite arbitrary and potentially harmful to people in rich and poor nations alike. If the Canadian government uses a VSL of $1 million, it will greatly underprotect its citizens, simply because Canada's VSL is so much higher. If Taiwan uses a VSL of $1 million, it will provide excessive protection, in the sense that its citizens are likely to lose more from regulation than they will gain.

The problem raises important dilemmas. What are the monetized costs of 100,000 worldwide deaths from climate change—deaths that include (let us make up some numbers) 80,000 people from poor countries and 20,000 from wealthy ones? The discussion thus far suggests that there is no sensible abstract answer to these questions; we need to know what, in particular, the answer is *for.* If a general question is asked, outside of any particular context, about the monetary value of some number of deaths in fifty years, that question is best left unanswered. The appropriate assessments of VSL, and variations across countries, depend on their intended use. If different numbers are meant to identify the actual monetary values of human lives, and to suggest that people in Canada are "worth" much more than people in Argentina or that poor people are "worth" less than rich ones, the numbers are ludicrous as well as offensive.

We should go further. If the different numbers are meant to suggest the appropriate amount that donor institutions should spend to reduce mortality risks, they make no sense at all. The fact that a poor person in a poor nation would be willing to pay $1 to eliminate a risk of 1/10,000, whereas a wealthy person in a wealthy nation would be willing to pay $100, cannot plausibly be used to defend the view that an international agency should devote its resources to the latter rather than the former. To illustrate this point, imagine choosing between two programs:

- Program A would eliminate (at a cost of $500) a 1/10,000 risk faced by fifty poor people in Costa Rica, each willing to pay $2 to eliminate that risk.
- Program B would eliminate (also at a cost of $500) a 1/10,000 risk faced by fifty wealthy people in Germany, each willing to pay $350 to eliminate that same risk.

We have no reason to think that a donor should prefer to save the Germans, even though their WTP is far higher than that of the Costa Ricans. In fact, Program A has much higher priority, because it would help people facing extreme deprivation. What is true at the individual level is true across nations as well.

But now consider a different issue. The government in a poor nation is deciding on appropriate policy to reduce workplace risks. What VSL should it use? Such a government would do well to begin by considering the admittedly low WTP of its own citizens. If citizens in a poor nation show a WTP of $8 to eliminate risks of

1/10,000, then their government does them no favors by requiring them to pay $50 or $100 for that protection. This is the sense in which VSL properly varies across nations, and in which citizens of poor nations have lower VSLs than citizens of wealthy ones.

If the government of India uses the American VSL of $6 million, on the theory that its citizens should not be valued less than those of wealthy nations, significant harm to the citizens of India will almost inevitably result. In the easy cases, the forced exchanges will be ludicrously harmful to the people whom they are supposed to help. Citizens of India will be required to pay much more than they want for regulatory protection against worst-case scenarios—and hence poor people will be expending money for risk reduction when they would much prefer to spend that money on something else. In the hard cases, the beneficiaries pay only a fraction of the cost, which will be mostly borne by others in the same nation. In such cases, a country like India has a dilemma. If India uses the American VSL of $6 million, it will probably be spending far too much of its money on risk reduction—or more precisely, on reducing the particular risks that happen to get onto the regulatory agenda. The result of the high VSL will be felt acutely and in many forms, including lower wages and more poverty. To be sure, the analysis will have to be different if the costs of risk reduction will be paid by people outside of India—for example, by wealthy nations. If so, people in India might be helped even if risk reduction is based on a high VSL.

Of course, the citizens of poor nations would almost certainly be helped most if they were given cash instead of risk reduction. If they were given cash, they could spend it however they wished. But if cash redistribution is not possible, regulatory benefits, provided for free or for a fraction of their cost, remain a blessing. The conclusion is that poor nations sensibly devote fewer resources to protecting people against worst-case scenarios than do wealthy nations—and that poor nations, attending to CBA, notice how much their citizens are willing to pay to prevent low-level risks. At the same time, it would be ludicrous to say that because people in poor nations have little to pay to prevent risks, wealthy people are under no obligation to help them. If welfare is our guide, serious risks, faced by countless people in poor nations, deserve special priority.

How, then, should global institutions, such as the Intergovernmental Panel on Climate Change, assess the monetary costs of risks faced by people all over the world? As I have suggested, the answer turns on the purpose of the assessment—on what issue the answer is supposed to address. We could obtain VSLs for every nation and aggregate the resulting amounts to obtain some kind of global figure, but what, exactly, would be the point of the aggregation? A more useful question is whether it would make sense for any particular nation to accept a particular way of responding to the problem of climate change, such as the Kyoto Protocol. For individual nations, a WTP that reflects the judgments of their own citizens is the best way to begin. The United States might use a figure of $6.1 million; India should use a lower figure; France should use a figure that is somewhere in between. The resulting calculations can provide a starting point for a judgment about whether a particular approach to climate change is in that particular nation's interest.

As we have seen, that judgment cannot resolve the question of what to do. The United States and Europe might believe that they have particular obligations to poorer nations, both because they are wealthy and because they are disproportionately responsible for the problem in the first place. But my goal in this chapter has not been to resolve any particular controversy. I have sought instead to explore how risks, and worst-case scenarios, might be translated into monetary equivalents. Of course, nations can often engage in an informal balancing of costs and benefits without attempting any such translation. In ordinary life, informal balancing tells us to ignore some worst-case scenarios and to pay careful attention to others. Well-being, not money, should be our guide, and the informal balancing is enough to show us what approach will promote our welfare, without bothering to monetize the goods that concern us. At most, monetized amounts are a proxy for what matters. And even when monetary equivalents are used, we should not put ourselves into a kind of mathematical straightjacket. Qualitative differences matter; we need to know what the numbers represent.

The most general conclusion is that cost-benefit analysis does not come close to telling regulators all that they need to know—but without it, they will know far too little. Let us now turn to the most vexing question raised by any effort at valuation: how to treat the future.

CHAPTER SIX

THE FUTURE

Suppose that a proposed regulation, designed to reduce some risk, will not produce benefits for many years. Suppose too that the government is interested in engaging in some form of cost-benefit analysis before it proceeds with the regulation. Everyone agrees that future monetary costs will be discounted, on the theory that a dollar today is worth more than a dollar in twenty years. But what should the government do about improved health or lengthened lives? Should these too be discounted, or should a death in 2025 be treated the same as a death today?

In terms of ultimate outcomes, the choice matters a great deal. If a government chooses not to discount, the calculation of benefits will shift dramatically from what it would be if the agency chose a discount rate of, for example, 10 percent. Suppose that a human life is valued at $8 million and that no discount rate is applied. If so, a life saved 100 years from now is worth the same expenditure today as a life saved now: $8 million. But at a discount rate of 10 percent, the same life would justify a current expenditure of only $581. For regulation whose effects would be felt centuries from now, any reasonable discount rate will reduce apparently substantial benefits to close to nothing. Worst-case scenarios in the distant future may not seem to be bad at all. If so, the result is absurd.

In the United States, the Office of Management and Budget suggests that agencies should prepare analyses using rates of both 3 percent and 7 percent, departing from its suggested 10 percent rate in the 1980s.[1] But even these lower numbers remain controversial. The midpoint—5 percent—would ensure that, if a single human life is valued at $8 million, one hundred deaths in one hundred years would be worth only $6.25 million today. But other things being equal, one hundred deaths today are not worse than one hundred deaths at some future date. The point has obvious implications for problems with long time horizons, such as climate change. If the most serious effects of climate change will be felt in 2100 or beyond, a decision to discount at any significant rate— even 3 percent—will dramatically reduce the monetized gain of emissions reduction strategies.[2] The deaths of millions of people two hundred years hence could be discounted into relative trivia. Any judgment about an international agreement—including the Kyoto Protocol and imaginable variations—will be much affected by our decisions about how to value the future.

Key questions are therefore: What discount rate, if any, should officials choose? Do life and health require some special discount rate—or no discount rate at all? Perhaps most important: What is the relationship between discount rates and the rights and interests of future generations?

In this chapter, I attempt to make progress on these questions. The eventual conclusion can be summarized in a Principle of Intergenerational Neutrality: The members of any particular generation should not be favored over the members of any other. But this claim does not dispose of the issue of discounting, and it hardly demonstrates that discounting is a bad idea. If we are engaged in cost-benefit analysis, refusing to discount will often injure, rather than promote, the interests of future generations. The Principle of Intergenerational Neutrality must be separated from the problem of discounting. To understand these claims, and their implications for the proper treatment of worst-case scenarios, we need to back up a bit.

Debates

Everyone agrees that *money* should be discounted. The simplest reason is that it can be invested and made to grow. A person is better off, financially, having $1,000 today than $1,000 in ten years, simply because $1,000 today, invested wisely, will be worth much more than $1,000 a decade hence. In addition to the investment value of money, people seem to have a "pure" time preference: They favor current consumption over future consumption. For both these reasons, discounting the future value of money is a widely accepted practice. But for life and health as such, discounting is greatly disputed in both theory and practice.

In one important case, a federal court said that discounting is necessary to provide an "apples to apples" comparison of costs and benefits—suggesting that government agencies are legally required to use the same discount rate for health and safety benefits as for dollars.[3] Other judicial decisions have insisted on careful explanations for whatever discount rates agencies choose.[4] Economists tend to believe that the argument for discounting life and health is obvious, though the consensus has started to unravel in the last decade, especially for problems with long-term time horizons, such as climate change.[5] Philosophers and lawyers are often skeptical about discounting. Philosophers have raised serious doubts about the idea that a future death or illness should be discounted in the same way as money. Lawyers as well have questioned that idea, suggesting that it depends on contentious empirical or normative assumptions.[6]

As I have suggested, the central problem is that a life in 2050 is not worth less than a life today. If ten people are killed twenty years hence, the outcome is no less bad than if ten people are killed tomorrow. Thus one critic asks: "What is wrong with discounting numbers of lives saved? One obvious problem is that death does not recognize human accounting conventions and death does not discount."[7] In the same vein, Ackerman and Heinzerling object that "the choice implicit in discounting is between preventing harms to the current generation and preventing similar harms to future generations. Seen in this way, discounting looks like a fancy justification for foisting our problems off onto the people who come after us."[8] They emphasize that with "a discount rate of five percent, for example, the death of a billion people 500 years from now becomes less serious than the death of one person today."[9]

Defenders of discounting have responded that a refusal to use a discount rate creates a number of logical and practical conundrums. For instance, a refusal to discount might require truly extraordinary sacrifices from the present for the sake of the (infinite) future. Should we really impoverish ourselves to protect those who will come much later? In one view, the "failure to discount would leave all generations at a subsistence level of existence, because benefits would be postponed perpetually for the future."[10] At the very least, a zero discount rate might produce rules and practices that ask the current generation to make apparently excessive sacrifices.

On the other hand, some people have argued that a failure to discount the monetized equivalent of regulatory benefits would actually lead to less regulation, not more. Suppose that regulators are indifferent to lives saved now or lives saved in the future but that they discount money at some positive rate. If so, it makes sense for them to delay life-saving expenditures indefinitely, simply because the cost-benefit ratio will always be better in the future.[11] If officials discount costs but not benefits, they will think: There is always a better later program, and that program should be funded first. Every program with a fixed starting date would be delayed, in favor of something in the future that will deliver more for less, because its costs are being discounted. How, exactly, would that approach help future generations?

In any case, defenders of discounting have argued that instead of discounting lives as such, regulators might simply use the future discounted (monetary) cost of *saving* lives at the time when the lives are saved—an approach that is mathematically identical and hence produces the same analysis as discounting.[12] A serious drawback is that the failure to use a discount rate will ensure that any cost-benefit analysis will ignore the opportunity cost of resources that are used for regulation; this could be a real problem for future generations, which might have benefited if those resources had been invested in a way that would have addressed their future needs. But these arguments have yet to convince the numerous critics of discounting, and rightly so. As we shall see, the relevant resources may not be "invested" for the benefit of future generations.

Responding to the controversy, some prominent analysts, including Kenneth Arrow, have distinguished between "descriptive" and "prescriptive" approaches.[13] Under descriptive approaches, the discount rate is chosen by examining the risk-free rate of return to capital. This is the standard approach of those who advocate discounting. Under prescriptive approaches, the discount rate is selected on the basis of ethical judgments about the duties of one generation to those that will succeed it. These approaches can lead to dramatically different rates. But this distinction presents one serious difficulty: Any "descriptive" approach must ultimately be defended in "prescriptive" terms. Whether the best prescriptive arguments require abandonment of what emerges from the preferred descriptive approach remains a serious question.

Building on Preferences

Some defenders of discounting have attempted to bracket the moral debates by investigating people's actual preferences in this domain.[14] They have tried to show that, through their preferences, people *do* discount future lives and the interests of future generations. According to an influential view, "a zero discount rate is inconsistent with the observable behavior of individuals, which is arguably the best guide for policy in a democratic state."[15] But the word "arguably" suggests the problem in this context: Why should the interests of future generations be determined by consulting the preferences of the present generation? Those preferences might well be self-serving and self-interested. Even if people express a (limited) degree of altruism in the present, that preference should not settle the moral entitlements of the future.

In any case, individual preferences in this context are not easy to identify, and they appear to change depending on how the question is framed. In an influential paper, the economist Maureen Cropper and her coauthors conclude that people are indifferent when asked to choose between saving one life today and saving 45 lives in 100 years—a conclusion that has concrete implications for the appropriate discount rate.[16] The conclusion was based on a study that asked people whether they would prefer a program that saves "100 people now" or one that saves a substantially larger number "100 years from now."

But other ways of framing the same problem yield radically different results.[17] Most people consider "equally bad" a single death from pollution next year and a single death from pollution in 100 years—a finding that implies no preference for members of the current generation. The question can even be framed in such a way as to show a *negative* discount rate—valuing those who will come later more highly than the present generation. In short, measurements of people's judgments about obligations to future generations are influenced by framing effects. For this reason, it is far from clear that judgments about discounting can be rooted in the actual preferences of the present—even if they should be controlling, as they should not be.

Health v. Money, Latent Harms vs. Future Generations

One of the most influential and elaborate treatments of these questions has been offered by Richard Revesz.[18] He makes two central arguments. First, he contends that the primary reasons for discounting future monetary benefits do not apply to risks to life and health. Money is discounted for two reasons. First, it can be invested; second, most people have a "pure" time preference for current over future consumption. But human lives cannot be invested, and a life lost twenty years hence cannot be "recovered" by investing some sum, or some person, in the present. (Human beings cannot be put in banks—or if they can, they are unlikely to grow there.) Nevertheless, Revesz acknowledges that people may well have a "pure" time preference that would treat a future risk as less troublesome than a present risk. One investigation of the empirical questions finds a real discount rate of about 2 percent, a figure that is in line with financial market interest rates for the period, adjusting for inflation.[19] Revesz argues that the existence of time preference justifies some discount rate for future harms that will occur to people now living.

To see the practical implication, consider the analysis of reducing arsenic levels in the water supply. In its rationale for regulation, the EPA treated an arsenic death in the future as equivalent to an arsenic death in the present—even though an arsenic death is likely to come, if it does come, decades after current exposure to arsenic.[20] In refusing to discount the latent harms from arsenic exposure, Revesz's argument suggests that the EPA's judgment is wrong, even arbitrary; some kind of discount rate is clearly appropriate.

But Revesz does not argue that the EPA should adopt a discount rate that is equivalent to the appropriate discount rate for money. He contends that, in the abstract, we have no reason to think that people have the same time preference for health risks as they have for dollars; and because no investment opportunity exists in the case of health, any discount rate for health risks is likely to be much smaller than the market rate of return typically used to discount money. In Revesz's view, the use of a market rate of return is likely to produce a significant undervaluation of regulatory benefits that will be enjoyed in the future. This is an important conclusion, because it suggests that current government practice should be substantially changed, in a way that would justify a number of regulations that cannot now satisfy a cost-benefit test.

Revesz also makes a distinction between latent harms and risks to future generations. For any person now living, an environmentally induced illness today is worse than an environmentally induced illness in twenty years; for this reason, some kind of discount rate makes a great deal of sense for latent harms. But for risks to future generations, Revesz believes that the argument for discounting is much more fragile. Why should the death of a ten-year-old in 2040 count less than the death of a ten-year-old today? Revesz concludes that we have no good answer to this question, and hence the standard idea of discounting is not properly applied to harms faced by members of future generations.

In its guidance to federal agencies, the OMB is alert to Revesz's concerns, but disagrees. It calls for the same discount rate for lives as for other goods, and briskly refers to opportunity costs: "It is true that lives saved today cannot be invested in a bank to save more lives in the future. But the resources that would have been used to save those lives can be invested to earn a higher payoff in future lives saved."[21] In any case, people prefer immediate health gains to equivalent health gains in the future. And because a failure to discount would produce "perverse" results, the OMB suggests that agencies should follow what it sees as a professional consensus, to the effect that future health effects, including both benefits and costs, should be discounted at the same rate. But the OMB blunders in suggesting that such a consensus exists.[22]

Discounting Money: The Last Generation

My principal interest here involves the rights of future generations. But we must first ask whether and how to discount risks and worst-case scenarios that will be faced by those now living. To separate this question from intergenerational issues, let us imagine that the question involves the practices of what is, in some part of the world, the Last Generation—a generation of living people who will have no successors. Should that generation engage in discounting?

For the Last Generation, this question is answered if we accept the proposition, now standard in the federal government, that statistical risks should be turned into monetary equivalents. When cost-benefit analysis is used, the government asks about people's willingness to pay to reduce statistical risks. When regulators are monetizing harms that will not occur for a long time (in the case of latent harms), the task is clear in principle. Regulators should work with people's *current* willingness to pay to eliminate risks that will not materialize until some time in the future. Both market evidence and contingent valuation studies can be enlisted to determine the appropriate values. The labor market, for example, exposes people not only to risks of immediate harm but also to risks of future harm, and the resulting evidence might be measured to obtain the appropriate values. In addition, it would be simple to design a contingent valuation study to determine people's current willingness to pay to avoid mortality risks of 1/100,000 that would be imposed five, ten, fifteen, and twenty years hence.

Of course, any such evidence would involve people's own discount rates—their willingness to pay less for future benefits than for present benefits. But in drawing on such evidence, government is not itself generating a special discount rate for "mortality" or "health." Instead, it is incorporating people's own judgments about how to deal with benefits that will be enjoyed in the future.

To be sure, determining the relevant values presents serious practical problems. Perhaps labor market studies are too "noisy" to permit confident judgments about current valuations of future risks. Perhaps people do not adequately understand the problem—and if they treat the future as if it were entirely unimportant, we might not want to use the resulting judgments for purposes of policy. These are important cautionary notes. But at least we can say that the general task is clear in principle: how to generate usable estimates of people's current willingness to pay to prevent future risks, with appropriate corrections for inadequate information and cognitive limitations.

Suppose, however, that regulators are interested not in *current* monetary valuation of latent harms but in *future* monetary valuations of such harms. The question might be, not how much people—part of the Last Generation—are now willing to pay to eliminate a risk that will be faced twenty years from now, but how much those same people will be willing to pay ten years hence to eliminate a risk that will occur either at that point or further out in their own future. Any judgments about the resulting amounts will be speculative, of course; for starters, we will have to project future income growth, which will increase valuations. But to know what the future will look like, we can make reasonable extrapolations from past changes over time, by comparing, say, the WTP in 1960 to the WTP in 1990. Once the relevant amounts are generated—and this is the key point—they will be monetary, and they must be discounted to present value.

To see how the analysis might work, imagine that the best estimate is that you will be willing to pay $150 for some good—say, a new tennis racquet—ten years from now. In deciding the value of your $150 in ten years, you will want to discount that amount to its present value. You would probably prefer to have $140 now than $150 in ten years, because the $140 can be invested and made to grow—so that a decade hence, you will be able to buy the same tennis racquet and have something left over. When discounting $150 in the future, or an amount that reflects people's monetary valuation of regulatory benefits in the future, regulators are doing nothing more controversial than discounting money. It is appropriate to discount the money that people will be willing to spend on refrigerators, automobiles, movies, books, education, and medicine; the same is true of the money that people are willing to spend to avoid risk.

To produce valuations for the Last Generation, we do not need to identify logical conundrums or implausible outcomes that seem to follow from a failure to discount. Only two steps are necessary: an appreciation of the theory that underlies current practice, and an understanding that what is involved, always, is money, and not life, health, or the environment as such.

Suppose that for the Last Generation we want to assign monetary values to a risk that will be faced in twenty years. Exposure to a certain level of arsenic in drinking water might impose no risk in the present, but a risk of 1/100,000 in twenty years. Suppose that ordinarily $8 million is the appropriate value of a statistical life— that is, suppose that people are willing to pay $80 to eliminate a 1/100,000 risk of mortality in the present. The empirical task is to elicit the correct monetary value now, to eliminate a risk that will come to fruition in twenty years. Almost surely, what we will elicit will be significantly less than $80; most people will think that facing a 1/100,000 mortality risk in twenty years is better than facing such a risk now.

If the issue is how much people in twenty years will be willing to pay to eliminate a risk of 1/100,000 twenty years from their own present, the resulting amount must be subject to the appropriate discount rate for money. It follows that any VSL in twenty years must be discounted too, since future money is worth only a fraction of current money because current money can be invested and made to grow.

The conclusion, then, is this: If we are asking about people's *current* valuations of risks that they will face in the future, we can simply elicit their current willingness to pay to reduce those future risks (with suitable corrections if people lack information or fail to treat the future with the seriousness that it deserves). If we are asking about people's *future* valuations of risks, we should try to estimate their willingness to pay in the future. These questions present serious challenges, but in neither case is the government itself discounting life or health as such.

Counterarguments

How might these arguments be resisted? It is true that national wealth tends to increase over time, and hence people will likely be wealthier in twenty years than they now are. Because they will be wealthier, they will demand more in return for being subjected to statistical risks. For this reason, use of the current VSL to calculate monetary amounts in the future likely produces unjustifiably low numbers.[23] But this is not a point against discounting. It simply suggests that the numbers that must be discounted are higher than regulators currently recognize. The proper analysis uses a multiplier for national income growth and any other relevant factors, and applies a discount rate from that point.

A different objection is that agencies are on fragile ground in using labor market studies to estimate VSL. Workers who accept a $60 premium to face a risk of 1/100,000 may be insufficiently informed or suffer from cognitive limitations. Perhaps the proper premium is $70, or $100, or $200. Perhaps the problem of insufficient information or bounded rationality is especially serious in the case of risks that will not materialize for a long time. Perhaps we cannot entirely trust either market evidence or contingent valuation studies that generate numbers for risks that will not be imposed for a decade or more. If so, we would have to rethink whatever numbers we have; but discounting itself would be unaffected. Our task would be to use the proper monetary amounts rather than the improper ones. So long as *any* monetary valuation is used, discounting generally follows. To repeat: When government discounts, what is being discounted is money, not the goods to which monetary amounts are assigned.

A separate objection would stress that in the future, technological, medical, and other changes will produce a stream of improvements with respect to health, safety, and the environment. Harms that we now project, holding current practices constant, might well not materialize, simply because posterity will be in a better position to prevent them. Perhaps climate change will produce less serious harm than we imagine, because adaptation will be possible, or because technology will be able to reduce warming. This objection is not implausible in itself, but it is not a claim about discounting. Certainly regulators who are projecting future harms should attempt to make an accurate projection, and accuracy requires an appreciation of technological innovation. But a judgment about such innovation should not be confused with the issue of discounting itself.

A more ambitious counterargument would suggest that the monetary values of human beings are not the proper basis for valuing some regulatory benefits. Consider, for example, the continued existence of an endangered species or the lives of wild horses, tigers, pandas, and elephants. As we saw in Chapter 5, aggregating people's willingness to pay to protect endangered species is not an adequate way to set a value on such animals. What is required is a more deliberative judgment, based on the exchange of reasons that can be offered on behalf of one or another outcome. But any method of valuation will necessarily include the explicit or implicit assignment of monetary values—even if those values are assigned in the democratic process, as citizens and representatives choose how to allocate scarce resources. So long as that monetary assignment is made, discounting is generally appropriate, because no one doubts that discounting money is appropriate.

Methuselah, Futureville, and Presentville

The argument thus far is meant to provide a background for the central question of intergenerational equity. Of course, the amounts spent by future generations involve money, and at first glance that money must be discounted, simply because it is money. But discounting might produce serious problems of intergenerational equity. The reason is that with discounting, cost-benefit analysis can lead the current generation to impose terrible burdens on future generations, leading to an overall welfare loss, a serious distributional problem, rights violations, or all three. If the present generation engages in CBA and discounts, it may enrich itself to the detriment of seriously disadvantaged people in the future who deserve to have decent lives.

To be sure, even without much worrying about their obligations to posterity, current generations will contribute a great deal to the well-being of those who will follow. The arc of human history, with its astounding improvements in wealth, health, and longevity, demonstrates that such contributions do occur over time.[24] In those terms, things have been getting much better for human beings, not worse. The best guess is that future generations will be healthier and more prosperous than our own. This point must be taken into account in any analysis of the obligations of the present generation. Unfortunately, we have no guarantee that the good trends will continue, in general or for particular risks. Environmental catastrophes could greatly reduce the well-being of those who will come later. To see the relevant considerations, consider a series of problems.

Methuselah   Suppose that society consists of only one person, who, it turns out, will live for a great many years, even centuries. Let us call him Methuselah. Suppose that Methuselah will face a set of health risks (none of them fatal) over time. Suppose that each risk of concern—those that involve a significant malady—is in the vicinity of 1/100 and that Methuselah is willing to pay $3,000 to eliminate each of these risks. According to standard assumptions, it is fully appropriate to discount, by the right amount, the monetary value of the relevant risks. If a 1/100 risk will be faced in 2020, it is worth not $3,000 but $3,000 discounted to present value. Methuselah can invest that discounted amount and watch it grow. His money is being discounted, not his health.

This conclusion might be questioned if Methuselah is seen as a series of selves extending over time and if an early self does not act as an appropriate agent for the later one. Perhaps Methuselah should be required to take steps to insure against serious harms in old age, especially if he has a problem with self-control. But if we indulge the assumption that Methuselah is a good agent for his later self, discounting is fully appropriate.

Paretoville   Suppose that everyone in a small town, Paretoville, faces a current risk of 1/100,000, and that every resident of Paretoville is willing to pay $50, but no more, to eliminate that risk. (The imaginary town is named after the economist Vilfredo Pareto, who is responsible for the idea of Pareto optimality, which occurs when no change in a social situation can make anyone better off without making at least one person worse off.) The mayor of Paretoville takes this figure very seriously and decides not to eliminate risks of 1/100,000 if the cost of doing so is greater than $50. Under plausible assumptions, involving adequate information and sufficient rationality, the mayor is properly using cost-benefit analysis in deciding how to proceed, and no objections can be raised from the standpoint of equity.

This is one of our easy cases from Chapter 5, in which every member of Paretoville pays, in full, for risk reduction; people should not be required to pay more than they wish, unless they suffer from inadequate information or bounded rationality, or doing so would inflict harms on third parties. In some regulatory contexts, these possibilities introduce serious complications, as we have seen; but we are assuming that they are absent in Paretoville. For the citizens of Paretoville, the argument for discounting is straightforward.

Dirtyville and Cleanville in Kaldorhicksiana   Two towns, Dirtyville and Cleanville, are adjacent to one another in the large and somewhat messy state of Kaldorhicksiana. (This imaginary town receives its name from the economists Nicholas Kaldor and John Hicks, who developed the idea of Kaldor-Hicks efficiency, which exists when those who gain could, in principle, compensate those who lose, while also leaving a surplus.)[25] Dirtyville engages in polluting activity that produces $60 in benefits to each of its 100,000 citizens. That activity creates a risk of 1/100,000, faced by each of the 100,000 citizens of Cleanville. Each citizen of Cleanville is willing to pay $50, but no more, to eliminate the risk of 1/100,000 caused by Dirtyville's polluting activity. On cost-benefit grounds, the polluting activity should be allowed; its value is $6 million, which is higher than its $5 million cost.

But this problem is different from the tale of Paretoville, because there is a distributional issue: The citizens of Cleanville are uncompensated losers. If we were committed to economic efficiency, we would want the polluting activity to continue, but the distributional problem complicates matters. The problem may be worse still, because monetized figures rather than direct measurements of welfare are involved. Perhaps the polluting activity actually creates a net welfare loss, with the citizens of Cleanville losing more, in terms of well-being, than the citizens of Dirtyville gain. Suppose, for instance, that the citizens of Cleanville are relatively poor. While they are willing to pay only $50 to eliminate a risk of 1/100,000, because of their relative poverty, they are nevertheless facing a huge welfare loss from subjection to that risk.

Presentville and Futureville   Presentville engages in polluting activity that produces $60 in benefits to each of its 100,000 citizens. But the polluting activity does not harm citizens of Presentville or any other current place; instead, it harms members of future generations. More particularly, the activity creates a risk that will materialize in one hundred years, in the town of Futureville—which, as it happens, is Presentville a century from now. In that time, the 1 million citizens of Futureville will face a death risk of 1/10,000—meaning that 100 people are expected to die. Let us venture an analysis of costs and benefits. If the lives of the people of Futureville are valued at $8 million, then the polluting activity should stop, because $800 million is far greater than $6 million. But if money is discounted at an annual rate of 7 percent, each of their statistical lives is worth only $581, and hence the polluting activity should continue, because $6 million is far greater than $58,100.

But on what premises does it make sense to refuse a $6 million (current) expenditure to save 100 future lives? Lives are not worth less because they are lived later. A refusal to make that $6 million expenditure will ensure overall welfare losses: Futureville loses much more in terms of well-being than Presentville gains. Such a refusal will also produce a distributional problem: Presentville is benefiting (to the tune of $6 million) at the expense of Futureville (in the form of 100 premature deaths). In light of the overall welfare losses and the serious distributional problem, cost-benefit analysis with discounting seems to be producing an unjustifiable outcome.

If all the people of Presentville and Futureville were treated as one giant person extending over time, then discounting would be appropriate. In that case, the various people would amount to just one person—Methuselah—who could invest the relevant resources and use them later. And we can imagine an intergenerational negotiation between the people of Presentville and the people of Futureville in which discounting would be part of a mutually beneficial trade.

For example, suppose the people of Presentville would agree not to squander or consume the benefits they receive from polluting but instead invest a relevant sum in trust for the people of Futureville, making them better off on balance. Perhaps the citizens of Futureville would receive a great deal of money, which they could use for improvements in health, in return for the risk that their ancestors have imposed on them. Those who emphasize the opportunity costs of investments as a reason for discounting implicitly appeal to the idea that future generations will in fact benefit from the investments that current generations make. Hence, discounting might be seen as a part of a (hypothetical) mutually beneficial intergenerational negotiation.

But that idea raises two serious difficulties. The first is conceptual: What is the set of background entitlements against which this purely hypothetical negotiation is occurring? No negotiation, even a hypothetical one, can be analyzed without some such entitlements. At first glance, the people of Presentville are literally dictators; they can decide to consume all existing resources, to ruin the environment, to impoverish posterity, even to remain childless and not create later generations at all. In the (hypothetical) negotiating process, are the people of Presentville permitted to threaten the (hypothetical) people of Futureville with nonexistence? With this kind of threat looming over them, how much will Futureville be able to extract in the negotiation? If Presentville is not permitted to threaten Futureville with nonexistence, is this because hypothetical people have some entitlement to be permitted to exist? (How many of them?) And if Presentville merely threatens Futureville with impoverishment and desperation, the people of Futureville will be in a singularly weak position to extract protection against individual risks of, say, 1/100,000. In short, the idea of a mutually beneficial deal raises serious conceptual difficulties. At the very least, we must identify some background entitlements on the part of both Presentville and Futureville against which they might bargain. To be plausible, any such specification will inevitably have to depend on an independent moral account of some kind—and that independent account, rather than a notion of intergenerational bargaining as such, will be doing the crucial work. I will explore such an account shortly; for the moment, let us simply notice that without it, we cannot speak of a mutually beneficial deal, and with it, we are not speaking of deals at all.

The second problem is pragmatic. Suppose that no mechanism exists to ensure that any mutually beneficial bargain will be enforceable; the citizens of Presentville might simply consume their resources instead of putting them in trust or otherwise using them in a way that will help Futureville. This problem could be solved with actual compensation from Presentville to Futureville. Perhaps Presentville will engage in action that produces 100 deaths but at the same time yields technological innovations that lengthen 1,000 or 10,000 lives. But the citizens of Futureville have no assurance that this will be the case. This practical problem raises a serious objection to those who defend discounting on the ground that it inevitably helps future generations, by ensuring that the relevant amounts will be invested and made to grow. Unfortunately, those amounts might not be invested at all.

Climate Change

Turn now from Presentville and Futureville to a more realistic example, involving climate change. Suppose that the primary victims of climate change will include poor people in India and Africa. Suppose that the planners concerned with climate change decide what to do by engaging in cost-benefit analysis and discounting the victims' costs to present value. If so, such victims will not be much helped, because no one is planning to invest the discounted sum to create a fund designed to compensate or to help them in the future. If future deaths, illnesses, and deprivations faced by poor citizens in India and Africa in 2100 are discounted to present value—at, say, a rate of 3 percent—those harms will be valued at a mere fraction of what they otherwise would be. How, exactly, does the resulting calculation benefit the victims of climate change?

As with the case of Presentville and Futureville, we can identify two major problems here. The first involves social welfare: If decisions are based on cost-benefit analysis with discounting, the losses might far exceed the gains, with the loss taking the form of a great deal of suffering and death. It is certainly plausible to think that climate change will inflict far more harm on future generations than greenhouse gas reductions would impose on the present—even if CBA with discounting argues against some such reductions. A revealing study, alert to this problem, shows that cost-benefit analysis with discounting would justify far less, in the way of greenhouse gas reductions, than would a utilitarian approach that gives equal weight to members of present and future generations.[26] In that calculation, CBA justifies a reduction of 16 percent in the short run and 23 percent in the long run, with a greenhouse gas tax that begins at $16 per carbon ton and rises to $76 by 2420. By contrast, a utilitarian approach would justify a 51 percent reduction, produced by a tax of $146 per carbon ton in the long run and rising to $636 over the next four centuries. Whatever our assessment of the particular numbers, cost-benefit analysis with discounting might produce an outcome that does not promote overall or aggregate well-being, however we might specify that contested concept.

An independent problem involves distribution: Those who are especially deprived will be greatly hurt, while those who are far less deprived will gain. The suffering imposed on those already facing serious deprivation is a reason for objection, even if less deprived people are gaining more than the more deprived people are losing.

As we have seen, discounting might be defended if the discounted amounts were invested and economic growth made it possible to take steps that would ease adaptation to warmer climates or spur technological innovation that would improve welfare in various ways. Technological innovations might mean that the problem of climate change will be less serious than it now appears, and what we see as premature deaths will end up at worst as mere illnesses. If the projected cost of anticipated harms is inflated, then of course the analysis must change; but this possibility does not justify discounting. The conclusion is that for climate change, cost-benefit analysis with standard discounting can produce decisions that are exceedingly hard to justify.[27]

The same is true for other problems with intergenerational dimensions. But the word "can" is important here. It is possible that cost-benefit analysis with discounting will produce excellent decisions with large overall welfare gains and no distributional problems at all. Suppose, for example, that the consequence of such analysis is to ensure investments that ultimately help everyone, including the most disadvantaged members of society. The only point is that we have no assurance that this will happen.

Your Rich Grandchildren

As I have noted, the course of human history suggests that future generations will be wealthier than our own. This point matters, for it does not make sense for the relatively poor present to transfer resources to the relatively rich future. This would be a perverse form of redistribution—akin to a transfer from Kenya or India to the United States and Germany. If future generations can be expected to be richer, that expectation must be part of the analysis of what equity requires. And if future generations can be expected to be richer, their anticipated wealth will be produced by some combination of the efforts of their predecessors, investments, and altruism—a point that compounds the concern about perverse redistribution.

For long-term problems, the question has been raised whether the current generation should provide "foreign aid" to posterity. Perhaps posterity is, in a sense, a foreign country. Thomas Schelling has pointed out that citizens of the developed world are not now willing to make significant sacrifices to help people in poor nations; he thinks that such citizens are extremely unlikely to make significant sacrifices to assist people in those same nations in the distant and probably less-poor future.[28]

But Futureville is not a foreign country. It consists to a large extent of Presentville's own descendents, and the risks its citizens face are a direct result of Presentville's own actions—both reasons to think that Presentville might have special obligations toward Futureville. The idea of "foreign aid" is a singularly poor fit for problems like that of climate change, in which environmental and health risks in some Futureville are a product of actions undertaken knowingly (and perhaps negligently or even recklessly) by some Presentville. In that event, the present might well be seen to have committed a kind of tort, and the claim for compensation is hardly a claim for some kind of subsidy or "foreign aid."

To give a stark example, imagine that present generations plant a bomb that will explode in two centuries. Is this a violation of the obligation to provide "foreign aid"? Environmental problems are rarely bombs, for they are usually not created with malice or with destructive goals; but if they result from activities that are projected to create risks, the analogy to foreign aid is unhelpful. This point has important implications for nuclear power; if nuclear waste disposal imposes serious dangers on future generations, present generations should take that point into account. Climate change must be analyzed similarly.

Intergenerational Justice

I have indicated that for some problems, future generations might well have a legitimate complaint if current generations follow the path indicated by cost-benefit analysis with discounting. But exactly what kind of complaint do they have?

We might be tempted to think of ethical obligations in compensatory terms, as in the idea that ethical obligations are satisfied if the present can make it worthwhile for future generations to run the risks to which it subjects them. But this idea turns out to be a false start, because we cannot know what the idea of compensation means in this context. Must the present compensate the future for each particular risk? That conclusion would be implausible. Surely it would be acceptable to impose a risk of 1/100,000 on 10 million future people if the very step that imposes that risk also eliminates a 1/1,000 risk that would be faced by 100 million future people (including the 10 million future people who are subjected to a new 1/100,000 risk).

At first glance, then, the goal should be to produce an overall "risk package" for which adequate compensation has been paid. But to what, exactly, is this overall risk package being compared? To a situation in which future generations face extreme poverty and catastrophic climate change? To a situation in which future generations do not exist at all? Do members of future generations have rights to exist? How many of them have such rights? As we have seen, these questions are closely connected with the difficulty of specifying the background entitlements against which any hypothetical bargaining occurs. In short, we have to identify the baseline against which any "compensation" must be paid, and the real work is being done by that baseline, not by the idea of compensation. The baseline must come from a more general account of the ethical obligations owed by the present to the future—and hence we are not speaking of compensation at all.

What might that account require? Some people believe that current generations are obliged not to make the environment worse than it is today.[29] On this view, current generations are environmental trustees; as such, they must follow a kind of environmental nondegradation principle. But environmental quality is not a unitary good; it is a heterogeneous set of goods with qualitative differences—including, for example, clean air, endangered species, clean water, wildlife in general, and aesthetic values. Some of these goods may well be in conflict with other goods.

A second problem is the selective focus on environmental quality. Suppose that the current generation sacrifices a remote island,

and, as a direct result of that action, it confers significant eco-nomic and other benefits on posterity, giving its members healthier, longer, and better lives. Is such a sacrifice so clearly unacceptable? Environmental quality is exceedingly important, but it is not the only important good, and intergenerational justice does not require subsequent generations to have the same level of (all dimensions of) environmental quality.

A more promising approach would insist on a Principle of Inter-generational Neutrality.[30] According to this principle, the decade of one's birth has no moral relevance, any more than does one's skin color or sex. Those who are born in 1950 violate their obligations if they treat those born in 2050 as worthy of less concern by virtue of their date of birth. In this spirit, John Rawls argues on behalf of a "just savings" principle, to be chosen by people behind a veil of ig-norance in which "they do not know to which generation they belong or, what comes to the same thing, the stage of civilization of their society."[31] The key point, for Rawls, is the extension of the device of the veil of ignorance to the intergenerational question. Rawls contends more particularly that his conception of justice—justice as fairness—ought to inform choices behind the veil. What is required, in this view, is a system of savings that will bring "about the full realization of just institutions and the equal liberties," with close attention to the "standpoint of the least advantaged of each generation."[32]

Adaptation of this approach to particular questions of risk regu-lation, and to the treatment of worst-case scenarios, is no simple matter. But in Rawls's approach, decisions based on cost-benefit analysis with discounting may well be morally objectionable if they ensure the imposition of devastating harm on the most disadvan-taged members of future societies. A key task is to consider the effects of various policies on the most disadvantaged people. Suppose that if greenhouse gas emissions are not reduced, the most disadvantaged members of future generations will be more disadvantaged than the most disadvantaged members of the present generation. If so, a refusal to reduce greenhouse gas emissions would be unacceptable—at least if restrictions on greenhouse gas emissions would not make the most disadvantaged members of the current generation more disadvantaged than the most disadvantaged members of future generations would be if such restrictions were not imposed.

And indeed, some debates over climate change devote attention to issues of exactly this sort. If "business as usual" would create extremely serious hardship for poor people in India and China, there is special reason not to continue with business as usual, or at least to provide funding to ease adaptation. But if emissions reduction requirements would impose serious strain on poor people in India and China—because such requirements would increase poverty and unemployment—there is good reason to hesitate before imposing those requirements.

In a later treatment, Rawls suggests that it is not useful to try to "imagine a (hypothetical and nonhistorical) direct agreement between all generations."[33] Instead, the parties, behind the veil of ignorance, might be "required to agree to a savings principle subject to the further condition that they must want all *previous* generations to have followed it." This savings principle counts as one of intergenerational neutrality, because it treats all generations the same. Such a principle might easily be used to orient analysis of climate change, ozone depletion, asteroid collisions, and other problems with intergenerational features.

Rawls himself emphasizes equal liberties and the situation of the most disadvantaged. He explicitly rejects utilitarianism, and his own approach is not welfarist. Rawls's approach will therefore be unacceptable to utilitarians, welfarists, and all others who reject his more general claims about what justice requires. But even after rejecting those claims, we might nonetheless agree that the veil of ignorance, and the idea of intergenerational neutrality, provide the right foundations for approaching the question of intergenerational equity. Indeed, the idea of intergenerational neutrality might easily provide the basis for approaches rooted in welfare or utility.

From the welfarist point of view, the goal should be to maximize social welfare over time. Welfarists would require current generations to give members of future generations exactly the same moral weight that they give to now-living people. It follows that the current generation should not engage in projects that lead to overall losses in well-being, measured after including the interests of all generations (with those interests themselves being given equal weight). Certainly, the current generation ought not to enrich itself through steps that condemn future generations to massive deprivation.

The veil of ignorance and the idea of intergenerational neutrality raise many questions, including population size: If we are committed to intergenerational neutrality, are we required to ensure that future generations have, or are able to have, certain numbers of members?[34] At first glance, what should matter is not population size but the level of well-being that actual people are able to have. But how does this conclusion bear on the obligations of current generations? I do not attempt to answer this question here. The point is that the Principle of Intergenerational Neutrality is the right place to start. It deserves to play an important role in the debate over endangered species and climate change—and it helps to explain why cost-benefit analysis with discounting can produce morally unacceptable decisions.

A Crude Response to the Intergenerational Problem

Refusing to discount is not a good way to fulfill the moral obligations of the present. Indeed, any such refusal might well hurt posterity. Those obligations are best discharged not by a zero discount rate but by asking the current generation to focus directly on what intergenerational neutrality requires it to do.

A refusal to discount is a singularly crude way of implementing the Principle of Intergenerational Neutrality. Suppose that the consequence of discounting is to increase investments, economic and otherwise, that lead to long-term benefits for the future. If so, then refusing to discount would be detrimental to future generations. If the generation born in the 1880s had impoverished itself, supposedly for our benefit, we would be less well off today, and it is most unlikely that we would be grateful for their sacrifice. The refusal to discount can also cause protective programs to be postponed, because without discounting it always makes sense to delay programs until the future, when the cost-benefit ratio is better. The conclusion is that the moral obligations of current generations must be uncoupled from the question of discounting, because refusing to discount is not an effective way of ensuring that those obligations are fulfilled. The moral issues should be investigated directly and independently.

In an optimistic view, current generations need not take special steps to protect the future. Some combination of market forces, economic development, and ordinary altruism tends to ensure that those who come later are, in all relevant respects, significantly better off than those who came before. Schelling has properly emphasized this point in suggesting that we should be wary about expending our own resources for the benefit of our wealthier descendents.[35] But such an optimistic view may be unrealistic for some problems, such as climate change. Suppose that climate change would impose truly catastrophic losses on the world as a whole, or at least on the most vulnerable members of the most vulnerable nations. If so, the current generation, committed to intergenerational neutrality, should take self-conscious steps to protect successor generations from the effects of climate change, no less than from the effects of ozone depletion.

A Brief Note on Sustainable Development

In recent years, a great deal of attention has been devoted to the topic of "sustainable development," an idea that has considerable force in international law.[36] Unfortunately, the idea of sustainability remains poorly defined. An influential report suggests that development is sustainable if it "meets the needs of the present without compromising the ability of future generations to meet their own needs"—a formulation that is not so far from that of intergenerational neutrality.[37] Focusing more narrowly on the environment, Edith Brown Weiss argues that each generation has a duty not to make the environmental quality of the planet worse and also to preserve the essential options available to future generations.[38] Robert Solow endorses a principle of intergenerational neutrality, defining sustainability to require each generation to have the capacity to attain the same levels of welfare as those that preceded it.[39] For the environmental context, this definition means that nonrenewable resources must be used so as not to make it impossible for future generations to acquire the same standard of living.

To the extent that the idea of sustainable development is meant to require a specific policy of preserving *environmental* goods, it offers a useful suggestion that current actions can produce short-run economic benefits while also creating long-term environmental problems. The suggestion is especially important in the face of potentially irreversible environmental change. But environmental protection can burden the future too, especially if it is extremely costly, and we have no abstract reason to believe that preserving a particular environmental amenity (a forest, a lake) is always better for posterity than other investments that do not involve the environment in particular (expenditures on basic research, reductions in national debt). In any case, economic growth can be good for the environment too, because it increases the resources available for protecting environmental amenities.

If the idea of sustainable development is designed to require present generations to take seriously the interests of those who will follow, it points in useful directions and may have considerable practical importance. The general conclusion is that the idea of sustainable development must be taken as a placeholder for a separate analysis, requiring specification and independent support, about what intergenerational equity requires. The Principle of Intergenerational Neutrality hardly answers every question, but it provides the right foundation for that analysis.

CONCLUSION

According to an old saying: "If you make a plan, God laughs. If you make two plans, God smiles."

The topic of worst-case scenarios is not exactly cheerful. Mental health professionals spend a lot of time dealing with those fixated on the worst that might happen. If you think about the worst possibilities, you might end up thinking about little else. To be sure, many people are paid a lot of money to think about bad outcomes. The group of worst-case specialists is large; it includes doctors, lawyers, military leaders, the secretary of defense, environmentalists, and those who work at insurance companies. But for most people most of the time, low-probability risks of disaster receive, and deserve, little attention.

A key reason is that attending to them can be so exhausting and unpleasant. Maybe God smiles on those who make special plans, but on most days, we can find much better things to do than to plan specially. Consider these words from a book on genetically modified organisms (GMOs): "What is the single greatest food-related threat to your health? Is it GMO's? Synthetic pesticides? Natural toxins? . . . None comes close. The greatest real damage is chronic anxiety over diet. Instead of worrying—almost always needlessly—over whether or not your food supply is safe, or if you're eating too much pesticide, or not getting enough fibre, or too much cholesterol, or too little polyunsaturated fat, simplify your life and diet. Eat balanced and varied meals . . . Enjoy your meals. Bon appétit."[1]

For most people, this is pretty good advice. And its underlying wisdom goes far beyond diet. A balanced and varied portfolio is the best protection against financial problems, and those who have a diverse portfolio ought not to waste their time on imaginable disasters. But those who suffer from obesity or high cholesterol levels would do well to watch their diet; and in many domains, occasional attention to the worst-case scenario has the virtue of enabling people to exercise far greater control over their lives. An appreciation of the worst that might happen, and of how people sometimes overreact and underreact, can be useful and even indispensable, simply because of the safeguards that it helps to provide.

Many people plan far too much—and many others far too little—for unlikely catastrophes. Usually the resulting errors are innocuous, but sometimes they produce either debilitating anxiety or real tragedy. The problems that beset individuals are replicated at the institutional level and most damagingly by governments. Excessively optimistic leaders may ensure that their countries face terrible military defeats, or that their citizens suffer unnecessarily from natural disasters, environmental harm, serious diseases, or famines.[2] Officials who focus on bad outcomes but neglect their probability, or who react excessively to recent incidents, waste a lot of time, money, and perhaps life itself—and divert attention from the most serious problems that people face. Saddam Hussein was a terrible tyrant and a danger to his people and to the world. But American deliberations over whether to go to war in Iraq were distorted by excessive concern with the worst-case scenarios if Saddam had remained in power. Abandoned hazardous waste dumps can be a genuine problem, but American governments have focused too much time and expense on that problem.

Often, public officials have two unfortunate incentives: to give undue attention to worst-case scenarios and to pay no attention to them at all. Sometimes their electoral prospects, or their overall popularity, depend on one or the other. Before the attacks of 9/11, almost all American officials neglected the need for better security at airports, not least because the public would have strongly resisted significant additional burdens on air travel. After 9/11, many officials know that if they emphasize the danger of terrorism, and the need for an aggressive posture, their popularity will increase. For President George W. Bush, and probably Republican candidates more generally, the electoral incentive has been strong and simple: to focus on the attacks of 9/11 and to center public attention on the risk of future attacks.[3] Fear is a powerful motivator, and with respect to terrorism, drawing attention to worst-case scenarios is very much in the self-interest of certain politicians.

We can find many parallels in American history. In an earlier era, for example, President Lyndon Johnson was aware that an emphasis on the risk of nuclear war would be damaging to his Republican opponent, Barry Goldwater. For this reason, the Johnson campaign televised a controversial advertisement featuring a little girl in a meadow, plucking the petals of a daisy, followed by a mushroom cloud. The ad ran only once, and Goldwater's name was not mentioned, but it vividly signaled the danger of nuclear conflict in a Goldwater presidency. According to Johnson's biographer, Robert Dallek, the "Mushroom Cloud" became the most famous political ad in television history.[4]

With respect to climate change, the political incentives have been altogether different. No vivid incidents or images have been able to stir the public imagination. The principal beneficiaries of greenhouse gas reductions either live elsewhere or are not yet born and hence cannot vote in favor of current leaders. Most politicians are unlikely to favor steps that would impose significant costs on current voters for the benefit of posterity.

We have seen that if a bad incident has occurred in the recent past, people are especially likely to focus on the worst-case scenario. If intense emotions are associated with a bad outcome, people might well neglect the question of probability altogether, focusing on that outcome instead. If people are outraged, above all because the incident is associated with an identifiable perpetrator (the Goldstein Effect), they will demand an especially strong response. When a terrible incident has occurred recently, and when it is highly salient, people's intuitions will often lead them to exaggerate the probability of another such incident. Whatever the statistical reality, people's reactions to a worst-case scenario will be dampened if they have no experience with its occurrence; if it is too abstract, image-free, or statistical to call up intense emotions; and if it is not associated with any particular face or any identifiable actor. Dampening will also occur if the bad outcome is not expected to occur for a long time—and if its victims are distant in either time or space.

Of course, well-organized groups, the media, and political leaders have power to influence the underlying dynamics. Worst-case scenarios can be made more or less vivid through words or pictures, and sometimes they come into view quite suddenly. The different American reactions to terrorism and climate change are at opposite ends of a continuum; many other risks can be placed toward one or another end. Depletion of the ozone layer, for example, is probably more vivid than climate change, because of the fear of skin cancer and the image of a "hole" in the "protective shield" around the earth. But for the ozone layer, the reaction of the world and of the United States was driven in part by a statistical analysis, showing that the risks were very high and that they could be reduced or even eliminated at an acceptable cost.

I have attempted to introduce a general framework for thinking about worst-case scenarios. The Precautionary Principle turns out to be flawed, not because it is vague (though it is), and not because it threatens to impede desirable economic development (though it does), but because it is paralyzing, forbidding the very steps that it requires. Troublesome worst-case scenarios are usually associated with all courses of action, including not only aggressive regulation and inaction but also everything in between. A preemptive war against a feared enemy is the simplest example, but the same is true for a host of problems involving safety, health, and the environment. We can take precautions against particular risks and particular bad outcomes, but we cannot take precautions against all of them at once, if only because efforts to do so will produce risks and worst-case scenarios of their own.

A Catastrophic Harm Precautionary Principle is far more useful. In its most modest form, that principle calls for close attention to both the magnitude and the probability of harm and hence to expected value. It demonstrates, for example, that a 1 percent chance of 10,000 deaths is not worth less attention than a 50 percent chance of 200 deaths. A mildly more aggressive version of the principle emphasizes that 10,000 deaths, from, say, a terrorist attack, are likely to be much worse, in their impact, than a simple exercise in multiplication might suggest. Those deaths will have ripple effects that include serious economic and noneconomic harm. As a small example, recall the fact that in the aftermath of the attacks of 9/11, many people switched from flying to driving—and that because driving is so much more dangerous than flying, thousands of people died as a result of the switch. This "social amplification of risk" suggests that special steps should be taken to prevent real catastrophes, even highly unlikely ones. When we create a margin of safety for certain large-scale harms, our behavior is akin to a purchase of insurance; whether the margin is worthwhile depends on what is lost and what is gained by insisting on it.

The idea of "expected value" can be controversial in this domain, and sometimes it will require a lot of thinking about our deepest commitments. (How much, for example, should we attend to risks to animals?) But in many cases, we can make a lot of progress in deciding what to do without resolving the most fundamental issues. In such cases, a focus on the magnitude and the likelihood of harm will be enough to enable us to identify the right course of action. In ordinary life, we often make the relevant judgments very quickly, and see either that the worst-case scenario deserves no concern (the airplane really isn't going to crash) or that we ought to take precautions. (It probably does make sense to have a colonoscopy after age fifty, even though it won't be a lot of fun.) Sometimes sensible judgments require us to go far beyond our intuitions; we need to be systematic about the underlying variables. For private and public institutions, a formal assessment of the expected value of both risks and precautions, including any margin of safety, is indispensable.

Once an endangered species is gone, it is gone forever; greenhouse gases stay in the atmosphere for a very long time. In ordinary life, people are willing to do and pay a great deal to preserve their options—in particular, to leave certain routes available as new knowledge accumulates. Some harms are irreversible or at least very difficult to reverse, and worst-case scenarios qualify as such partly for that reason. Some losses are not commensurable with others; what is lost is unique and deserves attention for that reason.

Building on such ideas, the Irreversible Harm Precautionary Principle suggests that regulators should be willing to take steps to preserve their future flexibility. If this point is taken together with an understanding of catastrophe, we can generate a working framework with which to approach a wide range of social threats.

The elaboration of any kind of Precautionary Principle requires attention to both what is gained and what is lost by precautions. Least contentiously, that assessment is qualitative as well as quantitative, and it does not require us to assign monetary amounts to the relevant variables. In deciding whether to take precautions against worst-case scenarios in daily life, sensible people engage in some such balancing; and they do not think about monetary equivalents. They ask about the likelihood of the worst case, its severity, the burdens and losses imposed by preventing it, and the worst-case scenarios associated with alternative courses of action. Well-functioning institutions, and their leaders, are not so very different. President Franklin Delano Roosevelt had an acute sense of how to handle the worst-case scenarios associated with both the Depression and the threat from Fascism. Unlike many other leaders, he was keenly aware that inaction had serious worst-case scenarios too. (His personal experience with polio probably heightened that awareness.[5])

More contentiously, I have argued that assigning monetary values to the key variables is essential in thinking about worst-case scenarios. Without being systematic about the costs and benefits of eliminating bad outcomes, progress can be difficult. To be sure, we need not be terribly enthusiastic about Richard Posner's effort to come up with a monetary figure for the extinction of the human race. (Happily, his figure—$600 trillion—is pretty high. But who would pay it?) For serious risks of 1/10,000 or 1/100,000, we can build on existing evidence to generate plausible figures for many bad outcomes. Few of us would be willing to pay $100,000, or $50,000, or even $10,000 to eliminate a risk of 1/100,000. If we want to respect individual autonomy or to protect social welfare, we might well start with people's actual practices when thinking about how, and how much, to reduce social risks.

The analysis must be changed when we are dealing with a wrongdoer, defined as someone who has intentionally, recklessly, or perhaps even negligently imposed serious risks on others. At the very least, intentional or reckless wrongdoers should be asked to stop, even if their victims are not willing to pay them a great deal to get them to stop. The proper analysis of terrorism does not depend on how much its victims are willing to pay terrorists. But for many situations having worst-case scenarios, we are dealing with the by-products of activities that are desirable or arguably so—building highways, driving cars, using heat and air-conditioning, providing health care, using cell phones. In such cases, asking about people's willingness to pay to eliminate worst-case scenarios is legitimate—certainly when they will themselves be paying for risk reduction. If people are not willing to pay more than $60 to eliminate a risk of 1/100,000, we do them no favors by requiring them to pay $150.

The question is different when those who will benefit from risk reduction pay little or none of the cost. Here as elsewhere, qualitative as well as quantitative information is important. We need to know not merely the benefits and costs, rendered in monetary terms, but also what those figures represent. Do they mean higher prices for consumers? Lower wages? More in the way of premature death and illness? Who, exactly, is suffering from these costs? Suppose, for example, that poor people in developing nations are willing to pay little for reductions in greenhouse gases, because they have so little money—and also that the cost of greenhouse gas reductions, to people in wealthy nations, would exceed the amount that poor people are willing to pay. In such circumstances, cost-benefit analysis seems to suggest that greenhouse gas reductions are not justified. But should the ultimate decision be based on that analysis? Surely it matters that those who are at risk are poor, while those who are asked to pay are wealthy. Surely it matters that the problem of climate change has been produced above all by wealthy nations. In any case, the beneficiaries in poor countries may well gain much more, in terms of overall welfare, than the losers in wealthy countries will lose in those terms—a point that bears on the proper analysis of many problems.

We can see, in this general light, that reasonable people doubted the Kyoto Protocol, because its benefits were projected to be relatively low to rich and poor alike, and because its costs were projected to be quite high. We can also see that with respect to climate change, complete inaction—and the obstructionist attitude of the United States under President Bush—are very hard to defend. In my view, the right approach would go well beyond the Kyoto Protocol, in the form of an international agreement with four central features: (1) fully global emissions trading, so as to drive down compliance costs; (2) sensible and nonarbitrary emissions limits, probably starting slowly and accelerating over time; (3) inclusion of the developing nations, including India and above all China, which is likely to be the world's leading greenhouse gas emitter in the near future; and (4) financial and technological assistance from the wealthy countries to poorer ones, to respond to the fact that wealthy countries have been largely responsible for the problem and are in any event in the best economic position to do something about it.

The most difficult point here is (2). Its specification depends on a judgment about the consequences of greenhouse gas emissions and of efforts to reduce them. Detailed information about the risks associated with climate change, and the likelihood of worst-case scenarios, is of course indispensable. We need to know the expense and burdens of emissions reduction—and to see who would bear that expense and face those burdens. Of particular importance is an analysis of the prospects for mitigating the problems that arise from warmer climates, in addition to reducing the likelihood of those problems through emissions reductions.

Point (4) raises its own challenges, including ethical ones. In any international agreement, how should the world allocate permission to emit greenhouse gases? Should permissions be distributed on a per capita basis, in a way that would provide substantial benefits to China and India, and generate significant opposition from the United States?[6] Or should nations, as such, have roughly uniform percentage reductions from whatever level of emissions they now generate, in a way that would favor the United States and generate significant opposition from China and India?

In terms of the future, the most important barrier to a serious response to climate change involves the incentives of both the United States and China. These two nations are the most serious sources of greenhouse gases, and China's emissions will soon exceed those of the United States by a large margin. At the same time, both the United States and China are not projected to be among the world's largest losers from climate change; India and Africa are far more vulnerable. Because the leading sources of the problem also have relatively less to lose from it, any serious response faces a significant obstacle. The obstacle might be overcome if the two nations can be persuaded that reductions will be less costly, or more beneficial, than current projections suggest. Or perhaps the two nations can be convinced that they have a moral obligation to protect the planet's most vulnerable people. The United States has long benefited from technologies that are imposing serious risks on disadvantaged people in India, Africa, and elsewhere. China is now doing the same. At a minimum, it makes sense to ask nations to contribute in a way that takes account of their past contributions to the current "stock" of greenhouse gas emissions, and also to allocate emissions rights in a way that is alert to the needs of those in poor nations.

For both monetary valuation and ethics, some of the most vexing questions are raised when future generations are at risk. I have argued for a Principle of Intergenerational Neutrality, which requires members of one generation to give equal weight to the interests of those who will follow. This principle helps to show that cost-benefit analysis with discounting can produce unacceptable outcomes. Nonetheless, the problem of discounting must be analyzed separately from that of intergenerational equity. A failure to discount the future might hurt, rather than help, those who will follow us, at least if it discourages investments that work to posterity's benefit.

For some problems, most obviously those of ozone depletion and climate change, the question of intergenerational equity must be tackled directly, by ensuring that the decisions of those now living do not unjustifiably imperil the prospects of those who will follow. Here as elsewhere, I have suggested that we can make a great deal of progress without answering the most difficult ethical questions, and without specifying precisely what is entailed by these ideas.

For some people, contemplation of worst-case scenarios, and of the right ways of handling them, is a central part of their job description. We delegate authority to them in the hope that they will do much better than those of us who must rely on intuitions, limited experience, and partial knowledge. Without an appreciation of human weakness, and of the best ways of counteracting it, their jobs cannot be done well. For most of us, worst-case scenarios rarely deserve sustained attention. Life is short, and we might as well enjoy it. But if we are alert, on occasion, to the worst that might happen, we should be able to enjoy life a lot longer.

NOTES

ACKNOWLEDGMENTS

INDEX

NOTES

Introduction

1. See Ron Suskind, *The One Percent Doctrine* 61–62 (New York: Simon & Schuster, 2006).

2. Issues of this kind are explored from a variety of perspectives in *Global Crises, Global Solutions* (Bjørn Lomborg ed.) (Cambridge: Cambridge University Press, 2004).

3. See, e.g., Elke Weber, "Experience-Based and Description-Based Perceptions of Long-Term Risk: Why Global Warming Does Not Scare Us (Yet)," 77 *Climatic Change* 103 (2006).

4. On incompletely theorized agreements in general, see Cass R. Sunstein, *Legal Reasoning and Political Conflict* (New York: Oxford University Press, 1996).

5. For relevant discussion, see Amartya Sen, *Development as Freedom* (New York: Random House, 1999); Martha Nussbaum, *Women and Human Development: The Capabilities Approach* (New York: Cambridge University Press, 2000).

1. Of Terrorism and Climate Change

1. Quoted in Alan H. Goldstein and Kate Braverman, "Bring on the Plague Years," *Salon* (October 28, 2004), available at http://archive.salon.com/tech/feature/2004/10/28/bioshield/index.html.

2. See Anthony Leiserowitz, "The International Impact of *The Day After Tomorrow*," 47 *Environment* 41 (2005); Anthony Leiserowitz, "Before and Af-

ter *The Day After Tomorrow:* A U.S. Study of Climate Change Risk Perception," 46 *Environment* 22 (2004).

3. See H. Gilbert Welch, *Should I Be Tested for Cancer? Maybe Not and Here's Why* (Berkeley: University of California Press, 2004).

4. *Sierra Club v. Sigler,* 695 F.2d 957 (5th Cir. 1983).

5. *Roberton v. Methow Valley Citizens Council,* 490 U.S. 332 (1989).

6. Kai T. Erikson, *Everything in Its Path: Destruction of Community in the Buffalo Creek Flood* 234 (New York: Simon & Schuster, 1976).

7. See Shelley E. Taylor, *Positive Illusions* 9–12 (New York: Basic Books, 1989).

8. *Id.*

9. Ian Shapira, "Long Lines, Even Longer Odds, Looking for a Lucky Number? How About 1 in 76,275,360?" *Washington Post,* April 12, 2002, p. B1.

10. See George A. Akerlof and William Dickens, "The Economic Consequences of Cognitive Dissonance," in George A. Ackerlof, *An Economic Theorist's Book of Tales* 123, 124–28 (Cambridge: Cambridge University Press, 1984).

11. See Garg H. McClelland et al., "Insurance for Low-Probability Hazards: A Bimodal Response to Unlikely Events," 7 *J. Risk & Uncertainty* 95 (1993).

12. See Jonathan Baron, *Thinking and Deciding* 255 (Cambridge: Cambridge University Press, 3rd ed., 2001).

13. See, e.g., Richard Posner, *Catastrophe: Risk and Response* 43–58, 75–86 (New York: Oxford University Press, 2005); Martin Rees, *Our Final Hour* (New York: Basic Books, 2003); Mark Maslin, *Global Warming* 83–101 (Stillwater, Minn.: Voyageur Press 2004); William Nordhaus and Joseph Boyer, *Warming the World: Economic Models of Global Warming* 87–89, 93–94 (Cambridge: MIT Press, 2000). The most detailed accounts can be found in the 2007 reports of the International Panel on Climate Change. See http://www.ipcc.ch/. On catastrophic impacts after the twenty-first century, see "Climate Change 2007: Impacts, Adaptation, and Vulnerability, Summary for Policymakers" 15, available at http://www.ipcc.ch/SPM13apr07.pdf.

14. See Posner, *supra* note 13, at 75–86; Robert Goodin, *What's Wrong with Terrorism?* 119 (noting one estimate of risk of a million deaths from efficient biological attack) (Cambridge: Polity, 2006). For a skeptical view, see John Mueller, *Overblown: How Politicians and the Terrorism Industry Inflate National Security Threats, and Why We Believe Them* 13–28 (New York: Free Press, 2006) (arguing that the catastrophic risks associated with terrorism are quite low).

15. See Nordhaus and Boyer, *supra* note 13, at 78–83. The risks associated

with climate change are of course greatly disputed, and any particular account threatens to go quickly out of date. One issue is the extent of warming; another is the damage, monetary and otherwise, associated with any particular level of warming. An especially comprehensive treatment can be found in *Stern Review: The Economics of Climate Change* 56–57 (2006), available at http://www.hm-treasury.gov.uk/independent_reviews/stern_review_economics_climate_change/sternreview_index.cfm (suggesting, for example, that 1–3 million more people will die from malnutrition at 3°C warming). For a valuable treatment of the relevant uncertainties here, see Robert S. Pindyck, "Uncertainty in Environmental Economics" (2006), available at http://www.aei-brookings.org/publications/abstract.php?pid=1142.

16. For a useful but inconclusive survey, see Henry Willis et al., *Estimating Terrorism Risk* (Santa Monica: Rand, 2005).

17. For one account, see Nordhaus and Boyer, *supra* note 13, at 88 (suggesting a 1.2% probability of a catastrophic impact with 2.5 degree Celsius warming and a 6.8% probability with 6 degree Celsius warming). This somewhat dated estimate was obtained by starting with a survey of relevant experts, using the median answer, and adjusting that answer upwards in accordance with more recent information. See *id*. Under the circumstances, with so much uncertainty and rapidly changing data, there is no basis for great confidence in the resulting figures. For reason to believe the risk of catastrophic warming is serious, see *Avoiding Dangerous Climate Change* (Hans Joachim Schellnhuber et al. eds.) (Cambridge: Cambridge University Press, 2006). For a much more systematic effort to assess probabilities of bad outcomes, see *Stern Review, supra* note 15, at 152–65, 195.

18. See Posner, *supra* note 13, at 49; Maslin, *supra* note 13, at 97 (noting projection of potential increase in malaria, by 2080s, of 260–320 million people); John Houghton, *Global Warming: The Complete Briefing* 178 (Cambridge: Cambridge University Press, 3d ed., 2004) (noting that "the potential impact of climate change on human health could be large" but that "the factors involved are highly complex; any quantitative conclusion will require careful study"). *Stern Review, supra* note 15, at 152–62, attempts to assess probabilities and to incorporate them into a general account of the costs of climate change.

19. See Deborah Small and George Loewenstein, "The Devil You Know: The Effect of Identifiability on Punitiveness" (unpublished manuscript 2004).

20. See Elke Weber, "Experience-Based and Description-Based Perception of Long-Term Risk: Why Global Warming Does Not Scare Us (Yet)," 77 *Climatic Change* 103 (2006).

21. See Robert Mendelsohn, "Perspective Paper No. 1.1," in *Global Crises, Global Solutions* 44, 44–47 (Bjørn Lomborg ed.) (Cambridge: Cambridge University Press, 2004); this position is rejected in many places, see, e.g., Houghton, *supra* note 18, at 227–30. See also *Stern Review, supra* note 15, at 2–4 (arguing against most aggressive responses but nonetheless describing economic consensus in favor of some kind of effort to reduce greenhouse gas emissions).

22. See Anthony Leiserowitz, "Communicating the Risks of Global Warming: American Risk Perceptions, Affective Images and Interpretive Communities," in *Communication and Social Change: Strategies for Dealing with the Climate Crisis* (S. Moser and L. Dilling eds.) (forthcoming); Anthony Leiserowitz, "Climate Change Risk Perception and Policy Preferences: The Role of Affect, Imagery, and Values, Climate Change," 77 *Climatic Change* 45 (2006).

23. *Id.*

24. *Id.*

25. http://www.pollingreport.com/enviro.htm.

26. Leiserowitz, *supra* note 22.

27. Gallup Poll News Service, "The Environment" (April 4–9, 2000).

28. See the summary and overview in *The New York Times,* April 23, 2006, at 14.

29. http://www.pollingreport.com/enviro.htm.

30. See Larry West, "Americans Would Support Higher Gas Tax to Reduce Global Warming" (2006), available at http://environment.about.com/od/environmentallawpolicy/a/gasolinetax.htm.

31. See Angus Reid Global Monitor, "Americans Review Possible Attack Scenarios" (August 4, 2005), available at http://www.angus-reid.com/polls/index.cfm/fuseaction/viewitem/itemID/8371.

32. See World Public Opinion.org, "Global Warming," available at http://americans-world.org/digest/global_issues/global_warming/gw2.cfm.

33. See *infra* notes 34, 39.

34. See "Most Think Global Warming Has Begun, But Differ with Scientists on Urgency" (June 15, 2005), available at http://abcnews.go.com/images/Politics/983a3GlobalWarming.pdf.

35. See Steven Brechin, "Comparative Public Opinion and Knowledge on Global Climatic Change and the Kyoto Protocol: The U.S. Versus the World?" 23 *International J. Sociology & Social Policy* 106, 110 (2003).

36. See Andrew Norton and John Leaman, *The Day after Tomorrow: Public Opinion on Climate Change* 4 (London: MORI Social Research Institute, 2004).

37. *Id.* at 5.

38. *Id.* at 6.
39. Stern Review, *supra* note 15, at 465.
40. For overviews, see White House Office of the Press Secretary, "Climate Change Fact Sheet" (May 18, 2005), available at http://www.state.gov/g/oes/rls/fs/46741.htm; and http://www.epa.gov/globalwarming/, in particular the reports mentioned at http://yosemite.epa.gov/oar/globalwarming.nsf/content/actions.html; "President Bush Discusses Global Climate Change" (June 11, 2006), available at http://www.whitehouse.gov/news/releases/2001/06/20010611–2.html; Daniel R. Abbasi, *Americans and Climate Change* 20–23 (New Haven, Conn.: Yale School of Forestry and Environmental Studies, 2006). On June 22, 2005, a 53–44 majority of the United States Senate approved a "sense of the Senate" resolution to the effect that "Congress should enact a comprehensive and effective national program of mandatory market-based limits and incentives on greenhouse gases that slow, stop and reverse the growth of such emissions." *Id.* at 20. One of the most aggressive legislative proposals to date, from Senators John McCain and Joseph Lieberman in 2003, would have capped greenhouse gas emissions at 2000 levels. The proposal was defeated by a vote of 55–43. For an overview, see US Senate Committee on Commerce, Science and Transportation, "Senate Casts Historic Vote on McCain-Lieberman Global Warming Bill" (October 30, 2003), available at http://commerce.senate.gov/newsroom/printable.cfm?id=214305; for an analysis, see Sergey Paltsev et al., "Emissions Trading to Reduce Greenhouse Gases in the United States: The McCain-Lieberman Proposal," available at http://web.mit.edu/globalchange/www/reports.html.
41. For a helpful outline, see Pew Center on Global Climate Change, "Analysis of President Bush's Climate Change Plan," available at http://www.pewclimate.org/policy_center/analyses/response_bushpolicy.cfm.
42. This in fact has been the experience of the United States between 1990 to 2004, with significant reductions in greenhouse gas intensity (by 21%) accompanied by significant growth in carbon dioxide emissions (by 19%). See Energy Information Administration, *Emissions of Greenhouse Gases in the United States 2004* at xii (2005).
43. See http://www.usgcrp.gov/.
44. White House Office of the Press Secretary, *supra* note 40.
45. *Id.*
46. Energy Information Administration, supra note 42, at ES-1; see also Energy Information Administration, *Emissions of Greenhouse Gases in the United States 2003* (2004) available at http://www.eia.doe.gov/oiaf/1605/1605a.html; US Environment Protection Agency, *US Emissions In-*

ventory 2006 (April 2006), available at http://yosemite.epa.gov/oar/globalwarming.nsf/content/ResourceCenterPublicationsGHGEmissions USEmissionsInventory2006.html.

47. See compilations of such voluntary reports at http://www.eia.doe.gov/oiaf/1605/frntvrgg.html. For an example of a voluntary report from General Motors Corporation, see General Motors Corporation, *Voluntary Reporting of General Motors Corporation United States Greenhouse Gas (GHG) Emissions for Calendar Years 1990–2002*, available at http://www.gm.com/company/gmability/environment/news_issues/news/ghgreport_2003.pdf.

48. See 42 U.S.C. § 13385 (requiring inventory of national aggregate emissions of each greenhouse gas for each calendar year for baseline period of 1987 through 1990, updated annually); 42 U.S.C. § 7651(k) (requiring monitoring and computing of aggregate annual total carbon dioxide emissions, to be made available to the public).

49. See James T. Hamilton, *Regulation through Revelation: The Origin, Politics, and Impacts of the Toxic Release Inventory Program* (New York: Cambridge University Press, 2005).

50. See   http://www.methanetomarkets.org/;   http://www.epa.gov/methanetomarkets/basicinfo.htm.

51. See Energy Information Administration, *supra* note 42, at iii–xx, showing that methane is a relatively small component of aggregate American contributions to climate change.

52. See www.rggi.org.

53. See http://www.seattle.gov/mayor/climate. For information on the Kyoto Protocol in general, see Nordhaus and Boyer, *supra* note 13; see also http://unfccc.int/2860.php.

54. See "West Coast Governors' Global Warming Initiative," available at www.ef.org/westcoastclimate.

55. See Energy Information Administration, *supra* note 42, at ix; Larry West, "Record Increase in U.S. Greenhouse Gas Emissions Sparks Global Controversy" (2006), available at http://environment.about.com/b/a/256722.htm.

56. In 2006, for example, 45% of Americans said that they worried "a great deal" about the possibility of future terrorist attacks, the same percentage that worried about "crime and violence," and a higher percentage than worried about the economy, hunger and homelessness, and the environment. See http://www.pollingreport.com/prioriti.htm.

57. *Id.*

58. See Program on International Policy Attitudes, "Terrorism," available

at http://www.americans-world.org/digest/global_issues/terrorism/terrorism_perception.cfm.

59. A 2002 study, involving students at Harvard University, found a "best estimate" mean of 294 deaths from terrorism in the next year, with an "upper bound" best estimate of 25,199. Interestingly, the upper bound estimates of "total fatalities due to all terrorism" were lower than the upper bound estimates of "total fatalities due to airplane terrorism"—a finding to which I will return. See W. Kip Viscusi and Richard Zeckhauser, "Sacrificing Civil Liberties to Reduce Terrorism Risks," 26 *J. Risk & Uncertainty* 99 (2003).

60. See http://www.pollingreport.com/terror4.htm.

61. See Mueller, *supra* note 14, at 2.

62. See Pew Research Center, "Americans taking Abramoff, Alito and Domestic Spying in Stride" (January 11, 2006), available at http://people-press.org/reports/display.php3?ReportID=267.

63. See Scott Wallsten and Katrina Kosec, "Economic Cost of the War in Iraq" (September 2005), available at http://aei-brookings.org/publications/abstract.php?pid=988.

64. See http://nationalpriorities.org/index.php?option=com_wrapper&Itemid=182.

65. See Nordhaus and Boyer, *supra* note 13, at 161. This highly disputed figure might turn out to be inflated if (for example) replacements for carbon dioxide have a diminishing cost as a result of technological innovation.

66. See http://www.ncsl.org/programs/press/2002/pdcongress.htm for an overview of domestic security legislation; the most prominent enactments include the USA Patriot Act, the Federal Aviation Security Act, and the Air Transportation Safety and System Stabilization Act.

67. For an early catalogue, see Office of Management and Budget, "Draft Report to Congress on the Costs and Benefits of Federal Regulations," 67 Fed. Reg. 15014 (March 28, 2002).

68. See Hamilton, *supra* note 49, at 177–91; Bruce Ackerman, John Millian, and Donald Elliott, "Toward a Theory of Statutory Evolution: The Federalization of Environmental Law," 1 *J. Law Economics & Organization* 313 (1985).

69. See Kevin Esterling, *The Political Economy of Expertise* (Ann Arbor: University of Michigan Press, 2004). For a parallel story with respect to ozone-depleting chemicals, see Richard Benedict, *Ozone Diplomacy* (New York: Oxford University Press, 1997); the evidence here is more complicated because a substantial segment of the public supported controls on such chemicals.

70. See Timur Kuran and Cass R. Sunstein, "Availability Cascades and Risk Regulation," 51 *Stanford Law Review* 683 (1998); Matthew Kahn, "Environmental Disasters as Regulation Catalysts? Exxon-Valdez, Love Canal, and Three Mile Island in Shaping U.S. Environmental Law" (unpublished manuscript 2006).

71. See Robert Percival et al., *Environmental Regulation* 387–93 (New York: Aspen, 2003); Aaron Wildavsky, *But Is It True?: A Citizen's Guide to Environmental Health and Safety Issues* (Cambridge: Harvard University Press, 1999). The ultimate response was a voluntary removal of Alar from the market, after EPA issued a preliminary determination to cancel all food uses of the substance. See Percival et al., *supra*, at 391.

72. See Max H. Bazerman and Michael D. Watkins, *Predictable Surprises* 15–42 (Cambridge: Harvard Business School Press, 2004).

73. See *id.* at 26–31, 128–29, and the suggestion that "the U.S. airline industry successfully resisted security improvements for decades, through its lobbying and campaign funding," *id.* at 128.

74. With respect to research, see Posner, *supra* note 13, at 53–57, including the suggestion that the research of many "global warming skeptics" has been "financed by the energy industries," and it "may not be very good research," *id.* at 53. With respect to regulation, see Robert Repetto, "Introduction," in *Punctuated Equilibrium and the Dynamics of Environmental Policy* 1, 17 (Robert Repetto ed.) (New Haven: Yale University Press, 2006); Lee Lane, "The Political Economy of U.S. Greenhouse Gas Controls," in *id.* at 162, 165–66.

75. *Id.* at 166 (quoting a speech by President Bush).

76. Thomas E. Drabek, *Disaster Evacuation Behavior: Tourists and Other Transients* (Boulder, Colorado: University of Colorado, 1996).

77. See Olivier Deschenes and Michael Greenstone, "The Economic Impacts of Climate Change: Evidence from Agricultural Output and Random Fluctuations of Weather" (January 2006), available at http://www.aei-brookings.org/publications/abstract.php?pid=1031; compare the suggestion in Nordhaus and Boyer, *supra* note 13, at 97, that "the economic impact of gradual climate change (that is, omitting catastrophic outcomes) is close to zero for a moderate (2.5 degree C) global warming." A more recent and different view is sketched in *Stern Review, supra* note 15, at 130 (offering optimistic and pessimistic cases for the United States, with pessimistic case involving a loss of 1.2% GDP for 3° C warming; the pessimistic case does not take full account of the effects of extreme weather events, such as hurricanes). Note that all of these conclusions do not come to terms with the economic effects on the United States

that would come from the very fact of serious economic harms in other nations.

78. See Robert Mendelsohn, *supra* note 21, at 44–47. Nordhaus and Boyer, *supra* note 13, at 98. This conclusion is vigorously challenged in Houghton, *supra* note 18, at 227–30 and *Stern Review, supra* note 15, at 193, 202–03 (arguing that a ten-year delay could make it impracticable to stabilize emissions at a desirable level). For the world in general, it is increasingly difficult to support the view that continued research is an adequate response. The International Panel on Climate Change concluded in 2007 that warming of the climate system "is unequivocal, as is now evident from observations of increases in global average air and ocean temperatures, widespread melting of snow and ice, and rising global average sea level." "Climate Change 2007: The Physical Science Basis, Summary for Policymakers," available at http://www.ipcc.ch/SPM13apr07.pdf, at 5.

79. For a superb and general discussion of precautions in the context of terrorism, see Jessica Stern and Jonathan Wiener, "Precaution against Terrorism," 9 *J. Risk Research* 393 (2006).

80. http://www.pollingreport.com/enviro.htm. See Lydia Saad, "Americans Still Not Highly Concerned about Global Warming" (April 7, 2006), available at http://poll.gallup.com/content/?ci=22291.

81. Leiserowitz, "Communicating the Risks," *supra* note 22.

82. For a contrary view, see US Global Change Research Program, "Climate Change Impacts on the United States: The Potential Consequences of Climate Variability and Change" (2000) available at http://www.usgcrp.gov/usgcrp/nacc/default.htm.

83. See Neal Feigenson et al., "Perceptions of Terrorism and Disease Risks: A Cross-National Comparison," 69 *Missouri Law Review* 991 (2004).

84. See Mueller, *supra* note 14, at 13–28.

85. See William D. Nordhaus and Joseph Boyer, *supra* note 13, at 127 (describing the net loss as "trivially small").

86. See *Stern Review, supra* note 15, at 193, 208.

87. See The Program on International Policy Attitudes, "Americans on the Global Warming Treaty," available at http://www.pipa.org/Online Reports/ClimateChange/GlobalWarming_Nov00/GlobalWarming_Nov00_rpt.pdf at Box 15.

88. *Id.*

89. *Id.* at Box 16.

90. *Id.*

91. W. Kip Viscusi and Joni Hirsch, "The Generational Divide in Support for

Climate Change Policies: European Evidence," 77 *Climatic Change* 121 (2006).

92. See Esterling, *supra* note 69.

93. See Nordhaus and Boyer, *supra* note 13, at 96–97.

94. See Deschenes and Greenstone, *supra* note 77; see also *supra* note 77 for other predictions of economic impacts.

95. See *supra* note 77.

96. See Wojciech Kopszuk et al., "The Limitations of Decentralized World Redistribution: An Optimal Taxation Approach," 30 *European Economic Review* 1051 (2005).

97. *Stern Review, supra* note 15, at 93–99, 128–31 (describing effects for various nations and regions and showing comparatively less, though still significant, vulnerability for United States).

98. Nordhaus and Boyer, *supra* note 13, at 161.

99. *Id.* at 161–63.

100. See UNFCCC, *Key GHG Data: Greenhouse Gas (GHG) Emissions Data for 1990–2003* 16–17 (2005).

101. See Bazerman and Watkins, *supra* note 72, at 84–87, 238–39; see also http://www.pollingreport.com/enviro.htm.

102. Thomas Schelling, "Intergenerational Discounting," in *Discounting and Intergenerational Equity* 99, 100 (Paul R. Portney and John P. Weyant eds.) (Washington, D.C.: Resources for the Future, 1999).

103. See Goodin, *supra* note 14, at 135.

104. See Bazerman and Watkins, *supra* note 72, at 15–41.

105. Goodin, *supra* note 14, at 135.

106. See Weber, *supra* note 20.

107. Paul Slovic, *The Perception of Risk* 414 (London: Earthscan, 2000).

108. See Weber, *supra* note 20.

109. See Joseph E. LeDoux, *The Emotional Brain* (New York: Simon & Schuster, 1996).

110. Weber, *supra* note 20.

111. Slovic, *supra* note 107, at 415–16.

112. *Id.*

113. *Id.*

114. *Id.* Compare student course evaluations. Among teachers, it is informal lore that when a particular class likes the instructor, the evaluation of all enumerated items will improve, including such items as course materials, even when they stay constant from year to year.

115. Abbasi, *supra* note 40, at 26.

116. Weber, *supra* note 20.

117. See *Judgment Under Uncertainty: Heuristics and Biases* (Daniel Kahneman, Paul Slovic, and Amos Tversky eds.) (New York: Cambridge University Press, 1982).

118. See Daniel Kahneman and Shane Frederick, "Representativeness Revisited: Attribute Substitution in Intuitive Judgment," in *Heuristics and Biases: The Psychology of Intuitive Judgment* 49–53 (Thomas Gilovich, Dale Griffin, and Daniel Kahneman eds.) (New York: Cambridge University Press, 2002).

119. See Amos Tversky and Daniel Kahneman, "Judgment Under Uncertainty: Heuristics and Biases," in *Judgment Under Uncertainty: Heuristics and Biases, supra* note 117, at 3, 11–14.

120. *Id.*

121. *Id.*

122. See W. Kip Viscusi, "Judging Risk and Recklessness," in *Punitive Damages: How Juries Decide* 171, 181–82 (Chicago: University of Chicago Press, 2002).

123. See Elke Weber et al., "Predicting Risk-Sensitivity in Humans and Lower Animals: Risk As Variance or Coefficient of Variation," 111 *Psychological Review* 430 (2004).

124. Slovic, *supra* note 107, at 40.

125. *Id.*

126. *Id.*

127. See Kathleen Tierney et al., *Facing the Unexpected* 161–66 (Washington, D.C.: Joseph Henry Press, 2001).

128. *Id.* at 162.

129. *Id.* at 161.

130. Ronald W. Perry and Marjorie R. Greene, "The Role of Ethnicity in the Emergency Decision-Making Process," 52 *Sociological Inquiry* 306, 326 (1982).

131. Hugh Gladwin and Walter Gillis Peacock, "Warning and Evacuation: A Night for Hard Houses," in *Hurricane Andrew: Ethnicity, Gender and the Sociology of Disasters* 52, 72 (Walter Gillis Peacock et al. eds.) (New York: Routledge 1997).

132. *Id.* at 159.

133. Ronald W. Perry, "The Effects of Ethnicity on Evacuation Decision-Making," 9 *International Journal of Mass Emergencies & Disasters* 47 (1991).

134. Steven J. Sherman et al., "Imagining Can Heighten or Lower the Perceived Likelihood of Contracting a Disease: The Mediating Effect of Ease of Imagery," in *Heuristics and Biases: The Psychology of Intuitive Judgment, supra* note 118, at 82.

135. See Feigenson et al., *supra* note 83.

136. Kahneman and Tversky emphasize that the heuristics they identify "are highly economical and usually effective" but also that they "lead to systematic and predictable errors." See Amos Tversky and Daniel Kahneman, "Judgment under Uncertainty: Heuristics and Biases," in *Judgment and Decision Making: An Interdisciplinary Reader* 38, 55 (Hal R. Arkes and Kenneth R. Hammond eds.) (New York: Cambridge University Press, 1986). Gerd Gigerenzer, among others, has emphasized that some heuristics can work extremely well, see Gerd Gigerenzer et al., *Simple Heuristics That Make Us Smart* (New York: Oxford University Press, 1999); Gerd Gigerenzer, *Adaptive Thinking: Rationality in the Real World* (New York: Oxford University Press, 2000), and used this point as a rejoinder to those who stress the errors introduced by heuristics and biases. For present purposes, it is not necessary to take a stand on the resulting debates. Even if many heuristics mostly work well in daily life, a sensible government can do much better than to rely on them.

137. See Bazerman and Watkins, *supra* note 72, at 91–93 (discussing effects of vividness).

138. Hamilton, *supra* note 49, at 184.

139. See *id.* at 178–91.

140. See James Dunn, "Automobile Fuel Efficiency Policy: Beyond the CAFE Controversy," in *Punctuated Equilibrium and the Dynamics of U.S. Environmental Policy, supra* note 74, at 197, 198.

141. See Rachel Carson, *Silent Spring* (Boston: Houghton Mifflin, 1962). For an overview of the influence of the book, see Thomas Hawkins, "Re-Reading Silent Spring," 102 *Environmental Health Perspectives* (1994), available at http://www.ehponline.org/docs/1994/102–6–7/spheres.html.

142. See Al Gore, "Introduction," available at http://clinton2.nara.gov/WH/EOP/OVP/24hours/carson.html.

143. See George Loewenstein and Jane Mather, "Dynamic Processes in Risk Perception," 3 *J. Risk & Uncertainty* 155 (1990).

144. *Id.* at 172.

145. See Goldstein and Braverman, *supra* note 1.

146. Gary Blasi and John T. Jost, "System Justification Theory and Research: Implications for Law, Legal Advocacy, and Social Justice," 94 *California Law Review* 1119 (2006).

147. See Mark J. Landau, "Deliver Us from Evil: The Effects of Mortality Salience and Reminders of 9/11 on Support for President George W. Bush," 20 *Personality & Social Psychology Bulletin* 1136 (2004); Thomas Pyszczynski et al., *In the Wake of September 11: The Psychology of Terror* (Washington, D.C.: American Psychological Association, 2003).

148. On the connection between hurricanes and climate change, see Houghton, *supra* note 18, at 4–6, 179, 183.

149. See http://www.pollingreport.com/enviro.htm.

150. See the summary in Baron, *supra* note 12, at 246–47.

151. *Id.*

152. Oswald Hober et al., "Active Information Search and Complete Information Presentation in Naturalistic Risky Decision Tasks," 95 *Acta Psychologica* 15 (1997).

153. Yuval Rottenstreich and Christopher Hsee, "Money, Kisses, and Electric Shocks: On the Affective Psychology of Risk," 12 *Psychological Science* 185 (2001).

154. See A. S. Alkahami and Paul Slovic, "A Psychological Study of the Inverse Relationship Between Perceived Risk and Perceived Benefit," 14 *Risk Analysis* 1086, 1094 (1994).

155. See George Loewenstein et al., "Risk as Feelings," 127 *Psychological Bulletin* 267 (2001).

156. See W. Kip Viscusi, "Alarmist Decisions with Divergent Risk Information," 107 *Economic J.* 1657 (1997).

157. *Id.*

158. See Mary Douglas, *Risk and Blame* (London: Routledge, 1992), for a general account of how particular sources of risk are blamed, and in particular pp. 9–14, for an emphasis on practices of blaming that have cultural sources, and that cannot be captured by exploring individual judgments about risk perception.

159. See Peter Sandman et al., "Communications To Reduce Risk Underestimation and Overestimation," 3 *Risk Decision & Policy* 93 (1998).

160. See Iris Bohnet et al., "Betrayal Aversion on Four Continents" (2006) available at http://papers.ssrn.com/sol3/papers.cfm?abstract_id=902370.

161. See, e.g., Tim Flannery, *The Weather Makers* (London: Allen Lane, 2006).

162. See Steven Brechin, *supra* note 35, at 123.

163. Abbasi, *supra* note 40, at 106.

164. *Id.*

165. *Id.*

166. See Hamilton, *supra* note 49, at 178–92.

167. See Joseph Henrich et al., "Group Report: What Is the Role of Culture in Bounded Rationality?" in *Bounded Rationality: The Adaptive Toolbox* 353–54 (Gerd Gigerenzer and Reinhard Selten eds.) (Cambridge: MIT Press, 2001), for an entertaining outline in connection with food choice decisions.

168. See Mary Douglas, *Purity and Danger* (New York: Prager, 1966).

169. See Dan Kahan and Donald Braman, "Cultural Cognition and Public

Policy," 24 *Yale Law & Policy Review* 149 (2006); Dan Kahan et al., "Fear of Democracy," 119 *Harvard Law Review* 1075 (2006).

170. The foundations of the approach can be found in Mary Douglas and Aaron Wildavsky, *Risk and Culture* (Berkeley: University of California Press, 1983).

171. See Cass R. Sunstein, *Laws of Fear: Beyond the Precautionary Principle* 94–102 (Cambridge: Cambridge University Press, 2005).

172. *Id.* at 166.

173. See Norton and Leaman, *supra* note 36, at 2.

174. Hence Michael Crichton's controversial best-seller, *State of Fear* (New York: Harper Collins Publishers, 2005), shows a strong understanding of cognitive and behavioral factors. (To avoid giving away the punchline, I offer no details.) The same is true of Al Gore's popular film, *An Inconvenient Truth* (2006).

175. See Hamilton, *supra* note 49, at 178–86; Repetto, *supra* note 74, at 9; William Brock, "Tipping Points, Abrupt Opinion Changes, and Punctuated Policy Change," in *Punctuated Equilibrium and the Dynamics of U.S. Environmental Policy, supra* note 74, at 47; Kahn, *supra* note 70; Thomas Birkland, *Lessons of Disaster: Policy Change After Catastrophic Events* (Washington, D.C.: Georgetown University Press, 2006); Thomas Birkland, *After Disaster: Agenda Setting, Public Policy, and Focusing Events* (Washington, D.C.: Georgetown University Press, 1997).

2. A Tale of Two Protocols

1. See Andrew E. Dessler and Edward A. Parson, *The Science and Politics of Global Climate Change: A Guide to the Debate* 10–11 (Cambridge: Cambridge University Press, 2006).

2. See Robert Percival et al., *Environmental Regulation: Law, Science, and Policy* 1047 (Boston: Aspen, 2003). See Scott Barrett, *Environment and Statecraft* 363 (New York: Oxford University Press, 2005). Indeed, an even earlier paper, from 1827, sketched the possible contribution of greenhouse gases. See James Houghton, *Global Warming: The Complete Briefing* 17 (New York: Oxford University Press, 3rd ed., 2004); Dessler and Parson, *supra* note 1, at 64–66. I refer to a scientific consensus, but of course there are dissenting voices. See, e.g., Nir Shaviv, "The Spiral Structure of the Milky Way, Cosmic Rays, and Ice Age Epochs on Earth," 8 *New Astronomy* 39 (2003) (arguing that cosmic rays are responsible for most of recent variations in global temperatures); Nir Shaviv and J. Veizer, "Celestial Driver of Phanerozoic Climate?" 13 *GSA Today* 4 (July 2003). A reply is Stefan Rahmstorf et al., "Cosmic Rays, Carbon Dioxide and Climate," in *Eos, Transactions of the American Geophysical Union* (January 27, 2004).

The International Panel on Climate Change concluded in 2007 that warming of the climate system "is unequivocal, as is now evident from observations of increases in global average air and ocean temperatures, widespread melting of snow and ice, and rising global average sea level." *Climate Change 2007: The Physical Science Basis, Summary for Policymakers,* available at http://www.ipcc.ch/SPM13apr07.pdf, at 5.

3. An illuminating discussion is Scott Barrett, "Montreal versus Kyoto: International Cooperation and the Global Environment," in *Global Public Goods: International Cooperation in the 21st Century* 192 (Inge Kaul et al. eds.) (New York: Oxford University Press, 1999). Barrett's analysis, drawn to my attention after this chapter was substantially complete, is very much in accord with that offered here, though Barrett places greater emphasis on the issue of compliance incentives, *id.* at 213, and also on the issue of "leakage," which occurs when polluting activity shifts from one nation to another.

4. See Dessler and Parson, *supra* note 1, at 20.

5. See Percival et al., *supra* note 2, at 1047.

6. Dessler and Parson, *supra* note 1, at 24.

7. *Id.* at 25.

8. *Id.* at 33.

9. Richard Benedick, *Ozone Diplomacy: New Directions in Safeguarding the Planet* 12 (Cambridge: Harvard University Press, 1991).

10. *Id.*

11. Dessler and Parson, *supra* note 1, at 33.

12. Benedick, *supra* note 9, at 28, 31.

13. 42 U.S.C. § 7457(b).

14. 43 Fed. Reg. 11301 (March 17, 1978).

15. Benedick, *supra* note 9, at 24.

16. *Id.*

17. Dessler and Parson, *supra* note 1, at 43.

18. *Id.* at 24–27, 33.

19. See James H. Maxwell and Sanford L. Weiner, "Green Consciousness or Dollar Diplomacy? The British Response to the Threat of Ozone Depletion," 5 *International Environmental Affairs* 19, 21 (1993).

20. Percival et al., *supra* note 2, at 1048. The shift in American policy appears to have had something to do with the replacement of Ann Gorsuch as administrator of the Environmental Protection Agency with William Ruckelshaus. See Dessler and Parson, *supra* note 1, at 115.

21. *Id.* at 117.

22. See Maxwell and Weiner, *supra* note 19, at 26.

23. *Id.*

24. *Id.*
25. Benedick, *supra* note 9, at 33.
26. See Dessler and Parson, *supra* note 1, at 251.
27. *Id.* at 252.
28. *Id.* at 127.
29. See James Hammitt, "Stratospheric-Ozone Depletion," in *Economic Analyses at EPA* 131, 157 (Richard Morgenstern ed.) (Washington, D.C.: Resources for the Future, 1997).
30. *Id.*
31. *Id.*
32. See 133 Cong. Rec. S 7750 (June 5, 1987).
33. Dessler and Parson, *supra* note 1, at 135–36.
34. See Benedick, *supra* note 9, at 63.
35. See Stephen J. DeCanio, "Economic Analysis, Environmental Policy, and Intergenerational Justice in the Reagan Administration: The Case of the Montreal Protocol," 3 *International Environmental Agreements: Politics, Law & Economics* 299, 302 (2003); Hammitt, *supra* note 29, at 155.
36. See Hammitt, *supra* note 29, at 68.
37. See Maxwell and Weiner, *supra* note 19, at 27.
38. Percival et al., *supra* note 2, at 1052.
39. Barrett, *supra* note 3, at 146.
40. *Id.* at 231.
41. *Id.* at 237.
42. For example, any monetary valuation of a human life is highly controversial, as is the adoption of a uniform number. For discussion, see DeCanio, *supra* note 35, at 304–06; Cass R. Sunstein, *Laws of Fear: Beyond the Precautionary Principle* (New York: Cambridge University, 2005).
43. An informative capsule summary can be found in Dessler and Parson, *supra* note 1, at 240–41.
44. *Id.* at 33.
45. See 143 Cong. Rec. S 5622 (June 12, 1997), available at http://www.nationalcenter.org/KyotoSenate.html.
46. George W. Pring, "The United States Perspective" in *Kyoto: From Principles to Practice,* 185, 196 (Peter D. Cameron and Donald Zillman eds.) (New York: Kluwer Law International, 2001).
47. *Id.* at 198.
48. See Richard Benedick, "Morals and Myths: A Commentary on Global Climate Policy," 109 *WZB-Mitteilungen Heft* 15, 15–16 (Sept. 2005).
49. *Pring, supra note 46,* at 205.
50. See Benedick, *supra* note 48, at 16.
51. See Percival et al., *supra* note 2, at 1072–73; Matthew Vespa, "Climate

Change 2001: Kyoto at Bonn and Marrakech," 29 *Ecology Law Quarterly* 395 (2002).

52. Percival et al., *supra* note 2, at 1073.

53. For illuminating discussions, see Nordhaus and Joseph Boyer, *Warming the World: Economic Models of Global Warming* (Cambridge: MIT Press, 2000); William R. Cline, "Climate Change," in *Global Crises, Global Solutions* (Bjørn Lomborg ed.) (Cambridge: Cambridge University Press, 2004). Frank Ackerman and Ian Finlayson, *The Economics of Inaction on Climate Change: A Sensitivity Analysis* (forthcoming 2007). See also P. Watkiss et al., "The Impacts and Costs of Climate Change," (Brussels: European Commission DG Environment, (September 2005), available at http://ec.europa.eu/environment/climat/pdf/final_report2.pdf; Claudia Kemfert, "Global Climate Protection: Immediate Action Will Avert High Costs," 1 *DIW Weekly Report:* 135 (2005). For a general account of current and future changes, see "Climate Change 2007: The Physical Science Basis, Summary for Policymakers," available at http://www.ipcc.ch/SPM13apr07.pdf. The authors project a warming of about 0.2° C per decade for the next two decades. *Id.* at 12. They also found that even if greenhouse gas concentrations were stabilized, "anthropgenic warming and sea level rise would continue for centuries due to the time scales associated with climate processes and feedbacks." *Id.* at 16.

54. Pring, *supra* note 46, at 194.

55. *Id.* at 196.

56. Wharton Economic Forecasting Associates, "Global Warming: The High Cost of the Kyoto Protocol, National and State Impacts" (1998), available at http://www.heartland.org/pdf/11399.pdf.

57. *Id.*

58. Nordhaus and Boyer, *supra* note 53. A relatively optimistic view of the costs of emissions reductions can be found in "Climate Change 2007: Mitigation of Climate Change, Summary for Policymakers," available at http://www.ipcc.ch/SPM040507.pdf. In the view of the authors, significant opportunities exist for mitigation with "net negative costs," meaning options with benefits, such as reduced energy costs, exceed their costs, not including the benefits of avoided climate change. *Id.* at 12. The median reduction in global Gross Domestic Product by 2030, for certain levels of stabilization, is below 1 percent. *Id.* at 16. It is reasonable, however, to think that this production is based on highly optimistic assumptions.

59. Nordhaus and Boyer, *supra* note 53.

60. For valuable overviews, see *Avoiding Dangerous Climate Change* (Hans Joachim Scellnhuber et al. eds.) (Cambridge: Cambridge University Press,

2006); Richard Tol, "The Marginal Damage Costs of Carbon Dioxide Emissions: An Assessment of the Uncertainties," 33 *Energy Policy* 2064 (2005); Nordhaus and Boyer, *supra* note 53; Cline, *supra* note 53; Ackerman and Finlayson, *supra* note 53.

61. Percival et al., *supra* note 2, at 1058. According to one account of current trends, warming of 2° to 3° C is anticipated within the next fifty years, see *Stern Review: The Economics of Climate Change* at vi (2006), available at http://www.hm-treasury.gov.uk/independent_reviews/stern_review_economics_climate_change/sternreview_index.cfm, and in the longer term, there is a greater than 50% change of warming in excess of 5° C. *Id.*

62. See Tol, *supra* note 60; Houghton, *supra* note 2; *Stern Review, supra* note 61, at 55–84. For a consensus account, see "Climate Change 2007: Impacts, Adaptation, and Vulnerability, Summary for Policymakers," available at http://www.ipcc.ch/SPM13apr07.pdf. The authors conclude that "many natural systems are being affected by" climate change, *id.* at 1, and that future effects are likely to include "an unprecedented combination of climate change, associated disturbances (e.g., flooding, wildfire, insects, ocean acidification, and other global change drivers," including pollution, *id.* at 5. Adverse health effects are projected for millions of people, including increased deaths as a result of heat waves, floods, storms, fires and droughts. *Id.* at 7. Particularly severe effects are expected for Africa, including adaptation costs of "at least 5–10% of Gross Domestic Product," *id.*

63. See Richard A. Posner, *Catastrophe: Risk and Response* (New York: Oxford University Press, 2005); *Avoiding Dangerous Climate Change, supra* note 60.

64. See *Stern Review, supra* note 61, at v, 152–65, 195 (exploring probabilities of very bad outcomes); Nordhaus and Boyer, *supra* note 53 (projecting a catastrophic risk of between 2 percent and 6 percent); Peter Challenor et al., "Towards the Probability of Rapid Climate Change," in *Avoiding Dangerous Climate Change, supra* note 60, at 55, 61 (projecting a risk of abrupt climate change, which is potentially catastrophic, at 30–40 percent).

65. See Nordhaus and Boyer, *supra* note 53, at 130–32 ($4 trillion): see also Posner, *supra* note 63, at 44 (noting but raising doubts about estimates of $4 trillion or $5 trillion). For a much more recent and systematic effort, see *Stern Review, supra* note 61, at i–xi (suggesting an anticipated 5% to 10% loss in global GDP from 5° to 6° C warming, with a 10% loss in poor nations). For a critical response, suggesting that the loss figures are inflated as a result of an unjustifiably low discount rate, can be found in William Nordhaus, "The *Stern Review* on the Economics of Climate Change" (November 17, 2006), available at http://

nordhaus.econ.yale.edu/SternReviewD2.pdf. Richard Tol has produced a number of highly illuminating papers on the costs and benefits of climate change and mitigation strategies; for a collection, see http://www.uni-hamburg.de/Wiss/FB/15/Sustainability/tol.html#publications.

66. See Posner, *supra* note 63, at 44.

67. See Ackerman and Finlayson, *supra* note 53.

68. See Houghton, *supra* note 2, at 188.

69. Kemfert, *supra* note 53; *Stern Review, supra* note 61, at x (projecting total losses between 5% and 20% of world GDP).

70. Nordhaus and Boyer, *supra* note 53, at 152.

71. See Cline, *supra* note 53, at 29.

72. See Nordhaus and Boyer, *supra* note 53, at 96–97. A pessimistic account for North American can be found at "Climate Change 2007: Impacts, Adaptation, and Vulnerability, Summary for Policymakers," available at http://www.ipcc.ch/SPM13apr07.pdf, at 9–10. The full report, justifying that pessimism, can be found at http://www.ipcc.ch.

73. See Olivier Deschenes and Michael Greenstone, "The Economic Impacts of Climate Change: Evidence from Agricultural Output and Random Fluctuations of Weather" (2006), available at http://www.aei-brookings.org/publications/abstract.php?pid=1031; see also note 77 in Chapter 1 for other predictions of economic impacts.

74. See Nordhaus and Boyer, *supra* note 53. Compare the discussion in *Stern Review, supra* note 61, at 130 (noting possible effects ranging from a loss of 1.2% GDP to a gain of 1% GDP from 3° C warming, and emphasizing that this assessment does not take full account of the effects of extreme weather events such as hurricanes).

75. Compiled on the basis of Nordhaus and Boyer 53, *supra* note, at 156–67.

76. See Posner, *supra* note 63. There is an analogous puzzle here about why California, in 2006, unilaterally adopted a significant restriction on greenhouse gases, roughly parallel to the restrictions in the Kyoto Protocol. See Felicity Barringer, "In Gamble, California Tries to Curb Greenhouse Gases," *New York Times,* Sept. 15, 2006, at p. 1. I return to this puzzle below.

77. See Ackerman and Finlayson, *supra* note 53. For a demonstrtion of how much turns on the discount rate, see William Nordhaus, "The Stern Review on the Economics of Climate Change" (2006), available at http://nordhaus.econ.yale.edu/recent_stuff.html.

78. Cline, *supra* note 53, at 31, suggests that the Kyoto Protocol would deliver worldwide benefits in excess of costs, while also suggesting that it accomplishes relatively little in reducing warming.

79. All data taken from: UNFCCC, Key GHG Data: Greenhouse Gas (GHG) Emissions Data for 1990–2003 submitted to the UNFCCC, at 16–17 (November 2005).
80. *Id.*
81. See "Rich Countries' Greenhouse Gas Emissions Ballooning," available at http://www.commondreams.org/headlines03/0610–07.htm.
82. UNFCCC, *supra* note 79, at 14.
83. See "Rich Countries' Greenhouse Gas Emissions Ballooning," *supra* note 81.
84. See Barrett, *supra* note 3. See Jack Goldsmith and Eric A. Posner, *The Limits of International Law* (Oxford: Oxford University Press, 2005); Jack Goldsmith, "Liberal Democracy and Cosmopolitan Duty," 54 *Stanford Law Review* 1667 (2003). See Maxwell and Weiner, *supra* note 19, at 37–38. See Wojciech Kopszuk et al., "The Limitations of Decentralized World Redistribution: An Optimal Taxation Approach," 30 *European Economic Review* 1051 (2005). I put to one side the possibility that the Kyoto Protocol could be defended as starting a process toward a better agreement, or that aggressive technology-forcing, on the part of the United States, might create innovation that would greatly help with greenhouse gas emissions. See Nordhaus and Boyer, *supra* note 53, at 175 (suggesting an international carbon tax, starting in the near term at under $15 per ton); Cline, *supra* note 53, at 37 (suggesting a higher carbon tax, starting at $150 per ton and increasing to $600 by 2100).
85. See Maxwell and Weiner, *supra* note 19, at 32–33.
86. See "Doing It Their Way," *The Economist* 22 (September 9–16, 2006) (reporting a shift in American opinion).
87. See Goldsmith and Posner, *supra* note 84. See Oona Hathaway and Ariel Lavinbuck, "Rationalism and Revisionism in International Law," 119 *Harvard Law Review* 1404 (2006).
88. See *Stern Review, supra* note 61, at 106 (noting significant vulnerability in China). Adverse effects for Asia are outlined in "Climate Change 2007: The Physical Science Basis, Summary for Policymakers," available at http://www.ipcc.ch/SPM13apr07.pdf.
89. Nordhaus and Boyer, *supra* note 53. More recent accounts can be found in "Climate Change 2007: Impacts, Adaptation, and Vulnerability, Summary for Policymakers," available at http://www.ipcc.ch/SPM13apr07.pdf, and in Stern Review, *supra* note 61.
90. Cline, *supra* note 53, and Ackerman and Finlayson, *supra* note 53, offer a picture of more serious monetized damage from climate change. Note also that Nordhaus and Boyer find that China and the United States are vulnerable to catastrophic climate change, with an expected GDP loss of 22.1% for both nations. Nordhaus and Boyer, *supra* note 53, at 90. A comprehensive treatment can be found in *Stern Review, supra* note 61, 104–06,

128–29. A general account can be found in "Climate Change 2007: Impacts, Adaptation, and Vulnerability," available at http://www.ipcc.ch/SPM13apr07.pdf, at 9–10.

91. See note 73 *supra.*

92. See "Doing it Their Way," *supra* note 86, at 22.

93. See Kevin A. Baumert et al., *Navigating the Numbers: Greenhouse Gas Data and International Climate Policy* 17–18 (World Resources Institute, 2005), available at http://www.oecd.org/dataoecd/28/43/36448807.pdf.

94. EIA, *International Energy Outlook 2006* at Table A10, available at http://www.eia.doe.gov/oiaf/ieo/pdf/ieoreftab_10.pdf.

95. See Jiahua Pan, "Common But Differentiated Commitments: A Practical Approach to Engaging Large Developing Emitters under L20" at 3 (September 20–21, 2004) (on file with author) (referring to cumulative emissions but emphasizing period of 1990–2000, when consequences were widely known).

96. See Dale Jamieson, "Adaptation, Mitigation, and Justice," in *Perspective on Climate Change: Science, Economics, Politics, Ethics* 217 (Walter Sinnott-Armstrong and Richard Howarth eds.) (Oxford: Elsevier JAI, 2005); Julia Driver, "Ideal Decision Making and Green Virtues," in *id.* at 249. For general discussion, see J. Timmons Roberts and Bradley C. Parks, *A Climate of Injustice* (Cambridge: MIT Press, 2006).

97. See Pan, *supra* note 95, at 4: "Countries with higher levels of national income . . . would be expected to carry a higher burden of mitigation."

98. See Driver, *supra* note 96.

99. I have touched only lightly on complex enforcement problems; it may be that the Montreal Protocol is not a good model in this regard. For discussion, see Barrett, *supra* note 3; David Victor, *The Collapse of the Kyoto Protocol and the Struggle to Slow Global Warming* (Princeton: Princeton University Press, 2001).

100. See Alan Carlin, Global Climate Change: "Is There A Better Strategy Than Reducing Greenhouse Gas Emissions?" *U. Pennsylvania Law Review* (forthcoming 2007).

101. See Nordhaus and Boyer, *supra* note 53, at 123–44. See Sheila M. Olmstead and Robert N. Stavins, "An International Policy Architecture for the Post-Kyoto Era," 96 *American Economic Review Papers & Proceedings* 35, 35–36 (2006). Barrett, *supra* note 3, at 379. A recent projection estimates the social cost of carbon at an average value of $12 per ton of carbon dioxide, with a range of less than $0 to $95 per ton. See "Climate Change 2007: Impacts, Adaptation, and Vulnerability, Summary for Policymakers," available at http://www.ipcc.ch/SPM13apr07.pdf, at 16.

102. See the excellent brief discussion in Jagdish Bhagwati, "Global Warming Fund Could Succeed Where Kyoto Failed," *Financial Times* (Aug. 16,

2006), available at http://www.ft.com/cms/s/7849f5b2–2cc3–11db–9845–0000779e2340.html, on which I draw here.

103. See *id.*

104. See *Stern Review, supra* note 61, at i–xviii; Cline, *supra* note 53; Ackerman and Finlayson, *supra* note 53. A response to the *Stern Review,* suggesting that the damage figures come from an unjustifiably low discount rate, can be found in William Nordhaus, "The *Stern Review* on the Economics of Climate Change" (November 17, 2006), available at http://nordhaus.econ.yale.edu/SternReviewD2.pdf. Detailed accounts of the anticipated damage can be found in the 2007 reports of the International Panel on Climate Change, available at http://www.ipcc.ch/.

105. See A. Denny Ellerman et al., *Markets for Clean Air: The U.S. Acid Rain Program* (Cambridge: Cambridge University Press, 1999).

106. See Nordhaus and Boyer, *supra* note 53, at 159.

107. See *id.*

108. *Id.;* for a clear and helpful summary, see in Nordhaus, *supra* note 104.

109. A counterargument is presented in Posner, *supra* note 63, on the ground that a sudden regulatory "shock" might be necessary and desirable as a way of spurring innovation.

3. Catastrophe

1. Some of the best work on the precautionary principle has been done by Jonathan Wiener. See, e.g., Jonathan Wiener, "Whose Precaution After All? A Comment on the Comparison and Evolution of Risk Regulatory Systems," 13 *Duke J. Comparative & International Law* 207 (2003); Jonathan B. Wiener and Michael D. Rogers, "Comparing Precaution in the United States and Europe," 5 *J. Risk Research* 317 (2002). For a valuable and somewhat technical discussion, see generally Christian Gollier and Nicolas Treich, "Decision-Making under Scientific Uncertainty: The Economics of the Precautionary Principle," 27 *J. Risk & Uncertainty* 77 (2003).

2. Quoted in Indur M. Goklany, *The Precautionary Principle: A Critical Appraisal of Environmental Risk Assessment* 5 (Washington, D.C.: Cato Institute, 2001).

3. Quoted in Bjørn Lomborg, *The Skeptical Environmentalist: Measuring the Real State of the World* 348 (Cambridge: Cambridge University Press, 2001).

4. Goklany, *supra* note 2, at 16.

5. "Final Declaration of the First European Seas At Risk Conference," at Annex I (Copenhagen, 1994), available at http://www.seas-at-risk.org/1mages/Microsoft%20Word%20-%20SAR%20shadow%20declaration%20for%204NSC.pdf.

6. See Amartya Sen, *Development as Freedom* (New York: Random House, 1999); Martha Nussbaum, *Women and Human Development: The Capabilities Approach* (New York: Cambridge University Press, 2000).

7. See Cass R. Sunstein, *Legal Reasoning and Political Conflict* (New York: Oxford University Press, 1996).

8. See, e.g., *Precaution, Environmental Science, and Preventive Public Policy* (Joel Tickner ed.) (Washington, D.C.: Island Press, 2003). This section draws extensively from Cass R. Sunstein, "Beyond the Precautionary Principle," 151 *U. Pennsylvania Law Review* 1003 (2003).

9. See Julian Morris, "Defining the Precautionary Principle," in *Rethinking Risk and the Precautionary Principle* 1–19 (Julian Morris ed.) (Oxford: Butterworth-Heinemann, 2000).

10. *Id.* A strong version is defended in Carolyn Raffensperger and Peter L. deFur, "Implementing the Precautionary Principle: Rigorous Science and Solid Ethics," 5 *Human & Ecological Risk Assessment* 933, 934 (1999).

11. See Lomborg, *supra* note 3, at 349 (explaining how misplaced "certainty" about the absence of harm played a key role in delaying preventative actions).

12. See http://www.wordspy.com/words/precautionaryprinciple.asp.

13. I explore this idea in detail in Cass R. Sunstein, *Laws of Fear: Beyond the Precautionary Principle* (Cambridge: Cambridge University Press, 2005), and I borrow in this section from the discussion there.

14. See Henry Grabowski and John Vernon, *The Regulation of Pharmaceuticals: Balancing the Benefits and Risks* 5–6 (Washington, D.C.: AEI, 1983); Kenneth I. Kaitin and Jeffrey S. Brown, "A Drug Lag Update," 29 *Drug Information J.* 361 (1995).

15. See Robert Percival et al., *Environmental Regulation* 1122–23 (Boston: Aspen, 2003).

16. See Judith P. Kelly et al., "Risk of Breast Cancer According to Use of Antidepressants, Phenothiazines, and Antihistamines," 150 *American J. Epidemiology* 861 (1999); C. R. Sharpe et al., "The Effects of Tricyclic Antidepressants on Breast Cancer Risk," 86 *British J. Cancer* 92 (2002).

17. Maurice Tubiana, "Radiation Risks in Perspective: Radiation-Induced Cancer among Cancer Risks" 39 *Radiation & Environmental Biophysics* 3, 8–10 (2000).

18. *Id.* For some counterevidence in an important context, see Lennart Hardell et al., "Further Aspects on Cellular and Cordless Telephones and Brain Tumours," 22 *International J. Oncology* 399 (2003) (discussing evidence of an association between cellular telephones and cancer).

19. See Benoit Morel et al., "Pesticide Resistance, the Precautionary Principle, and the Regulation of Bt Corn: Real Option and Rational Option Approaches to Decisionmaking," in *Battling Resistance to Antibiotics and*

Pesticides 184–86 (Ramanan Laxminarayan ed.) (Washington, D.C.: Resources for the Future, 2003).

20. See Kym Anderson and Chantal Nielsen, "Golden Rice and the Looming GMO Debate: Implications for the Poor" (2004), available at http://papers.ssrn.com/sol3/papers.cfm?abstract_id=508463.

21. See *id.;* see also Goklany, *supra* note 2, at 30–41 (discussing environmental and health benefits of engineered crops).

22. Ralph Keeney, "Mortality Risks Induced by Economic Expenditures," 10 *Risk Analysis* 147 (1990) (explaining results that "suggest some expensive regulations and programs intended to save lives may actually lead to increased fatalities"); Randall Lutter and John F. Morrall III, "Health-Health Analysis: A New Way to Evaluate Health and Safety Regulation," 8 *J. Risk & Uncertainty* 43, 49 table 1 (1994).

23. See Keeney, *supra* note 22, at 155.

24. Robert W. Hahn et al., *Do Federal Regulations Reduce Mortality?* 7 (Washington, D.C.: AEI, 2000).

25. See Kenneth S. Chapman and Govind Hariharan, "Do Poor People Have a Stronger Relationship between Income and Mortality Than the Rich? Implications of Panel Data for Health-Health Analysis," 12 *J. Risk & Uncertainty* 51, 58–63 (1996).

26. See Lutter and Morrall, *supra* note 22.

27. See David Vogel, "The Hare and the Tortoise Revisited: The New Politics of Consumer and Environmental Regulation in Europe," 33 *British J. Political Science* 557, 570–71 (2003) (attributing Europe's increased enthusiasm for precautionary regulation to a sense of urgency created by past regulatory failures).

28. See Wiener and Rogers, *supra* note 1.

29. See Poul Harremoës, *The Precautionary Principle in the 20th Century: Late Lessons from Early Warnings* (London: Earthscan Publications, 2002).

30. Allan Mazur, *True Warnings and False Alarms* 2 (Washington, D.C.: AEI, 2004).

31. *Id.* at 97.

32. See Richard H. Thaler, *Quasi Rational Economics* 143 (New York: Russell Sage Foundation, 1991) (finding that "losses loom larger than gains"); Daniel Kahneman, Jack L. Knetsch, and Richard H. Thaler, "Experimental Tests of the Endowment Effect and the Coase Theorem," 98 *J. Political Economy* 1325, 1328 (1990); Colin Camerer, "Individual Decision Making," in *The Handbook of Experimental Economics* 587, 665–70 (John H. Kagel and Alvin E. Roth, eds.) (Princeton, N.J.: Princeton University Press, 1995).

33. See, e.g., Frank Ackerman and Lisa Heinzerling, *Priceless: On Knowing the*

Price of Everything and the Value of Nothing 230 (New York: New Press, 2004).

34. 42 U.S.C. § 7409(b)(1). See *American Petroleum Institute v. Costle*, 665 F.2d 1176, 1186 (D.C. Cir. 1981) ("In setting margins of safety the Administrator need not regulate only the known dangers to health, but may 'err' on the side of overprotection by setting a fully adequate margin of safety."").

35. See Matthew E. Kahn, "The Beneficiaries of Clean Air Act Regulation," 24 *Regulation* 34, 37 (Spring 2001).

36. See Goklany, *supra* note 2, at 13–27; Cass R. Sunstein, *Risk and Reason: Safety, Law and the Environment* 14 (New York: Cambridge University Press, 2002).

37. See Goklany, *supra* note 2, at 55.

38. See Elke Weber et al., "Predicting Risk-Sensitivity in Humans and Lower Animals: Risk As Variance or Coefficient of Variation," 111 *Psychological Review* 430 (2004).

39. On the other hand, we can often find risks of such ascertainable probabilities, see Richard Wilson and Edmund Crouch, *Risk-Benefit Analysis* (Cambridge: Harvard University Press, 2001).

40. One hundred and four were at the University of Alabama Law School and seventy two were at the University of Chicago Law School.

41. Daniel J. Fiorino, "Technical and Democratic Values in Risk Analysis," 9 *Risk Analysis* 293, 295 (1989).

42. *Id.* at 295. See also J. D. Robinson, M. D. Higgins, and P. K. Bolyard, "Assessing Environmental Impacts on Health: A Role for Behavioral Science," 4 *Environmental Impact Assessment Review* 41, 48–49 (1983).

43. See generally *The Social Amplification of Risk* (Nick Pidgeon et al. eds.) (Cambridge: Cambridge University Press, 2003).

44. See Gerd Gigerenzer, "Out of the Frying Pan Into the Fire: Behavioral Reactions to Terrorist Attacks," 26 *Risk Analysis* 347 (2006).

45. Daniel Kahneman and Amos Tversky, "Prospect Theory: An Analysis of Decision Under Risk," in *Choices, Values, and Frames* 17, 28–38 (Daniel Kahneman and Amos Tversky eds.) (New York: Cambridge University Press, 2001); Amos Tversky and Daniel Kahneman, "Advances in Prospect Theory: Cumulative Representations of Uncertainty," in *id.* at 44, 64–65.

46. See *id.*

47. On these issues, see Duncan Luce and Howard Raiffa, *Games and Decisions* 20–21 (New York: Wiley, 1957).

48. See George Akerlof and William T. Dickens, "The Economic Consequences of Cognitive Dissonance," in *An Economic Theorist's Book of Tales* (New York: Cambridge University Press, 1984).

49. See W. Kip Viscusi and Joel Huber, "Hyperbolic Discounting of Public Goods," NBER Working Paper 11935 (2006).

50. W. Kip Viscusi, "Rational Discounting for Regulatory Analysis," *U. Chicago Law Review* (forthcoming 2007).

51. Frank H. Knight, *Risk, Uncertainty, and Profit* (Boston: Houghton Mifflin Co., 1933); see also Luce and Raiffa, *supra* note 47, 275–86.

52. See Knight, *supra* note 51; Paul Davidson, "Is Probability Theory Relevant for Uncertainty? A Post-Keynesian Perspective," 5 *J. Economic Perspectives* 129 (1991). Some people object that uncertainty does not exist because it is always possible for decision-makers to produce probability assignments by proposing a series of lotteries over possible outcomes; but such assignments have no epistemic credentials if not rooted in either theory or repeated experiences, and many risk-related problems, such as those involving global warming, are in that category. I take up this point in detail below.

53. On ignorance and precaution, see Poul Harremoës, "Ethical Aspects of Scientific Incertitude in Environmental Analysis and Decision Making," 11 *J. Cleaner Production* 705 (2003).

54. For a technical treatment of the possible rationality of maximin, see Kenneth Arrow and Leonid Hurwicz, "An Optimality Criterion for Decision-Making Under Ignorance," in *Uncertainty and Expectations in Economics: Essays in Honor of G. L. S. Shackle* (C. F. Carter and J. L. Ford eds.) (Oxford: Blackwell, 1972); for a nontechnical overview, see Jon Elster, *Explaining Technical Change* 185–207 (Cambridge: Cambridge University Press, 1983).

55. See John C. Harsanyi, "Morality and the Theory of Rational Behavior," in *Utilitarianism and Beyond* 40 (Amartya Sen and Bernard Williams eds.) (Cambridge: Cambridge University Press, 1982).

56. See Richard A. Musgrave, "Maximin, Uncertainty, and the Leisure Trade-Off," 88 *Quarterly J. Economics* 625, 626–28 (1974).

57. See, e.g., Elster, *supra* note 54, at 188–205.

58. See Stephen Gardiner, "A Core Precautionary Principle," 14 *J. Political Philosophy* 33 (2006). For the work on which Gardiner draws, see John Rawls, *A Theory of Justice* 132–39 (Cambridge: Harvard University Press, rev. ed., 1999).

59. *Id.* at 134.

60. *Id.* Rawls draws in turn on William Fellner, *Probability and Profit: A Study of Economic Behavior along Bayesian Lines* 140–42 (Homewood, Ill.: R. D. Irwin, 1965). He offers a somewhat revised defense of maximin in John Rawls, "Some Reasons for the Maximin Criterion," 64 *American Economic Review* 141 (May 1974).

61. See Elster, *supra* note 54, at 203.

62. See Richard T. Woodward and Richard C. Bishop, "How to Decide When Experts Disagree: Uncertainty-Based Choice Rules in Environmental Policy," 73 *Land Economics* 492, 505 (1997).

63. See, e.g., Musgrave, *supra* note 56; Kenneth J. Arrow, "Some Ordinalist-Utilitarian Notes on Rawls' *Theory of Justice*," 70 *J. Philosophy* 245 (1973); J. C. Harsanyi, "Can the Maximin Principle Serve as a Basis for Morality? A Critique of John Rawls' Theory," 69 *American Political Science Review* 594 (1975).

64. Musgrave, *supra* note 56, at 627.

65. See Milton Friedman, *Price Theory* 282 (Chicago: Aldine Pub. Co., 1976). See also Jack Hirshleifer and John G. Riley, *The Analytics of Uncertainty and Information* 10 (Cambridge: Cambridge University Press, 1992): "In this book we disregard Knight's distinction, which has proved to be a sterile one. For our purposes risk and uncertainty mean the same thing. It does not matter, we contend, whether an 'objective' classification is or is not possible. For, we will be dealing throughout with a 'subjective' probability concept (as developed especially by Savage, 1954): probability is simply degree of belief . . . [Because we never know true objective probabilities, d]ecision-makers are . . . never in Knight's world of risk but instead always in his world of uncertainty. That the alternative approach, assigning probabilities on the basis of subjective degree of belief, is a workable and fruitful procedure will be shown constructively throughout this book. For the purposes of the analysis by Hirshleifer and Riley, the assignment of subjective probabilities may well be the best approach. But the distinction between risk and uncertainty is not sterile when regulators are considering what to do but lack information about the probabilities associated with various outcomes."

66. See Stephen F. LeRoy and Larry D. Singell, Jr., "Knight on Risk and Uncertainty," 95 *J. Political Economy* 394 (1987) (arguing, against many critics, that Knight's work supported the idea of subjective probabilities). For a clear explanation of why uncertainty exists, see Elster, *supra* note, at 193–99, 199 ("One could certainly elicit from a political scientist the subjective probability that he attaches to the prediction that Norway in the year 3000 will be a democracy rather than a dictatorship, but would anyone even contemplate acting on the basis of this numerical magnitude?").

67. See Elster, *supra* note 54, at 195–99.

68. *Id.*

69. John Maynard Keynes, *A Treatise on Probability* 214 (London: Macmillan and Co., 1921).

70. *Id.*

71. See Henry Willis et al., *Estimating Terrorism Risk* 17 (Santa Monica: Rand, 2005).

72. Richard A. Posner, *Catastrophe: Risk and Response* 49–50 (New York: Oxford University Press, 2005). Judge Posner's view seems increasingly out of date, with current efforts to generate probabilities for various climate change scenarios. See, e.g., Nicholas Stern, *The Economics of Climate Change: The Stern Review* 161–89 (Cambridge: Cambridge University Press, 2007).

73. See William D. Nordhaus, "Expert Opinion on Climatic Change," 82 *American Scientist* 45, 47 (1994).

74. See *Stern Review: The Economics of Climate Change* (2006), available at http://www.hm-treasury.gov.uk/independent_reviews/stern_review_economics_climate_change/sternreview_index.cfm; John Houghton, *Global Warming: The Complete Briefing* (Cambridge: Cambridge University Press, 3d ed., 2004).

75. See Daniel Ellsberg, "Risk, Ambiguity, and the Savage Axioms," 75 *Quarterly J. Economics* 643, 651 (1961).

76. See Luce and Raiffa, *supra* note 47, at 284.

77. See *id.;* Isaac Levi, "On Indeterminate Probabilities," 71 *J. Philosophy* 391 (1974).

78. One hundred and seventy-three law students were surveyed; seventy-one were from the University of Chicago, and one hundred and two were from the University of Alabama. Interestingly, the answers from the two groups were essentially identical.

79. See, e.g., Arrow and Hurwicz, *supra* note 54 (suggesting the rationality of either maximin or maximax (maximizing the best-case scenario)). See, e.g., Luce and Raiffa, *supra* note 47, 286–97.

80. See Adrian Vermeule, *Judging Under Uncertainty* 173–75 (Cambridge: Harvard University Press, 2006); Elinor Mason, "Consequentialism and Principle of Indifference," 6 *Utilitas* 316 (2004).

81. See Mason, *supra* note 80.

82. See Luce and Raiffa, *supra* note 47, at 286–97.

4. Irreversibility

1. See W. David Montgomery and Anne E. Smith, "Global Climate Change and the Precautionary Principle," 6 *Human & Ecological Risk Assessment* 399, 400 (2000). In its 2007 report, the International Panel on Climate Change offered a range of best estimates, from various scenarios, of between 1.8° C and 4.0° C (3.2–7.2° F) warming by 2100. See "Climate Change 2007: The Physical Science Basis, Summary for Policymakers," available at http://www.ipcc.ch/SPM13apr07.pdf, at 13. Notably, constant year 2000 concentrations would produce 0.6° C warming by 2100.

2. See generally Benoit Morel et al., "Pesticide Resistance, the Precautionary

Principle, and the Regulation of Bt Corn: Real Option and Rational Option Approaches to Decisionmaking," in *Battling Resistance to Antibiotics and Pesticides* 184 (Ramanan Laxminarayan ed.) (Washington, D.C.: Resources for the Future, 2003) (proposing option theory as an analytical framework for the Precautionary Principle and applying that framework to the issue of commercializing Bt corn); Justus Wesseler, "Resistance Economics of Transgenic Crops under Uncertainty: A Real Options Approach," in *id.* at 214 (discussing pest resistance as an irreversible cost of transgenic crops).

3. See Scott Farrow, "Using Risk-Assessment, Benefit-Cost Analysis, and Real Options to Implement a Precautionary Principle," 24 *Risk Analysis* 727, 728 (2004).

4. See, e.g., Robert Mendelsohn, "Perspective Paper 1.1," in *Global Crises, Global Solutions* 44, 47 (Bjørn Lomborg ed.) (Cambridge: Cambridge University Press, 2004); Wilfred Beckerman, *Small Is Stupid* 102–03 (London: Duckworth, 1995). The cautious approach of the Bush administration can be understood though not defended in this light. See "Global Climate Change Policy Book" (Feb. 2002), available at www.whitehouse.gov/news/releases/2002/02/climatechange.html; Chuck Hagel and Frank Murkowski, "High Costs of Kyoto," *Washington Post,* Jan. 29, 2000, at A17. Nordhaus and Boyer find, in an admittedly dated discussion, that extremely little is lost by a ten-year delay in emissions reductions. See William D. Nordhaus and Joseph Boyer, *Warming the World: Economic Models of Global Warming* 127 (Cambridge: MIT Press, 2000) (describing the net loss as "trivially small"). For a technical discussion, see Alistair Ulph and David Ulph, "Global Warming, Irreversibility and Learning," 107 *Economic J.* 636 (1997).

Despite the complexities here, recent evidence does suggest that evidence of serious harm is unmistakably clear and that waiting and research are exceedingly difficult to defend. See "Climate Change 2007: The Physical Science Basis, Summary for Policymakers," available at http://www.ipcc.ch/SPM13apr07.pdf, at 5; Nicholas Stern, *The Economics of Climate Change: The Stern Review* (Cambridge: Cambridge University Press, 2007). William Nordhaus, "The Stern Review on the Economics of Climate Change" (2006), available at http://nordhaus.econ.yale.edu/recent_stuff.html, urges far less aggressive measures than those urged by Stern, but he reflects the consensus that waiting and research are unjustified.

5. See Graciela Chichilnisky and Geoffrey Heal, "Global Environmental Risks," 7 *J. Economic Perspectives* 65, 80 (1993).

6. See David A. Dana, "Existence Value and Federal Preservation Regulation," 28 *Harvard Environmental Law Review* 343, 345 (2004); Charles J.

Cicchetti and Louis J. Wilde, "Uniqueness, Irreversibility, and the Theory of Nonuse Values," *American J. Agricultural Economics* 1111, 1121, 1121–22 (1992).

7. See *Ohio v. U.S. Department of the Interior*, 880 F.2d 432, 464 (D.C. Cir. 1989).

8. Cicchetti and Wilde, *supra* note 6, at 1122 (noting Weisbrod's analogy of such amenities to public goods, in that "individuals who may never purchase the commodity still hold a value for the option to do so"). The independent use of option value is, however, challenged in various places. See, e.g., A. Myrick Freeman III, *The Measurement of Environmental and Resource Values* 249–51 (Washington, D.C.: Resources for the Future, 2003) (suggesting that "what has been called an option value is really just the algebraic difference between the expected values of two different points on a WTP [willingness to pay] locus").

9. See *Ohio v. U.S. Department of the Interior*, 880 F.2d 432, 464 (D.C. Cir. 1989).

10. See, e.g., 60 Fed. Reg. 29914, 29928 (June 6, 1995); 60 Fed. Reg. 28210 (May 30, 1995); 59 Fed. Reg. 1062, 1078 (January 7, 1994). But see 69 Fed. Reg. 68444 (November 24, 2004) (doubting whether option value should be recognized as separate from other values).

11. See Frank Ackerman and Lisa Heinzerling, *Priceless: On Knowing the Price of Everything and the Value of Nothing* 185 (New York: New Press, 2004).

12. For a helpful overview, see Richard C. Bishop, "Option Value: An Exposition and Extension," 58 *Land Economics* 1 (1982).

13. See Tom Copeland and Vladimir Antikarov, *Real Options: A Practitioner's Guide* 12–13 (London: Texere, 2001).

14. See Richard Brealey and Stewart Myers, *Principles of Corporate Finance* 565 (Boston: McGraw-Hill, 2003).

15. See generally Cass R. Sunstein, *One Case at a Time* (Cambridge: Harvard University Press, 1999).

16. See Kenneth J. Arrow and Anthony C. Fisher, "Environmental Preservation, Uncertainty, and Irreversibility," 88 *Quarterly J. Economics* 312 (1974). This essay has produced a large literature, some of it summarized and cited in Anthony C. Fisher, "Uncertainty, Irreversibility, and the Timing of Climate Policy" (2001), available at http://stephenschneider.stanford.edu/Publications/PDF_Papers/timingFfisher.pdf.

17. Arrow and Fisher, supra note 16, at 319.

18. See Anthony C. Fisher, "Uncertainty, Irreversibility, and the Timing of Climate Policy" 9 (2001), available at http://stephenschneider.stanford.edu/Publications/PDF_Papers/timingFfisher.pdf. A helpful treat-

ment can also be found in Robert S. Pindyck, "Uncertainty in Environmental Economics" (2006), available at http://www.aei-brookings.org/publications/abstract.php?pid=1142.

19. See Richard Posner, *Catastrophe: Risk and Response* 161–62 (New York: Oxford University Press, 2005). A more technical discussion to the same effect is contained in Chichilnisky and Heal, *supra* note 5, emphasizing the need for a distinctive approach to "risks that are poorly understood, endogenous, collective, and irreversible." *Id.* at 67. For a more detailed treatment of option value and irreversibility, see *id.* at 76–84.

20. Posner, *supra* note 19, at 161–62.

21. *Id.* at 162.

22. See Chichilnisky and Heal, *supra* note 5, at 76.

23. See Avinash K. Dixit and Robert S. Pindyck, *Investment Under Uncertainty* 6 (Princeton: Princeton University Press, 1994) ("When a firm makes an irreversible investment expenditure, it exercises, or 'kills,' its option to invest. It gives up the possibility of waiting for new information to arrive that might affect the desirability or timing of the expenditure, and this lost option value is an opportunity cost that must be included as part of the investment.").

24. *Id.*

25. See, e.g., Ling Zhong, "Note, Nuclear Energy: China's Approach Towards Addressing Global Warming," 12 *Georgetown International Environmental Law Review* 493 (2000). It is of course possible to urge nations to reduce their reliance on coal or nuclear power and move instead toward alternatives that would be preferable on risk-related grounds, such as solar power. For general discussion, see *Renewable Energy: Power for a Sustainable Future* (Godfrey Boyle ed.) (Oxford: Oxford University Press, 1996); Allan Collinson, *Renewable Energy: Facing the Future* (London: Cloverleaf, 1991); Dr. Dan E. Arvizu, "Advanced Energy Technology and Climate Change Policy," 2 *Florida Coastal Law J.* 435 (2001). But these alternatives pose problems of their own, involving feasibility and expense.

26. Fisher, *supra* note 16, at 11.

27. Good discussions can be found in Elizabeth Anderson, *Value in Ethics and Economics* (Cambridge: Harvard University Press, 1993); Joseph Raz, *The Morality of Freedom* (Oxford: Oxford University Press, 1985).

28. See remarks of Vernon L. Smith in *Global Crises, Global Solutions* 630, 635 (Bjørn Lomborg ed.) (Cambridge: Cambridge University Press, 2004).

29. Remarks of Thomas C. Schelling in *id.* at 627.

30. Remarks of Vernon L. Smith in *id.* at 630, 635.

31. See, e.g., William R. Cline, "Climate Change," in *id.* at 13, 56, 57. Cline

emphasizes that both the slowness of political processes and the gradual nature of climate change make it nearly impossible to make such changes "on a dime." *Id.*

32. See generally Juan Almendares, "Science, Human Rights, and the Precautionary Principle in Honduras," in *Precaution, Environmental Science, and Preventive Public Policy* 55 (Joel A. Tickner ed.) (Washington, D.C.: Island, 2003) (discussing advantages to Third World countries offered by the precautionary principle).

33. See, e.g., Jon Elster, *Ulysses and the Sirens: Studies in Rationality and Irrationality* (Cambridge: Cambridge University Press, rev. ed., 1986).

34. See David A. Dana, "A Behavioral Economic Defense of the Precautionary Principle," 97 *Northwestern University Law Review* 1315 (2003).

35. See, e.g., *Thomas v. Peterson*, 753 F.2d 754, 764 (9th Cir. 1985).

36. See *Save Our Ecosystems v. Clark*, 747 F.2d 1240, 1250 (9th Cir. 1984). For a general discussion, see Zygmunt J. B. Plater, "Statutory Violations and Equitable Discretion," 70 *California Law Review* 524 (1982).

37. *Weinberger v. Romero-Barcelo*, 456 U.S. 305 (1982).

38. *Amoco Production Co. v. Village of Gambell*, 480 U.S. 531 (1987).

39. *People of Village of Gambell v. Hodel*, 774 F.2d 1414, 1424 (9th Cir. 1985) (emphasis in original), rev'd in part, vacated in part, sub nom. *Amoco Production Co. v. Village of Gambell*, 480 U.S. 531 (1982).

40. For a general discussion, see Leslye A. Herrmann, "Injunctions for NEPA Violations: Balancing the Equalities," 59 *U. Chicago Law Review* 1263 (1992).

41. See, e.g., *New York v. NRC*, 550 F.2d 745, 762 (2d Cir. 1977); *Conservation Society v. Secretary of Transportation*, 508 F.2d 927, 933 (2d Cir. 1974); *United States v. 27.09 Acres of Land*, 737 F. Supp. 277, 283–84 (S.D.N.Y. 1990); *Stand Together Against Neighborhood Decay v. Board of Estimate*, 690 F. Supp. 1192, 1200 (E.D.N.Y. 1988).

42. See *Sierra Club v. Marsh*, 872 F.2d 497, 503–04 (1st Cir. 1989).

5. Money

1. The developments discussed in this paragraph are traced in Cass R. Sunstein, *Risk and Reason: Safety, Law and the Environment* (Cambridge: Cambridge University Press, 2002).

2. See Cass R. Sunstein, "The Arithmetic of Arsenic," in *id* at 153.

3. See Cass R. Sunstein, *The Cost-Benefit State: The Future of Regulatory Protection* 145 (Washington, D.C.: American Bar Association, 2002).

4. The best overview is W. Kip Viscusi and Joseph Aldy, "The Value of a Statistical Life: A Critical Review of Market Evidence Throughout the World," 27 *J. Risk & Uncertainty* 5 (2003).

5. See Richard L. Revesz, "Environmental Regulation, Cost-Benefit Analysis, and the Discounting of Human Lives," 99 *Columbia Law Review* 941, 962–74 (1999).

6. See Sunstein, *supra* note 1, at 177.

7. An especially valuable discussion of these issues can be found in Matthew Adler and Eric A. Posner, *New Foundations for Cost-Benefit Analysis* (Cambridge: Harvard University Press, 2006).

8. See Frank Ackerman and Lisa Heinzerling, *Priceless: On Knowing the Price of Everything and the Value of Nothing* (New York: New Press, 2004).

9. See Adam Burgess, *Cellular Phones, Public Fears, and a Culture of Precaution* (Cambridge: Cambridge University Press, 2004).

10. See Richard A. Posner, *Catastrophe: Risk and Response* (New York: Oxford University Press, 2004).

11. Ackerman and Heinzerling, *supra* note 8, at p. 234.

12. The most well-known is John F. Morrall III, "A Review of the Record," *Regulation* 25, 30, Table 4 (November/December 1986). For an updated treatment, see John F. Morrall III, "Saving Lives: A Review of the Record," 27 *J. Risk & Uncertainty* 221 (2003).

13. David M. Driesen, *The Economic Dynamics of Environmental Law* (Cambridge: MIT Press, 2003), offers a powerful criticism of cost-benefit analysis insofar as it offers a static account of both costs and benefits and fails to see that regulation and other forces often produce innovation, thus reducing the expense of environmental protection. I believe that this argument is best taken as a reason for skepticism about existing figures about likely costs, rather than as an attack on cost-benefit analysis as such. See Matthew Adler, "Cost-Benefit Analysis, Static Efficiency, and the Goals of Environmental Law," 31 *Boston College Environmental Affairs Law Review* 591 (2004).

14. John D. Leeth and John Ruser, "Compensating Wage Differentials for Fatal and Nonfatal Injury Risk by Gender and Race," 27 *J. Risk & Uncertainty* 257 (2003).

15. But see Howard Margolis, *Dealing with Risk* (Chicago: University of Chicago Press, 1999), for a challenge to this account of the lay/expert division in risk perceptions.

16. Note, however, that the "Not In My Backyard Syndrome"—known in the trade as NIMBY—suggests that many people will make self-serving judgments about the proper location of environmentally risky activities. This point is related to the suggestion, developed below, that people tend to become intuitive cost-benefit analysts when both the benefits and the costs of environmental regulation are on-screen.

17. Ackerman and Heinzerling, *supra* note 8, at 227.

18. A different set of issues is raised by the risks associated with use of cell phones while driving. Here there is much stronger evidence of serious hazards. For one overview, see Robert Hahn and James Prieger, "The Impact of Driver Cell Phone Use on Accidents" (July 2004), available at http://www.aei-brookings.org/publications/abstract.php?pid=806.

19. Burgess, *supra* note 9, at 1.

20. *Id.* at 2.

21. *Id.* at 88–89.

22. *Id.* at 222.

23. See Martin Rees, *Our Final Hour* 120 (New York: Basic Books, 2003).

24. See William Nordhaus and Joseph Boyer, *Warming the World* (Cambridge: MIT Press, 2000).

25. See Frank Ackerman and Ian Finlayson, *The Economics of Inaction on Climate Change: A Sensitivity Analysis* (forthcoming 2007).

26. Posner, *supra* note 10, at 221. There are, however, many current efforts to generate probabilities for various climate change scenarios. See, e.g., Nicholas Stern, *The Economics of Climate Change: The Stern Review* 161–189 (Cambridge: Cambridge University Press, 2007).

27. *Id.* at 222.

28. Ackerman and Heinzerling, *supra* note 8, at 193.

29. Burgess, *supra* note 9, at 272.

30. Price Fishback and Shawn Everett Kantor, *A Prelude to the Welfare State* (Chicago: University of Chicago Press, 1998).

31. See Allan Gibbard, "Risk and Value," in *Values at Risk* 97 (Douglas MacLean ed.) (Totowa, N.J.: Rowman & Allanheld, 1986), for a valuable discussion of how cost-benefit analysis might be taken as "a rough surrogate for expected total intrinsic-reward maximization." To the same general effect, defending CBA on welfare grounds, see Adler and Posner, *supra* note 7; Matthew Adler and Eric A. Posner, "Implementing Cost-Benefit Analysis When Preferences Are Distorted," 29 *J. Legal Studies* 1105 (2000); Matthew Adler and Eric A. Posner, "Rethinking Cost-Benefit Analysis," 109 *Yale Law J.* 167 (1999).

32. See Ronald Dworkin, *Sovereign Virtue* (Cambridge: Harvard University Press, 2002).

33. See Richard A. Epstein, "A Theory of Strict Liability," 2 *J. Legal Studies* 151 (1973); Richard Posner, *Economic Analysis of Law* 175–82 (New York: Aspen Publishers, 4th ed., 1992).

34. See William Bessette, *The Mild Voice of Reason* (Chicago: University of Chicago Press, 1992).

35. Amartya Sen, *Rationality and Freedom* 287 (Cambridge: Harvard University Press, 2001).

36. *Id.* at 289.
37. See Jon Elster, *Sour Grapes* (Cambridge: Cambridge University Press, 1983); Martha Nussbaum, *Women and Human Development* (Cambridge: Cambridge University Press, 2001).
38. See George A. Akerlof, *An Economic Theorist's Book of Tales* 123–37 (Cambridge: Cambridge University Press, 1984).
39. Daniel T. Gilbert and T. D. Wilson, "Miswanting," in *Thinking and Feeling: The Role of Affect in Social Cognition* 178 (Joseph P. Forgas ed.) (Cambridge: Cambridge University Press, 2000); Timothy D. Wilson and Daniel T. Gilbert, "Affective Forecasting," 35 *Advances in Experimental Social Psychology* 345 (June 2003).
40. For general discussion, see Daniel Kahneman, "A Psychological Perspective on Economics," 93 *American Economic Review Papers & Proceedings* 162 (2003); Daniel Kahneman et al., "Back to Bentham? Explorations of Experienced Utility," 112 *Quarterly J. Economics* 375, 379–80 (1997).
41. I develop this point in Cass R. Sunstein, *Laws of Fear: Beyond the Precautionary Principle* (New York: Cambridge University, 2005).
42. See *id.*
43. See Matthew E. Kahn, "The Beneficiaries of Clean Air Act Regulation," 24 *Regulation* 34 (Spring 2001).
44. See, e.g., Louis Kaplow and Steven Shavell, "Why the Legal System Is Less Efficient Than the Income Tax in Redistributing Income," 23 *J. Legal Studies* 667, 667 (1994).
45. *Id.* at 27–28.
46. Cf. Intergovernmental Panel on Climate Change, *Third Assessment Report: Climate Change 2001: Mitigation* 483 (finding that "[t]he VSL is generally lower in poor countries than in rich countries"), available at http://grida.no/climate/ipcc_tar/wg3.
47. See John Broome, "Cost-Benefit Analysis and Population," 29 *J. Legal Studies* 953, 957 (2000) (noting that this conclusion is a product of "a money-metric utility function to represent a person's preferences," an approach that Professor Broome rejects). In the easy cases, I suggest that a money-metric utility function is not absurd, and it is not quite absurd in the hard cases either. See Intergovernmental Panel on Climate Change, *supra* note 46, at 483: "The VSL is generally lower in poor countries than in rich countries, but it is considered unacceptable by many analysts to impose different values for a policy that has to be international in scope and decided by the international community. In these circumstances, analysts use average VSL and apply it to all countries. Of course, such a value is not what individuals would pay for the reduction in risk, but it is an 'equity adjusted' value, in which greater weight is given to the WTP of

lower income groups. On the basis of EU and US VSLs and a weighting system that has some broad appeal in terms of government policies towards income distribution, Eyre et al. (1998) estimate the average world VSL at around 1 million Euros (approximately US$1 million at 1999 exchange rates)."

6. The Future

1. For the 7% rate, see Office of Management and Budget, "Benefit-Cost Analysis of Federal Programs," 57 Fed. Reg. 53520 (Nov. 10, 1992); for a more recent suggestion that agencies use both 3% and 7%, see "Circular A-4" 33–34 (September 17, 2003), available at http://www.whitehouse.gov/omb/inforeg/regpol.html.

2. For an illuminating discussion, see Frank Ackerman and Ian Finlayson, *The Economics of Inaction on Climate Change: A Sensitivity Analysis* (forthcoming 2007). See also William Nordhaus, "The Stern Review on the Economics of Climate Change" (2006), available at http://nordhaus.econ.yale.edu/recent_stuff.html (showing immense importance of discount rate to value of emissions reductions).

3. *Corrosion Proof Fittings v. EPA*, 947 F.2d 1201 (5th Cir. 1991).

4. *Natural Resources Defense Council, Inc. v. Herrington*, 768 F.2d 1355, 1410–14 (D.C. Cir. 1985); *Northern California Power Agency v. FERC*, 37 F.3d 1517 (D.C. Cir. 1994).

5. See Robert W. Hahn, "The Economic Analysis of Regulation: A Response to the Critics," 71 *U. Chicago Law Review* 1021, 1026–27 (2004); John J. Donohue III, "Why We Should Discount the Views of Those Who Discount Discounting," 108 *Yale Law J.* 1901 (1998). Various positions are presented in *Discounting and Intergenerational Equity* 99, 100 (Paul R. Portney and John P. Weyant eds.) (Washington, D.C.: Resources for the Future, 1999), with recognition of some of the underlying complexities. See the introduction by Paul R. Portney and John P. Weyant, which stresses in particular "the unease even the best minds of the profession feel about discounting, due to the technical complexity of the issues and to their ethical ramifications," *id.* at 5. See also Robert S. Pindyck, "Uncertainty in Environmental Economics" (2006), available at http://www.aei-brookings.org/publications/abstract.php?pid=1142.

6. Tyler Cowen and Derek Parfit, "Against the Social Discount Rate," in *Justice Between Age Groups and Generations* 144, 148 (Peter Laslett and James S. Fishkin eds.) (New Haven: Yale University Press, 1992); Derek Parfit, *Reasons and Persons* 357 (Oxford: Oxford University Press, 1984). See Sidney Shapiro and Robert Glicksman, *Risk Regulation at Risk: Restoring a Pragmatic Approach* 118–19 (Stanford: Stanford University Press,

2003); Frank Ackerman and Lisa Heinzerling, "Pricing the Priceless," 150 *U. Pennsylvania Law Review* 1553, 1570–73 (2002); Frank Ackerman and Lisa Heinzerling, *Priceless: On Knowing the Price of Everything and the Value of Nothing* (New York: New Press, 2004). See Richard L. Revesz, "Environmental Regulation, Cost-Benefit Analysis, and the Discounting of Human Lives," 99 *Columbia Law Review* 941 (1999). Valuable discussions can be found in Daniel Farber, "From Here to Eternity: Environmental Law and Future Generations," 2003 *U. Illinois Law Review* 289 (2003); Daniel Farber, *Eco-Pragmatism: Making Sensible Environmental Decisions in an Uncertain World* (Chicago: University of Chicago Press, 1999).

7. See Richard W. Parker, "Grading the Government," 70 *U. Chicago Law Review* 1345, 1374 (2003).

8. See Ackerman and Heinzerling, "Pricing the Priceless," *supra* note 6, at 1571.

9. *Id.*

10. See David Pearce and R. Kelly Turner, *Economics of Natural Resources and the Environment* 223–24 (Baltimore: Johns Hopkins University Press, 1990).

11. Emmett B. Keeler and Shan Cretin, "Discounting of Life-Saving and Other Nonmonetary Effects," 29 *Management Science* 300 (1983). Ackerman and Heinzerling discuss this claim and reject it, see *Priceless, supra* note 6, at 193–94, in part on the ground that allowing numerous current deaths would be politically unacceptable; but the claim is one of the logical implications of refusing to discount, and the fact that it entails a politically unacceptable outcome does not mean that it is wrong.

12. John F. Morrall III, "Saving Lives: A Review of the Record," 27 *J. Risk & Uncertainty* 221 (2003).

13. See Kenneth J. Arrow et al., "Intertemporal Equity, Discounting, and Economic Efficiency," in *Climate Change 1995: Economic and Social Dimensions of Climate Change* 125 (J. P. Bruce et al. eds.) (Cambridge: Cambridge University Press, 1996); William R. Cline, "Discounting for the Very Long Term," in *Discounting and Intergenerational Equity, supra* note 5, at 131, 135, 137–39.

14. See Raymond J. Kopp and Paul R. Portney, "Mock Referenda and Intergenerational Decisionmaking," in *Discounting and Intergenerational Equity, supra* note 5, at 87.

15. *Id.*

16. Maureen L. Cropper et al., "Preferences for Life Saving Programs: How the Public Discounts Time and Age," 8 *J. Risk & Uncertainty* 243, 244, 254 (1993).

17. Shane Frederick, "Measuring Intergenerational Time Preference: Are Future Lives Valued Less?" 26 *J. Risk & Uncertainty* 1 (2003).

18. See Revesz, *supra* note 6.
19. Michael J. Moore and W. Kip Viscusi, "Discounting Environmental Health Risks: New Evidence and Policy Implications," 18 *J. Environmental Economics & Management* S-59, S-61 (1990).
20. 66 Fed. Reg. 6976, 7013 (January 22, 2001) (codified at 40 C.F.R. pts. 9, 141, and 142).
21. See Circular A-4, *supra* note 1, at 35.
22. See *id.*
23. See Revesz, *supra* note 6; Dora L. Costa and Matthew E. Kahn, "The Rising Price of Nonmarket Goods," 93 *American Economic Review Papers & Proceedings* 227, 229 tbl.1 (2003) (suggesting a likely current value of $12 million). In the context of arsenic regulation, the EPA also noted in its sensitivity analysis that the appropriate adjustment would increase the VSL from $6.1 million to $6.7 million. See 66 Fed. Reg. 6976, 7012 (Jan. 22, 2001) (codified at 40 C.F.R. pts. 9, 141, and 142). Note also that wealthier people might not merely be willing to spend more because they are wealthier; certain goods, such as environmental protection, might be especially appealing to wealthier people, whose preferences and tastes might change as a result of their relative wealth.
24. See remarks of Vernon Smith, in *Global Crises, Global Solutions* 630, 635 (Bjørn Lomborg ed.) (Cambridge: Cambridge University Press, 2004); remarks of Thomas Schelling, in *id.* at 627.
25. A good discussion can be found in Matthew Adler and Eric A. Posner, *New Foundations for Cost-Benefit Analysis* (Cambridge: Harvard University Press, 2006).
26. See Richard B. Howarth, "Against High Discount Rates," in *Perspectives on Climate Change: Science, Economics, Politics, Ethics* 99, 103–07 (Walter Sinnott-Armstrong and Richard B. Howarth eds.) (Oxford: Elsevier JAI, 2005).
27. See *id.*
28. Thomas Schelling, "Intergenerational Discounting," in *Discounting and Intergenerational Equity, supra* note 5, at 99, 100.
29. Edith Brown Weiss, "Intergenerational Equity: A Legal Framework for Global Environmental Change," in *Environmental Change and International Law: New Challenges and Dimensions* 385 (Edith Brown Weiss ed.) (Tokyo: United Nations University Press, 1991).
30. A principle of this sort underlies the illuminating discussion in Howarth, *supra* note 26.
31. John Rawls, *A Theory of Justice* 254 (Cambridge: Harvard University Press, rev. ed., 1999).
32. *Id.* at 258.

33. *Id.* at 274.
34. On these questions, see Derek Parfit, *supra* note 6.
35. See Schelling, *supra* note 28.
36. See Revesz, *supra* note 6, at 1009–1014; *Sustainable Development* (Julian Morris ed.) (London: Profile, 2002); *Models of Sustainable Development* (Sylvie Faucheux et al. eds.) (Cheltenham, UK: Edward Elgar, 1996).
37. See World Commission on Environment and Development, *Our Common Future* 43 (Oxford: Oxford University Press, 1987).
38. Edith Brown Weiss, *supra* note 29. Brown Weiss's account, like Solow's, goes well beyond what is required by Rawls's just savings principle.
39. Robert Solow, "An Almost Practical Step Toward Sustainability," 19 *Resources Policy* 162 (1993).

Conclusion

1. Alan McHughen, *Pandora's Picnic Basket* 264 (New York: Oxford University Press, 1999).
2. See Dominic Johnson, *Overconfidence and War* (Cambridge: Harvard University Press, 2004).
3. See Gary Blasi and John T. Jost, "System Justification Theory and Research: Implications for Law, Legal Advocacy, and Social Justice," 94 *California Law Review* 1119 (2006); Mark J. Landau, "Deliver Us From Evil: The Effects of Mortality Salience and Reminders of 9/11 on Support for President W. Bush," 20 *Personality & Social Psychology Bulletin* 1136 (2004); Thomas Pyszczynski et al., *In the Wake of September 11: The Psychology of Terror* (Washington, D.C.: American Psychological Association, 2003).
4. Robert Dallek, *Lyndon B. Johnson: Portrait of a President* (New York: Oxford University Press, 2004).
5. See Cass R. Sunstein, *The Second Bill of Rights: FDR's Unfinished Revolution and Why We Need It More than Ever* (New York: Basic Books, 2004).
6. An argument to this effect is made in Dale Jamieson, "Adaptation, Mitigation, and Justice," in *Perspectives on Climate Change: Science, Economics, Politics, Ethics* 217, 230–33 (Walter Sinnott-Armstrong and Richard B. Howarth eds.) (Oxford: Elsevier JAI, 2005).

ACKNOWLEDGMENTS

Many colleagues provided invaluable help with this book. For special thanks, I would like to single out Bruce Ackerman, Matthew Adler, Elizabeth Emens, Martha Nussbaum, Eric Posner, Richard Posner, Adam Samaha, David Strauss, Adrian Vermeule, and David Weisbach. Additional thanks to Richard Posner for reading the entire manuscript at the final stage. I am also grateful to participants in a superb seminar devoted to Chapter 2 at the Woodrow Wilson School of Princeton University, and in particular to Robert Keohane, my commentator on that occasion; I regret that I have not been able to respond adequately to all of the questions raised there, and especially to Keohane's excellent suggestions. Thanks to Rachael Dizard and Matthew Tokson for outstanding research assistance. Superb referee reports, producing many changes and additions, and some happy deletions, were provided by Max Bazerman, Jonathan Baron, and an anonymous reader. Thanks too to my editor, Michael Aronson, for encouragement and very wise counsel. Susan Wallace Boehmer made innumerable improvements, both substantive and stylistic, in the manuscript; many thanks for her labor, speed, and patience.

I dedicate this book to a wonderful friend, Bill Meadow, with whom I have been playing racquet sports (squash and tennis) for about a quarter century—sometimes once a week, sometimes twice, sometimes three times, sometimes more. Racquet sports teach you a lot about worst-case scenarios. I have learned a great deal from Bill, about sports, risk, and how to approach life.

I have drawn here on a number of previously published essays, most of which were produced with an eye toward this book, but which were also able to stand on their own. In many cases, however, I have greatly altered both the exposition and the argument, and some of the changes have been fundamental. The relevant essays include "On the Divergent American Reactions to Terrorism and Climate Change," 107 *Columbia Law Review* 103 (2007); "Of Montreal and Kyoto: A Tale of Two Protocols," 31 *Harvard Environmental Law Review* 1 (2006); "Irreversible and Catastrophic," 91 *Cornell Law Review* 841 (2006); "Cost-Benefit Analysis and the Environment," 115 *Ethics* 351 (2005); and "On Discounting the Future: Money, Risk, and Intergenerational Equity," 74 *University of Chicago Law Review* 171 (2007) (with Arden Rowell). I am especially grateful to Arden Rowell for help with some of the arguments in Chapter 6 and for permission to draw on our joint work here; she should not be held responsible for errors that my discussion may have introduced. In a few places, I have also drawn on the discussion in *Laws of Fear: Beyond the Precautionary Principle* (Cambridge: Cambridge University Press, 2005); readers interested in the Precautionary Principle in general might consult the discussion there.

Index